Intra-African Pentecostalism and the Dynamics of Power

"Nigerian Pentecostal churches and their diasporic communities in Europe and the USA have received much attention. Amos Chewachong provides an insightful perspective on robust evangelistic practices in other African countries. By examining Winner's Chapel in Cameroon, Chewachong illuminates the intersection of missionary activity and Nigerian control and examines strategies of cultural homogenization. This book ably addresses the implications of Nigeria's religious influence, the strategies of Pentecostal growth, and issues of mission, power, and empowerment."

—**Emma Wild-Wood**, professor of African religions and world Christianity, University of Edinburgh

"Scholarship on the vibrant phenomenon of African Pentecostalism has been fascinated with the complex dynamics between religious, economic, and political power, especially in relation to the continuing hegemony wielded by the Global North in the Global South. By examining the expansion of the Nigerian Pentecostal church, Winners' Chapel, into neighboring Cameroon, this book breaks exciting new ground by showing how these dynamics also play out in an intra-African context."

—**Brian Stanley**, professor emeritus of world Christianity, University of Edinburgh

"Chewachong's provocative study offers a refreshingly disruptive perspective on the politics of indigeneity within continental African Pentecostalism. Through a nuanced examination of the missional strategies of Winners' Chapel—a leading Nigerian Pentecostal movement—and its expansion into the Republic of Cameroon, Chewachong illumines the complex interplay of power dynamics, religious leadership, and identity politics within African Pentecostalism. An essential reading, Chewachong's text provides a rich understanding of the dynamic interplay between spiritual and temporal powers within contemporary African Christianity."

—**Eric Lewis Williams**, director, Office of Black Church Studies, assistant professor of theology and Black church studies, The Divinity School, Duke University

"This book is a much-needed corrective to scholarship on Christian migration, which is largely focused on "reverse mission" and the reshaping of Christianity in the West. Its focus on a Nigerian-originated Pentecostal denomination in Cameroon reminds us that migration and mission are not just from the West to the Rest—or the reverse, but from Everywhere to Everywhere. Amos Chewachong highlights the complexity of intra-African transnational dynamics and unearths the intertwined nature of mission and power within African neo-Pentecostalism."

—**Dr Alexander Chow**, co-director, Centre for the Study of World Christianity, University of Edinburgh

Intra-African Pentecostalism and the Dynamics of Power

The Nigerian Winners' Chapel in Cameroon

Amos B. Chewachong

Foreword by Brian Stanley

WIPF & STOCK · Eugene, Oregon

INTRA-AFRICAN PENTECOSTALISM AND THE DYNAMICS OF POWER
The Nigerian Winners' Chapel in Cameroon

Copyright © 2024 Amos B. Chewachong. All rights reserved. Except for brief quotations in critical publications or reviews, no part of this book may be reproduced in any manner without prior written permission from the publisher. Write: Permissions, Wipf and Stock Publishers, 199 W. 8th Ave., Suite 3, Eugene, OR 97401.

Wipf & Stock
An Imprint of Wipf and Stock Publishers
199 W. 8th Ave., Suite 3
Eugene, OR 97401

www.wipfandstock.com

PAPERBACK ISBN: 978-1-6667-3567-3
HARDCOVER ISBN: 978-1-6667-9300-0
EBOOK ISBN: 978-1-6667-9301-7

VERSION NUMBER 11/12/24

Scripture quotations taken from the Holy Bible, New International Version®, NIV®. Copyright © 1973, 1978, 1984, 2011 by Biblica, Inc.™ Used by permission. All rights reserved worldwide.

To my late father, Mr. Wachong Daniel Che., a devoted educationist whose lifelong dedication to teaching and discipline shaped the lives of countless students, including mine. Your commitment to the value of education and the rewards of hard work will forever inspire me. Though you left us in 2021, your legacy remains deeply embedded in my heart and this work.

And to my mother, Cecilia Bei Wachong, whose unwavering discipline and nurturing spirit provided the foundation for my growth and success. Your steadfast guidance and care allowed me to dream big and pursue my goals with focus and determination.

This monograph is a tribute to both of you.

Contents

List of Figures | ix
Abbreviations | xi
Foreword by Brian Stanley | xiii
Acknowledgments | xvii
Introduction | xxi

Chapter One: Power, Identity, and Transnational Dynamics | 1
Chapter Two: Shifting Paradigms in African Pentecostalism | 26
Chapter Three: The Phenomenology of Pentecostal Power | 63
Chapter Four: The Strategic Rise of Winners' Chapel in Cameroon | 91
Chapter Five: Power, Persuasion, and Pentecostalism | 111
Chapter Six: The Socioeconomic Impact of Winners' Chapel | 157
Chapter Seven: Dynamics of Mission and the Politics of Pentecostal Power | 195

Bibliography | 215
Index | 231

List of Figures

4.1. Statistics of Winners' Chapel Congregations in Cameroon | 101

4.2. The Administrative Structure of Winners' Chapel in Cameroon | 104

6.1. Borehole Project of Winners' Chapel Ndogbong-Douala | 163

Abbreviations

AGIP: Africa Gospel Invasion Programme
AIC: African Independent (or Initiated) Church
CMFI: Christian Missionary Fellowship International
CNPS: Caisse Nationale de Prévoyance Social
CoP: Church of Pentecost
CPU: Cameroonian Pastors Union
DOMI: David Oyedepo Ministries International
DPH: Dominion Publishing House
LFCW: Living Faith Church Worldwide
LFWOC: Living Faith World Outreach Centre
MFM: Mountain of Fire and Miracles Ministries
NCMP: National Citizens Movement Party
PCC: Presbyterian Church in Cameroon
PFN: Pentecostal Fellowship of Nigeria
RCCG: Redeemed Christian Church of God
SCOAN: Synagogue Church of All Nations
SNEC: The National Water Supply Company of Cameroon
WCC: World Council of Churches
WMA: World Mission Agency
WOFBI: Word of Faith Bible Institute
ZAOGA: Zimbabwe Assemblies of God Africa

Foreword

RECENT YEARS HAVE WITNESSED a veritable avalanche of scholarly publications on Pentecostal varieties of Christianity in the global South, and in Africa in particular. Pentecostalism has usurped theologies of liberation as the most popular topic within scholarship on world Christianity. Why, therefore, should we take notice of yet another research monograph on African Pentecostalism? The title of Amos Chewachong's book suggests a two-fold answer:

First, this is a study of "intra-African" Pentecostal Christianity. Much recent work has situated African Pentecostalism within an ongoing argument and discourse about the global dimensions of religious transnationalism. On one side of the argument are those scholars who trace the external origins of Pentecostalism in Africa to successive waves of mission initiatives from the United States or Britain, beginning with the Azusa Street revival of 1904 and extending to the more recent contribution of "Word of Faith" or prosperity gospel teaching to the extraordinary proliferation of African "neo-Pentecostal" churches, most notably in Ghana and Nigeria. Many, though not all, of the scholars who emphasize the externality of African Pentecostal origins then situate their narrative within a wider discourse about the continuing economic and ideological dependency of Africa on transnational currents of influence and control running from the Global North to the Global South. On the other side of the argument are those who interpret African Pentecostalism as an authentic expression of African religiosity, restoring to Christianity the openness to the realm of invisible spiritual power that it largely lost in Europe and North America as a result of Enlightenment rationalism.

For such scholars, the transnational dimension of the narrative is most clearly revealed in the migrant and missionary expansion of African neo-Pentecostal churches to the cities of Europe and North America. Without denying the continuing existence of neo-colonial controls wielded by the North over the South, they highlight the "reverse mission" that is bringing African perspectives on spiritual power to urban populations in the global North.

Both sides of these arguments have their merits, and they seem destined to continue. What both parties to this discourse have in common, however, is a tendency to juxtapose Africa as a continent with the global North—or, sometimes, simply with the United States as its most powerful representative—as the two poles of the transnational relationship. Amos Chewachong's book reminds us of the obvious but neglected truth that transnationalism does not necessarily mean trans-continentalism. Africa has its own vibrant centers of both economic and religious flourishing, which have created its own internal networks of mission and migration. By examining the expansion of the Nigerian neo-Pentecostal church Winners' Chapel into neighboring Cameroon, the author has reset the terms of the current discourse about the transnational dimensions of African Pentecostal Christianity.

The second aspect of this book's title that points to its originality is the simple word "power." In itself, the focus on power is not, of course, unprecedented. Analyses of the dynamics of power within religious organizations are legion. From its earliest days, Pentecostalism has been about the rediscovery of Christianity as a faith premised on the transformative power of the Holy Spirit, bringing to ordinary lay believers, female as much as male, the capacity to confront the quotidian challenges of sickness, impoverishment, and evil spiritual forces. Nevertheless, what existing scholarship on African neo-Pentecostalism has tended to underplay is the ambiguity that surrounds the relationship between the extraordinary spiritual power typically attributed to the prophet, apostle or bishop who is or was the founder of most neo-Pentecostal churches, and the managerial or organizational strategies that are needed to transmit and preserve that power once the church enters a different geographical or temporal sphere. How can the peculiar spiritual charisma of the founder be communicated to congregants who may reside in a different region or even country, and whose interface with the founder's uniquely anointed ministry is a purely electronic one? Can such power be reliably accessed through a television screen or a cell phone? Equally, can it be reliably accessed through the mediation of his appointed missionary representatives, or will there inevitably be progressive dilution of the charisma? These questions will become still more pressing once the founder has passed from the scene: What structural mechanisms and hierarchies of church office will therefore need to be instituted in preparation for that day when the founder of such a church can no longer minister, no longer accomplish works of power? Ultimately the strategies required to transmit unique spiritual charisma across the boundaries of space and time are more than managerial ones—they require a theology of apostolic succession and an ecclesiology designed to preserve faithful transmission of the original pneumatic tradition.

Some of the most fascinating aspects of Chewachong's narrative of Bishop David Oyedepo's strategies of missionary leadership relate to questions such as these. Oyedepo has committed the church of which he is lifelong president to a missionary mandate that extends beyond Nigeria to the entire African continent, and in principle to the whole world. Such global ambition in mission, however, demands quite elaborate structural architecture if the intended geographical diffusion is not inevitably to lead to diffusion of the original vision revealed to Oyedepo. Chewachong demonstrates how, viewed from the perspective of Cameroonian converts who have been persuaded of the spiritual authenticity of Oyedepo's vision and ministry, the resulting ecclesial architecture can appear politically and ethnically oppressive, as a structure designed to perpetuate Nigerian hegemony over its smaller and less wealthy neighbor. Measures that are defended as necessary to preserve and transmit spiritual power can thus appear as forms of domination. This is not, of course, the first time in Christian history that such conundrums have surfaced. The parallel that Chewachong draws on with Roman Catholic ecclesiology is intended, not as a piece of anti-Catholic propaganda, but as a pointer toward fruitful analysis. African neo-Pentecostalism exhibits a number of intriguing parallels with traditional pre–Vatican II Catholicism, in its increasing use of certain material objects as holy vehicles of spiritual power, in its development of theories of apostolic succession, and in its admission that some form of "temporal power" is necessary in order to preserve the integrity and independence of apostolic truth as it is handed down across the centuries and communicated across national frontiers.

Amos Chewachong's book thus deserves a wide readership, not simply among those primarily interested in the changing face of African Christianity, but also much more broadly. The multiple ironies and ambiguities of power—both spiritual and temporal—are part of the stuff of Christian history and will remain so for the future.

Brian Stanley
Professor Emeritus of World Christianity
University of Edinburgh
August 2024

Acknowledgments

IN THE JOURNEY OF crafting this book, I stand on the shoulders of many who have guided, supported, and journeyed with me, and to whom I owe my deepest gratitude.

First and foremost, I give thanks to God, whose providence directed my steps to the University of Edinburgh when my initial plans to study Faith and Globalization at Durham University did not come to fruition. This divine redirection not only provided the opportunity to pursue my academic aspirations but also allowed me the experience of serving in full-time ministry with the Church of Scotland.

I am especially grateful to the scholars whose mentorship has shaped my intellectual journey. Professor Brian Stanley, your unwavering support and supervision during my PhD at the University of Edinburgh have been pivotal. Your encouragement, careful reading of my manuscripts, and continual mentorship inspired me to see this book to completion, for which I am forever indebted. I am thankful to Professor Afe Adogame of Princeton Theological Seminary. Your mentorship during my master's program at Edinburgh laid the foundation for this academic pursuit, and it was your introduction to PhD studies that opened the door to this path. Your course on "Religion and the New African Diaspora" ignited my curiosity about Pentecostal dynamics, guiding the trajectory of my research. In fond remembrance, I extend my heartfelt gratitude to the late Professor Andrew Walls, my secondary PhD supervisor, whose profound insights left an indelible mark on my work. May his soul rest in eternal peace. I also wish to acknowledge Dr. Elizabeth Koepping, whose critical reflections on world Christianity during my master's studies significantly shaped my theological thinking.

To Paul Oliver, whose friendship began during our academic journeys at Edinburgh, my heartfelt thanks. Your initial surprise at my command of English led to a lasting bond, and your thoughtful feedback on my thesis helped sharpen not only my linguistic expression but the clarity of my arguments. Your encouragement throughout this process has been invaluable. I am deeply appreciative of my colleagues—Eric Williams, Prasad Philips, Michael Tete, Amid Elabo, and Sara Afshari. Your companionship, along with your intellectual curiosity and investment in my work, fueled the momentum necessary to bring this monograph to life. Our shared journey has been a source of strength and inspiration.

The Presbyterian Church in Cameroon, my spiritual and intellectual home, played an instrumental role in shaping both my faith and my academic journey. From my early theological education at the Presbyterian Theological Seminary in Kumba, to my time as a young pastor, the church has been a guiding force in my life. I am deeply grateful to moderator emeritus of the PCC the Very Rev. Dr. Festus Asana, whose administration initially permitted me to pursue further studies abroad from 2012. To the community at my church in Newport-On-Tay, I extend my deepest gratitude for your understanding and generosity in allowing me the necessary leaves of absence to focus on completing this book.

I would like to express my appreciation to the Rt. Rev. Dr. Fonki Samuel Forba, moderator of the PCC, whose leadership entrusted me with the role of coordinator of the church's congregations in Europe and the Gulf missionary field. This appointment enabled me to continue living abroad, while my appointment as visiting lecturer for world Christianity at the Presbyterian Theological Seminary has allowed me to continue carrying out further research. My sincere gratitude to Mr. Ndive Ngole Mbuayo, financial secretary of the PCC, and Professor Colin Vincent of Newport-On-Tay Church. Your financial contributions were instrumental in making the publication of this monograph possible. To Mr. Elangwe Peter Nanje, my dear friend and brother, I owe an immense debt of gratitude. Your wise counsel guided my decision to pursue further education in Great Britain, and your boundless generosity made the journey possible. Your kindness has left an indelible mark on my life and this work.

Thanks to the members and leaders of Winners' Chapel in Cameroon. Your openness in granting me interviews and welcoming me into your services provided invaluable insights. My deepest thanks to the

Nigerian missionaries serving in Cameroon and the Cameroonian pastors of Winners' Chapel, whose generosity of time and resources allowed me to gain a deeper understanding of your work and values.

Finally, I am profoundly grateful for my family—my wife, Florence, and our children, Larry-Craig, Talitha-Zerah Amosons, Reuel-Gilead, Arielle-Amora Amosons, and Anna-Danielle Amosons. Your understanding, sacrifices, and the joy you brought into my life during study breaks have been a constant source of strength.

To each and every one of you, I offer my deepest appreciation. Your contributions have been vital to the realization of this work, and your influence will forever be cherished.

Introduction

Pentecostal and charismatic expressions of Christianity, with their deep-rootedness in African cultures and their heartfelt spirituality, have found increasingly diverse landscapes to navigate, especially in the contemporary era of globalization. This faith is not just a religious phenomenon, but a display of human magnetism and deeply personal encounters with God. Pentecostalism has increasingly become a sociocultural force, influencing migrations, identity formations, and power dynamics across borders.

Leading sociologists and scholars of World Christianity have noted the impassioned expansion of African Pentecostalism into the northern hemisphere. The concept of "reverse mission," or the "Southernization of European Christianity," highlights this reverse missionary flow, where the once-evangelized now take on the mantle of evangelists to the new Dark Continent of Europe. However, the dynamics of this transnational religious movement have shifted intriguingly because of the flows of the Christian faith within Africa itself. What drives African Pentecostal movements to traverse their own continent, creating a unique theater of evangelism where Africa is both the sender and the receiver?

To shed light on this circuitous weaving of faith, culture, and power, this book examines the Nigerian Pentecostal movement, Winners' Chapel, and its power dynamics in Cameroon. Employing a qualitative research methodology, we study the character, motivations, and implications of such transnational movements, with Winners' Chapel serving as our primary lens. The title of this book, *Intra-African Pentecostalism and the Dynamics of Power*, encapsulates the core themes, the spread of

African Pentecostalism and the complicated power play within the continent. While the study of religious transnationalism has recently gained scholarly traction, a significant gap remains in understanding the power dynamics underlying these transnational religious endeavors. How do these movements ensure loyalty to the mother church? How is their vision transmitted, received, and adapted across national borders? And in the midst of this, how does a charismatic leader like Bishop Oyedepo, the linchpin of Winners' Chapel, maintain his position as the church's spiritual fulcrum? Drawing upon the widely accepted premise that Pentecostal movements have a strong inclination towards transnational missions, this book situates this theme in an intra-African context and attempts to dissect the subtle and often intricate dance between mission, power, loyalty, and identity.

We will explore the transference of religious practices from Nigeria to external branches of Winners' Chapel elsewhere in sub-Saharan Africa, and the resulting complex dynamics that ensue. This includes the church's strategies to ensure allegiance to the mother institution and its founder, and the role of mediation and media in sustaining this allegiance. Central to our narrative is Bishop Oyedepo, the driving force behind Winners' Chapel. His role, seen through both spiritual and temporal prisms, offers profound insights into the nature of power within transnational religious movements. This exploration is distinct from other scholarly works. Instead of focusing on the reverse missionary trend where African Pentecostalism makes its mark on European or North American shores, this study focuses on intra-African dynamics. It uncovers the subtle nuances, conscious and unconscious choices within Oyedepo's brand of Christianity, and its broader implications for the African Christian landscape. Thus, the importance of this book lies in its attempt to enrich the expanding academic discourse on African Pentecostalism. It not only adds to existing literature but also unveils the often-overlooked tensions, alignments, and resistance between founders and followers within intra-African Pentecostal movements. In doing so, it aims to provide a clearer understanding of the complex power dynamics inherent within the relationship of transnational religious actors and their counterparts in the receiving nations, painting a comprehensive picture of Pentecostalism's role in shaping Africa's spiritual and socio-cultural fabric.

The book's interdisciplinary outlook considers theoretical and methodological issues, balancing theory with case studies and personal stories to demonstrate how faith, culture, power and politics interweave in intra-African Pentecostalism. The first chapter of the book, on "Power, Identity, and Transnational Dynamics," offers a general introduction to the major themes. Through the immersive narrative of a personal sojourn to Winners' Chapel in Douala, the largest city in Cameroon, the interaction between global aspirations of the church and the resonant echoes of local cultures is vividly depicted. The complexity of the phenomenon of Reverse Mission is also unraveled, offering a fresh perspective on a historical narrative that was once predominantly Western-driven. It challenges traditional paradigms and introduces the reader to multi-dimensional facets of Pentecostal expansion, backed by entrepreneurial zeal and a profound belief in spiritual mandates. The link between global aspirations and local cultures revealed in this chapter is not merely a rhythmic swaying to gospel tunes; it reveals a sophisticated choreography of power, identity, and politics. The subsequent chapters offer a panoramic view of the evolving contours of African Pentecostalism.

However, as chapter 2 reveals, the rise of African Pentecostalism is not without its challenges. The prosperity gospel's allure and the symbiotic relationship between politics and faith demand a critical examination. These new power structures and their palpable socioeconomic impacts further underscore the dichotomy between the spiritual and the temporal, questioning the essence of faith in a materially driven world. Chapter 3 introduces us to the ethereal nature of Pentecostal power, blending the traditional with the contemporary and spotlighting figures like Bishop Oyedepo who stand at the confluence of spiritual and temporal power. Yet, this power also poses pertinent questions, unraveling tensions that lie within the fabric of belief. Chapter 4 traces the journey of Winners' Chapel in Cameroon, analyzing the strategic rise of the church, which remains firmly rooted in Nigeria yet is now blooming in Cameroonian soil. This strategic entrenchment is emblematic of a broader vision—one that aspires to transcend Africa's borders. In chapter 5, the intricate dynamics of intra-African Pentecostalism come to the fore, with regional giants like Nigeria shaping the continent's religious pulse. This chapter unpacks the subtle yet persuasive dynamics of soft power, spotlighting how religious entities sculpt beliefs and influence adherents. Chapter 6, with its exploration of Winners' Chapel's socioeconomic endeavors, adds yet another dimension to the narrative. It sheds light on how churches are not mere spiritual havens but have evolved into sites of socioeconomic support and activity, impacting their local communities in profound ways. Yet, it also nudges the reader to discern where the balance lies between empowerment and dependence. Concluding with chapter 7, the book takes the reader back into the heart of religious transnationalism. It revisits the phenomenon of "reverse mission" and presents it as a powerful testament to the shifting epicenters of world Christianity, underscoring Africa's rising influence in charting the course of Christian faith worldwide. As noted earlier, the phenomenon of African Pentecostal churches actively evangelizing in the traditional strongholds of Christianity, such as Europe and North America, implies a significant saturation and maturity of the Christian faith within the African continent. This development allows for an exportation of a distinctly African interpretation of Christianity to these regions. However, the continued expansion of African Pentecostal movements, such as those from Nigeria, across the African continent raises intriguing questions about the dynamics of their missionary activities. This situation presents a complex scenario where Africa serves as both a stage for the gospel and a source of its dissemination. I have characterized this scenario as a "reversal of the reverse mission." Traditionally, the term "reverse mission" has been used to describe the phenomenon where the once "missionized" become missionaries themselves, often evangelizing in the lands of those who originally brought them the faith. In this context, the "reverse mission in reverse" would imply a scenario where these new centers of Christianity (like African nations) are not only sending missionaries to the historical heartlands of the faith but are simultaneously strengthening and expanding their evangelical efforts within their own and neighboring regions. The "reverse mission in reverse" in this context involves understanding African Pentecostalism as a multi-directional movement. It is not just about the flow of missionary work from the "Global South" to the "Global North" but also encompasses a vigorous evangelical outreach within the "Global South" itself. The concept of "reverse mission in reverse" acknowledges the dynamic and complex nature of contemporary Christian missionary activities, especially as practiced by African Pentecostal churches, which challenge traditional paradigms of evangelism and mission work. The book takes its readers on a thought-provoking journey through the complex layers of faith, power, and identity within African Pentecostalism.

The insights and narratives shared in this book spring from extensive research in Cameroon conducted as part of my PhD studies in the University of Edinburgh from 2013 to 2017, an exploration that I have passionately continued to this day. While the perspectives offered are primarily grounded in the viewpoints of local actors, they are blended with external sources that help to interpret these viewpoints and relate them to wider themes in the study of religion. A distinct feature of this book is the prioritization of practitioners' narratives, their experiences, life lessons, expressions, and the realities they confront in an evolving global landscape. Interestingly, though the central subject is a Nigerian church, the voices that resonate most prominently are those of the Cameroonians. This intentional focus stems from the book's mission: to explore the operations of a Nigerian Pentecostal Church set against the backdrop of Cameroon, examining how such a transnational institution navigates cultural diversity in a foreign, albeit neighboring, land.

Chapter One

Power, Identity, and Transnational Dynamics

On Sunday, September 20, 2015, at approximately 7:30 a.m., I left the Royal Palace Hotel, situated in Ancient Road, Bonaberi, Douala, in search of the Winners' Chapel congregation rumored to be in the area. A local motorbike driver transported me a short distance to the right of the hotel and dropped me off near several roadside shops to my left. He instructed me to find the church concealed behind these establishments. I followed a narrow alley, flanked by additional shops on either side, eventually arriving in front of a former cinema hall, known as Cinema Fouato. This building now serves as the spiritual home of three different churches: two are Nigerian transnational Pentecostal churches, the Redeemed Christian Church of God and Winners' Chapel International, while the third is the Brazilian Pentecostal Church "God is Love," headquartered in São Paulo.

As I walked toward the buildings, I was approached by a well-dressed young man and woman. Both of them handed me a flyer, cordially inviting me to their respective churches in the vicinity. It was at this point that I realized there were multiple churches in the area. Upon examining the flyer, I discovered that I was being invited to the Redeemed Christian Church of God. However, my objective was to attend Winners' Chapel. While I was in the midst of explaining my intention, I looked up and noticed the signage for Winners' Chapel displayed on the roof of the adjacent building to my right. Bishop Oyedepo's iconic image overshadowed the sign post, immediately capturing my attention. I turned toward the direction of Winners' Chapel, but the two ushers from the Redeemed Christian Church of God persisted, insisting that it was divine providence that had brought me to them. They asserted that I might miss out on blessings from their congregation if I chose otherwise. Nevertheless, I remained steadfast in my resolve to attend Winners' Chapel and promptly made my way toward the church.

Winners' Chapel Bonaberi occupies a modest hall situated to the right of the main entrance to the Cinema Hall. In 2021, the church boasted a seating capacity of approximately three hundred worshipers. On the day of my visit, ushers were stationed outside the church and along the pews inside. These ushers, dressed in black skirts and white shirts for women and black trousers for men, warmly greeted incoming congregants, directing some to front-row seats. Upon identifying myself as a first-time visitor, a female usher promptly escorted me to a front-row seat, declaring that I was welcomed to the "home of signs and wonders." Shortly thereafter, a tall, Brown-skinned man, likely in his early forties, approached from the row to my left and greeted me. His Nigerian accent revealed his origin. Approximately thirty minutes into the service, following some announcements and spirited praise and worship, the man who had greeted me earlier stepped up to the podium to deliver the sermon. He was the senior pastor of the Bonaberi branch. The pastor had relocated to Cameroon from South Africa after previously serving in Swaziland and Ghana and was nearing the end of his two-year term as a missionary to Cameroon. He led the Bonaberi congregation as their senior pastor, overseeing six Cameroonian assistant pastors. In stark contrast, the Nigerian Redeemed Christian Church of God and the Brazilian God is Love Pentecostal Church in the same vicinity were each led by Cameroonian pastors.

Upon visiting the headquarters of Winners' Chapel Cameroon in Ndogbong-Douala the following Sunday, I discovered that the national pastor (or overseer of all the church's work in Cameroon) was Nigerian, while all assistant pastors were Cameroonian. The sermons delivered during my visits to both Bonaberi and Ndogbong had been prepared in Nigeria by Bishop Oyedepo, the founder and leader of the church, who claims to receive prophetic revelations from God weekly. These revelations are employed to craft sermons disseminated to all church branches as a matter of policy. The testimonies shared in the churches and distributed on flyers for evangelism predominantly featured Nigerian Christians who had experienced supernatural breakthroughs in healing, finance, and other significant areas of their lives. These stories had been reproduced in Cameroon for Cameroonian audiences to learn from and emulate, with the hope of attaining favor from God and similar miraculous rewards.

Following the Ndogbong service, I inquired why the church in Cameroon used Nigerian testimonies and declarations instead of those from their own congregations. In response, my interlocutors explained that Winners' Chapel constituted a singular entity regardless of location-whether in Cameroon, Kenya, Ghana, or elsewhere. All members considered themselves part of one church under the direct spiritual authority of their founding bishop, David Oyedepo. They regarded themselves as his spiritual children, transcending geographic boundaries and temporal constraints.[1] Another member expressed that the Cameroonian church, being relatively new, needed to draw strength from the mother church in Nigeria and benefit from the grace of Bishop Oyedepo. Testimonies and supernatural experiences from Nigeria were seen as empowering, showcasing how the bishop's spiritual authority operated.[2] These responses and perceptions echo the concept of cultural homogenization, where cultural diversity diminishes as a result of the widespread dissemination of cultural symbols—comprising not just physical artifacts but customs, ideas, and values.

Francis Steven Mickus, in his exploration of cultural homogenization within the Star Trek universe, provides a nuanced critique of how the franchise depicts the process of achieving unity through the amalgamation of distinct cultural identities into a singular, monolithic culture. The critique is particularly centered around the idea that while the narrative of Star Trek valorizes diversity and the coexistence of multiple cultures, it simultaneously, and perhaps unwittingly, showcases a universe where the complexity of real cultural interactions is simplified into a more homogenized whole for the sake of unity.[3] This tension between celebrating diversity and the practical implications of achieving interplanetary (or intercultural) unity provides a rich framework for examining the phenomenon of transnational Pentecostalism, specifically through the lens

1. Personal interview with Kum Tegha (pseudonym), Douala (Sept. 20, 2016).
2. Personal interview with Fabian Bong (pseudonym), Douala (Sept. 20, 2016).
3. Mickus, "Culture of One," 368–88.

of the Nigerian Winners' Chapel church's expansion into Cameroon. Winners' Chapel embodies a form of cultural homogenization similar to what Mickus describes. The church, under the spiritual leadership of Bishop Oyedepo, operates on the principle of a singular, unified religious culture that transcends geographical, national, and cultural boundaries. This unity is maintained through the sharing of testimonies and declarations from the Nigerian mother church, which are used in congregations worldwide. This practice suggests a deliberate effort to maintain a cohesive and unified church identity, one that prioritizes the spiritual authority and cultural practices of the Nigerian headquarters over local expressions of faith.

The transnational expansion of Nigerian Pentecostal churches into Cameroon underscores not only the evangelization of the gospel but also an underlying politics of power. This outreach represents an attempt to carve out a distinct space in the religious marketplace, where faith, narratives, and leadership dynamics converge. The emphasis on Nigerian narratives in Cameroon, while indicative of a universal church ethos, also subtly suggests a hierarchical model where the Nigerian experience is positioned as superior or more authentic. The implication here is two-fold: On the one hand, it fosters a sense of unity and shared identity among believers across borders, but on the other, it runs the risk of overshadowing local experiences and beliefs. This dynamic intertwines religious evangelism with cultural homogenization, thereby raising pertinent questions about the balance between global outreach and local integration. However, they also provide valuable insights into the fundamental ideological tenets of the mission within Winners' Chapel or the Living Faith Church Worldwide.

The Living Faith Church Worldwide

The Living Faith Church Worldwide (LFCW), a.k.a. Winners' Chapel International, is a product of the vision of David Oyedepo, who claims to have received a mandate from God to save mankind from suffering and pain. In Nigeria, the church is registered as Living Faith Church Worldwide (LFCW) with the Corporate Affairs Commission,[4] but it is popularly known as Winners' Chapel. In Cameroon, the church is not

---

4. The Corporate Affairs Commission is the Nigerian government agency responsible for the registration of companies and non-profit organizations.

registered with the government but the application for registration, which is currently being processed, gives the church's name as "World Mission Agency Inc." Some official documents of the church have two names: "World Mission Agency Inc." and Winners' Chapel International, Cameroon.[5] This difference in nomenclature between the church in Nigeria and the one in Cameroon is raising concerns to the extent that some Cameroonian pastors believe there is no Winners' Chapel in Cameroon despite its significant presence and representation through missionaries from Nigeria.

However, the church is popularly called Winners' Chapel in Cameroon. The name visibly conveys the philosophy of action and theology of the LFCW as being those of a church primarily concerned with the success and empowerment of its members. The founder and leader of Winner's Chapel prefers his organization to be known and called LFCW.[6] The LFCW is one branch of David Oyedepo Ministries International (DOMI). The others are The African Gospel Invasion Programme (AGIP), the Dominion Publishing House (DPH), Faith Academy, Covenant University, Gilead Medical Centre, and the Word of Faith Bible Institute (WOFBI).[7] This book examines the emergence and power dynamics of the Winners' Chapel of the DOMI conglomerate in Cameroon and the ways in which the founding bishop has interpreted his mandate for the church across the world.

The Mandate of Bishop Oyedepo

An understanding of the emergence and power dynamics of Winners' Chapel in Cameroon is only possible when grounded in an examination of the vision and mission of its founder, who has been the main architect of the unfolding dynamics of the church from its inception. This vision and mission are summarized by Oyedepo in a monograph entitled *The Mandate: Operational Manual, Living Faith Church Worldwide aka Winners' Chapel International*.[8] The book records revelations

---

5. Letter addressed to the president of the Republic of Cameroon, dated September 3, 2014, obtained by the author, by Clement Simon Mbambad, "Exercise Illegal et non-respect de la Legislation Camerounaise par La Congregation Religieuse World Mission Agency INC-Winners' Chapel International au Cameroun."

6. Kuponu, "Living Faith Church," 18.

7. Kuponu, "Living Faith Church," 18.

8. Oyedepo, *Mandate*.

which Oyedepo claims to continually receive from God, instructing him on how to manage and organize various aspects of his church organization. According to Oyedepo, the beginning of Winners' Chapel was never a human conception but a divine mandate which resulted from an eighteen-hour encounter with the Lord on May 2, 1982. In that encounter, God instructed Oyedepo to liberate the world from all oppressions of the Devil through the preaching of the word of faith. This encounter provided a vision for his mission in which God revealed the plight of humanity as fraught with all kinds of perplexities. It also envisaged the bishop as responsible for resolving the situation through the preaching of the word of faith in local and global contexts. The global picture of Winners' Chapel is implied in the name Winners' Chapel International, and there is no doubt that Oyedepo perceives his mission as one in which his spiritual power needs to be appropriately transmitted from Nigeria to other places where he has established churches, in order to maintain and sustain the mandate which God bestowed on him. This explains why the bishop has historically used Nigerian missionaries to lead Winners' Chapel churches beyond Nigeria. The evidence is in the fact that by the close of the 1990s, a branch of Winners' Chapel had been established in the capital cities of about thirty African countries, with Nigerian pastors posted from Lagos as leaders.[9]

Winners' Chapel prototypically represents the new megachurches of the African neo-Pentecostal or charismatic type, which occupy diverse spaces in local and global contexts. It has a dominant social visibility through a network of churches in over three hundred cities and towns spread across thirty-six states and the Federal Capital territory of Nigeria. It has also established congregations in more than thirty-five other countries,[10] including Cameroon, where the church continues to wield considerable influence from Nigeria.

The history of emergence, spread, and power dynamics of Winners' Chapel in Nigeria and across international boundaries illustrates what André Corten and Ruth Marshall-Fratani describe as a burgeoning and complex tapestry of international Pentecostal connections. These

---

9. Matthews Ojo, "Nigerian Pentecostalism and Transnational Religious Networks in West African Coastal Regions," in Fourchard et al., *Entreprises Religieuses Transnationales*, 405. Also see Kuponu, "Living Faith Church."

10. Matthews Ojo, "Nigerian Pentecostalism and Transnational Religious Networks in West African Coastal Regions," in Fourchard et al., *Entreprises Religieuses Transnationales*, 405.

networks see a swift and fervent exchange of congregants, finances, beliefs, and iconography, challenging any attempt to trace them back to a single origin or final point.[11] The movement and establishment of Nigerian neo-Pentecostal churches into new host-territories is a captivating subject for further exploration. For instance, the Redeemed Christian Church of God has showcased a historical capacity to weave networks, reaching into Ghana, Benin, and other African nations by holding major religious convocations in Nigeria. The strategic dissemination of doctrine, homilies, and news through printed materials, alongside the placement of representatives, has cemented the bonds between the originating church and its international offshoots.[12]

Nigerian missionaries are casting their nets widely, seeding and nurturing congregations far beyond Africa's borders. They are bolstered by a belief that Nigeria's demographic significance in Africa may be part of a divine plan for them to evangelize the continent.[13] These churches are finding fertile ground in other African nations by advocating their version of Christianity as not only superior but also as a salve for the socio-political and cultural upheavals prevalent across the continent.

Many scholars and observers of African Pentecostalism might recognize the pattern following my analysis and would identify with my brief overview of my encounter with the Winners' Chapel: their repurposing of former cinema halls for worship, and the co-habitation of different Pentecostal churches within one building vying for new members as if in a religious marketplace. They have seen how these churches welcome newcomers, emphasize exuberant worship, and are founded on prophetic visions claimed by their leaders. However, what demands more scholarly attention is the calculated approach of transnational neo-Pentecostal churches in dispatching missionaries to establish and lead their faith communities within Africa. The interplay of the spiritual authority wielded by founding leaders and the earthly organizational frameworks through missionaries, as well as the nuances in how sermons are crafted and transmitted from the main church to its branches for preaching, have not been thoroughly examined in existing research.

---

11. Corten and Fratani, *Between Babel and Pentecost*, 1.

12. Olufunke Adeboye, "Transnational Pentecostalism in Africa: The Redeemed Christian Church of God, Nigeria," in Fourchard et al., *Entreprises Religieuse Transnationales*, 453.

13. Ayuk, "Portrait of a Nigerian Pentecostal Missionary," 121, citing Grady Lee, "Nigeria's Miracle," *Charisma and Christian Life* (2002) 38–49.

Transnational Pentecostal Dynamics

Much of the literature on religious transnationalism focuses on the migration of Christianity's epicenter to the majority world and the sending of missionaries from the global South to the global North, known as the "reverse mission." Some scholars talk about the "gospel's return" from erstwhile heathen nations to Christianity's former heartlands in Europe and North America.[14] The evidence is in the increasing number of churches and missionaries from Africa and the global South in Western territories. For example, London's largest church is Nigerian, and many Cameroonian, Kenyan, and Ghanaian churches and missionaries are found in various parts of Europe and the USA. I am a case in point—an ordained minister of the Presbyterian Church in Cameroon now serving as parish minister for Newport-On-Tay Church of Scotland, a predominantly Scottish Presbyterian congregation where my family are the only African contingent.

There is considerable evidence that the missionary trajectory has shifted, with fewer individuals leaving the Western world for the global South and more making the opposite journey. This shift suggests that developed nations like the USA and others in Europe no longer exclusively control the missionary enterprise. Instead, missionaries are now emerging from Africa, Asia, Latin America, and other parts of the global South to evangelize or re-Christianize the North. One of the reasons for sending missionaries from the Western world to the global South may be to provide theological training, teaching, and empowerment of local leadership rather than solely for evangelistic purposes, as was the case before. Given their deeper understanding of their culture and available human resources, Africans can make more effective evangelists to their people. In this context, evangelism might no longer be the primary need of Christians from the majority world, as they are already more engaged in it than ever before.[15]

The shift in Christianity's center from the global North to the global South suggests that African countries no longer need missionaries, given the saturation of Christianity in the continent, despite Muslim influences, especially in the North and parts of West and Central Africa. Consequently, the movement of missionaries across Africa reveals a significant

---

14. Jenkins, *Next Christendom*. Also see Rebecca Catto, "Reverse Mission: From the Global South to Mainline Churches," in Goodhew, *Church Growth in Britain*, 91–103.

15. Yeh, *Twenty-First Century Mission*, 19.

evolution within world Christianity. An example of this profound missionary enterprise is David Oyedepo's Winners' Chapel, where church practices in Nigeria are transmitted to Cameroon. This phenomenon, alongside other transnational religious transactions through media, prompts questions about the motivations for cross-border exchanges in a continent that has become the new theater of global Christianity, where missionaries are both produced and dispatched.

Previous studies of Pentecostal transnationalism reveal that Nigerian-based independent Pentecostal churches and their networks across Africa have a thriving exchange of Pentecostal products.[16] These products, such as recorded audio and video cassettes, religious-themed home video films, and devotional literature, are produced in Nigeria and distributed widely to other African countries. Through these products, Nigerian Pentecostal culture continues to permeate other African nations, and their products have become tangible resources for strengthening their networks and are rich sources for spiritual nourishment.[17]

From Missionary Expansion to Entrepreneurship

Two distinct eras have significantly influenced the understanding of religious transnationalism in Africa and the evolution of Pentecostal mission objectives. The first phase, from the late 1970s to the late 1980s, was marked by an intent to expand missionary outreach across Africa. The aspiration to liberate Africans from the shackles of sin and demonic influences initiated the creation of networks to accomplish missionary goals. In achieving this, Nigerian Pentecostal churches catalyzed the indigenous and grassroots growth of Pentecostalism in other African nations without directly asserting control.[18]

The subsequent phase, starting from the mid-1980s, witnessed the transition of African Pentecostal churches toward an entrepreneurial approach, leading to financial investment in new "mission fields." This

16. Matthews Ojo, "Nigerian Pentecostalism and Transnational Religious Networks in West African Coastal Regions," in Fourchard et al., *Entreprises Religieuses Transnationales*.

17. Matthews Ojo, "Nigerian Pentecostalism and Transnational Religious Networks in West African Coastal Regions," in Fourchard et al., *Entreprises Religieuses Transnationales*.

18. Matthews Ojo, "Nigerian Pentecostalism and Transnational Religious Networks in West African Coastal Regions," in Fourchard et al., *Entreprises Religieuses Transnationales*.

investment was not solely for missionary purposes but also aimed at generating profit. By the late 1990s, the emergence of additional neo-Pentecostal churches further transformed the African religious landscape. Established Pentecostal churches aimed to strengthen their presence within their religious domain and safeguard their congregations from shifting to newly founded churches. To fulfill these needs, they adopted marketing techniques to cater to the religious and spiritual demands of their potential constituents.[19]

The entrepreneurship-inspired religious networking led Nigerian charismatic churches to thwart the rise of emerging charismatic organizations in other West African nations by sending missionaries to establish or take over branches of their churches outside Nigeria, thereby preserving their influence. Powerful Pentecostal churches like Winners' Chapel International and the Redeemed Christian Church of God successfully employed media resources to connect with their followers and consolidate their power and influence in their new "mission fields."[20]

One of the most prominent shifts in the twenty-first-century dynamics of Christian missions is the evolution of negotiation between the local and the global. In the 1970s and 1980s, this negotiation primarily occurred between American and Nigerian models and other African models within the African continent. In the twenty-first century, the negotiation is increasingly between Nigeria and Ghana and other African countries.[21]

This book's central argument is about the deep-rooted connection between neo-Pentecostal principles within the existing global frameworks of transnational power and the capacity of religion to shape the socio-cultural and spiritual experiences of individuals in transit. Although the subject of religious transnationalism is the focus of renewed critical thinking, there is an evident lack of comprehensive analysis informed by power dynamics, specifically concerning the complexities inherent in African transnational Pentecostalism.

19. Matthews Ojo, "Nigerian Pentecostalism and Transnational Religious Networks in West African Coastal Regions," in Fourchard et al., *Entreprises Religieuses Transnationales*.

20. Matthews Ojo, "Nigerian Pentecostalism and Transnational Religious Networks in West African Coastal Regions," in Fourchard et al., *Entreprises Religieuses Transnationales*.

21. Matthews Ojo, "Nigerian Pentecostalism and Transnational Religious Networks in West African Coastal Regions," in Fourchard et al., *Entreprises Religieuses Transnationales*.

The book starts from the premise that Pentecostal churches and their founders have a penchant for transnational missionary praxis. While this concept has been extensively discussed in existing literature, noticeable gaps persist. The following chapters will provide a detailed yet comprehensive examination of the intricate interweaving of mission and power, alongside the ever-evolving vision of transitional churches. These include contrived processes aimed at ensuring loyalty to the mother church and its founder within external branches. The exploration will analyze the transmission of practices from Winners' Chapel's Nigerian headquarters to its branches in Cameroon, and the transnational followers' willingness to accept and incorporate these practices.

I am aware of the immense diversity within Pentecostalism, but it will be wearisome to use a term like Pentecostal/Charismatic or neo-Pentecostalism at every turn to differentiate between one form from the other. I will streamline the use of the term "Pentecostal" for simplicity, unless otherwise necessary to make a particular point. The focus will be on Winners' Chapel, employing practical examples from the church to substantiate the argument concerning African Pentecostal Transnationalism. While these examples may not be uniformly representative of transnational Pentecostal churches, I will nevertheless argue that they are prototypical enough to substantiate my argument. The central contention of this book is that there is an overarching trajectory of power in transnational Pentecostalism in Africa. While familiar to those versed with the intricacies of power within Pentecostalism, this contention underscores an often underexplored relationship between spiritual authority and temporal power structures. In the context of Winners' Chapel devotees in Cameroon, the prevalence and influence of Nigerian missionaries is anchored on the perceived potency of Nigerian Christianity, and their clergy are widely viewed as more spiritually adept than other religious figures on the continent.

The role of Nigerian missionaries as holders of temporal power tasked with implementing the church's policies in Cameroon; their perceived command over biblical texts and the art of preaching; coupled with the belief in their ability to manifest the sought-after miracles, has led to their acceptance among Cameroonians. Their appeal lies in their apparently compelling ability to meet the spiritual needs of the Cameroonian populace. Moreover, Bishop Oyedepo's skilful use of the media to connect with followers worldwide and the widespread endorsement of his leadership both locally and transnationally shows how technology fortifies transnational religious organizations. This technological prowess enhances the immediacy and intensity of devotees' interaction with their spiritual leader, thus facilitating their active participation in the church's day-to-day operations.

Transnational religious practices represent one dimension of transnational activity in which adherents of Pentecostal movements engage. In contrast to studies of diaspora or global religion, analyses of transnational religion focus on the everyday experiences of a transnational organization in at least two locations. Firstly, they explore transnational religious practices of ordinary individuals by focusing on concrete expressions of religious beliefs, practices, and organizational intricacies[22] as defined by the leader, and how these are embedded in broader social and spiritual power hierarchies. Secondly, these analyses produce maps of horizontal ties[23] that link individual members to spiritual leaders, and religious social movement actors, both in the originating and host countries, and situate these localized ties within the context of global cross-border connections in which they are embedded.

For those who are unfamiliar with the missionary operations and transnational dynamics of Pentecostal churches like the Winners' Chapel, the careful planning and execution of transnational engagements can easily be taken for granted. However, the strategies employed to achieve and maintain control of the Nigerian mother church over its Cameroonian daughter church are deliberate and reveal its intentionality toward achieving missionary goals.

Nigerian missionaries deployed to Cameroon fulfill their religious duties alongside indigenous Cameroonian pastors, a dynamic that frequently results in complex intersections of allegiances and contention. While Cameroonian pastors may at times challenge the authority of the Nigerian missionaries, a strong sense of loyalty often characterizes their relationship. Accusations of favoritism and marginalization levied by native Cameroonian pastors against Nigerian missionaries reveal the convoluted pathways both parties navigate within the new "mission field." These dynamics underscore how transnational missionary practice is entwined within power structures that can, at times, result in the alienation of less advantaged participants.

---

22. Levitt, "You Know, Abraham Was," 847–73.
23. Levitt, "You Know, Abraham Was," 847–73.

Social scientists may readily identify such manipulations of power, as well as the pre-eminence of Nigerian leadership, due to their ostensible associations with power and monetary influence. However, many overlook how these power structures and transnational practices can empower church members and workers. In some instances, they can even serve as a catalyst for the rise of Cameroonian indigenous pastors and the establishment of independent ministries originating from Winners' Chapel.

Bishop Oyedepo's deliberate strategy of exporting his version of Christianity from Nigeria to other African countries, along with the deployment of missionaries to safeguard his influence abroad, exemplifies a transformative shift in missionary direction. African churches are now creating and exporting missionaries not only to the Western world but also within Africa, a continent already replete with Christianity. The missionary practices of other Nigerian Pentecostal churches corroborate the evidence of an emerging missionary orientation. Thus, while the Redeemed Christian Church of God (RCCG) commits strategically to establishing churches within a five-minute walking distance in every city and town of developing countries, and a five-minute driving distance in every city and town of developed countries, thereby staking a claim for Christ in every nation, the Living Faith Church Worldwide a.k.a. Winners' Chapel International pledges to cultivate and elevate humanity by awakening the divine potential inherent in people of all races and nations. Their objective is to liberate the entire world from all forms of oppression, both spiritual and physical, through the teachings and preaching of the word of faith.

Consequently, Nigerian-founded churches are actively negotiating religious spaces in both local and transnational contexts to accomplish their goals. Nigerian pastors have further asserted that they have been divinely called to deliver salvation not only to the rest of Africa but also to the entire world. This claim echoes earlier precedents of an imperial theology.

Imperial Theology

When European powers, driven by an imperial theology, expanded their territories, they did so with an understanding that they were divinely mandated to civilize, evangelize, and transform the newly encountered societies. The concept of imperial theology originated in the backdrop of European colonialism from the mid- to the late nineteenth century and materialized during an era when African and Asian territories were predominantly colonized by European powers. These industrializing nations viewed the African and Asian continents as pools of raw materials, inexpensive labor, and territories primed for future settlement.

Religious imperialism embodies the ways in which religious convictions and practices were used to validate and support imperial power hierarchies. This strategy encompassed the religious dominance and regulation of colonized populations, frequently through the enforcement of European religious doctrines and the suppression of native spiritual customs. Imperial theology was designed for empire building, legitimized by a narrow and exclusive interpretation of the Judeo-Christian concept of the covenant. This interpretation positioned election as an exclusive vocation of Western Christendom within God's salvific plan. Western societies regarded themselves as divinely chosen, set apart to spread Christianity and "civilize" the world in preparation for God's kingdom.[24] The outcome of this theological perspective was a shift and transformation of theological principles into ideological categories underpinning political supremacy. This resulted in the "domestication" of God's universal covenant of grace with humanity in Christ, the territorialization of God's kingdom, the "politicization" of evangelism, and the "imperialization of the symbols of Christ."[25]

In the context of African Pentecostalism, echoes of imperial theology can be discerned. One manifestation of this is the adoption of a prevailing theological schema, such as religious discourses that perpetuate power dynamics within the movement and confer unmitigated power to an elite few. For instance, numerous Pentecostal leaders leverage rhetoric that renders them spiritually irreplaceable, concurrently crafting hierarchical constructs within their churches that safeguard their power and authority. These leaders demand obedience, submission, and fiscal contributions from their followers, who may constitute the economically marginalized. This can reflect colonial power dynamics, casting leaders in the role of "colonizers" and congregations as the colonized.

In a parallel and fascinating twist of earlier European imperial theologies, these Nigerian-founded churches are exhibiting a similar missionary zeal but claiming a distinct motivation and context. According to

---

24. Abraham Akrong, "Deconstructing Colonial Mission—New Missiological Perspectives in African Christianity," in Adogame et al., *Christianity in Africa*, 63–74.

25. Abraham Akrong, "Deconstructing Colonial Mission—New Missiological Perspectives in African Christianity," in Adogame et al., *Christianity in Africa*, 63–74.

them, rather than imperial expansion for material gain, their churches are engaged in a spiritual and religious expansion, emphasizing their divine call to deliver salvation and liberation. The ambition of having a church within a specific walking or driving distance in cities worldwide mirrors an aspiration to create a global spiritual empire. This spiritual empire is characterized by the teachings and preaching of the word of faith, aiming for universal liberation from all forms of oppression.

The efforts, as driven by Nigerian pastors and churches, suggest an evolution and recontextualization of the imperial theology narrative. The direction has shifted from the West to the South, specifically from Europe to Africa, and one wonders whether the impetus in intra-African Pentecostalism is different. European colonialism was largely propelled by the desire for economic enrichment and geopolitical power. However, religious institutions and missionaries frequently held a more altruistic or divinely ordained perspective on the purpose of imperial expansion. Despite these lofty Christian principles, the actual practice of European colonialism rarely lived up to them. Similarly, Nigerian Pentecostal churches argue that they are motivated by a spiritual mission to convert Africa to Christianity, but the evidence suggests that they might inadvertently be bolstering Nigeria's political, economic, and religious hegemony across the continent.

In essence, while the motivations may differ, the echoes of imperial theology can be discerned in the global ambitions of Nigerian churches. The question that emerges is: How will this modern iteration impact world Christianity, interfaith relations, and the geo-spiritual landscape? It showcases the changing face of religious dissemination in the twenty-first century and the pivotal role Africa, once a recipient, now plays as a significant exporter of faith-based movements. It also reveals how specific powerful individuals are being privileged in the religious realm, thereby undermining the primary objective of the mission mandate.

The classical mission mandate, found in Matt 28:18–20, affirms: "All authority on earth has been given to me. Therefore, go and make disciples of all nations, baptizing them in the name of the father, the Son and the Holy Spirit and teaching them to obey everything I have commanded you." This mandate affirms that mission begins with God sending his Son, Jesus Christ, as the means by which God reveals himself to humanity (*missio Dei*). The authority to make disciples is self-authenticating since disciples are made in the name and by the authority of God in Christ. The Gospel of John employs concepts like "abundant life" and "light" to express the multifarious nature and objectives of salvation. However, when the goals of disciple-making are extricated from the broader, multifaceted dimensions of salvation in Christ, the mission mandate becomes vulnerable to ideological manipulations. True Christian discipleship is rooted in aligning oneself with the teachings of Christ. It is about a personal journey of faith, where each follower of Christ is called to reflect on his words and live by them. No single disciple holds the authority to demand blind obedience from others; instead, each individual's connection with the teachings of Christ should guide their path.

The assertive influence of some African transnational Pentecostal churches, alongside their claims to indispensability and spiritual supremacy, can precipitate a devaluation or outright dismissal of local spiritual practices and cultural expressions in host countries. In instances where this occurs, it has led to a form of cultural and religious imperialism. Indigenous beliefs, traditions, and pastors of the church in these territories have been regarded as inferior or incongruous with the imported Pentecostal theology and its facilitators. Consequently, local religious practices and expressions have been marginalized.

The readiness of adherents of Winners' Chapel in Cameroon to adopt Nigerian transnational church practices, their affirmation of Bishop Oyedepo's spiritual power, and the accompanying temporal power structures personified by the missionaries unveils the magnitude of Pentecostal influence. This demonstrates how churches can skillfully employ religious ideologies to persuade transnational audiences to partake in and yearn for their spiritual offerings.

In the field of public diplomacy, the capacity of influential entities to induce others to emulate their example or desire their possessions is termed "soft power." Soft power encapsulates the shaping of others' preferences via attraction and appeal. It entails the strategic employment of cultural influence by dominant countries to advance their national interest within the global sphere in manners that simultaneously mirror the interests of other entities. Yet, an important question remains: How does the religious demography of host territories resonate with and shape the trajectory of transnational Pentecostalism?

Pentecostalism in Cameroon

The emergence of Pentecostalism in Cameroon is traced to the 1940s, when missionaries from Nigeria first introduced classical Pentecostal groups with origins in Europe. The first Pentecostal church to be established was the Apostolic Church of British origin in the late 1940s by I. O. Oyoyo, a Nigerian missionary. For many years the church remained in the Anglophone part of Cameroon, but after the Pentecostal boom following the democratization process of the early 1990s, it became national with congregations throughout the country.[26] The Full Gospel Mission was the second Pentecostal church to be introduced to Cameroon. Its creation was pioneered by Werner Knorr, a German missionary, who originally went to Nigeria but, in the late 1950s, migrated to Cameroon and with the help of his Nigerian assistants established the first Full Gospel Mission church in Muténgéné in 1961.[27] The church gained recognition in 1969 and has since spread to the ten regions of Cameroon. The Full Gospel Mission is arguably the largest Pentecostal church in Cameroon.[28] Its congregations have also been established in Chad and the Central African Republic.[29]

One of the first Pentecostal churches to be established without a foreign missionary initiative was the *Vraie Eglise de Dieu*, in 1959, by Nestor Toukea. In the mid-1990s the church claimed to have more than two hundred congregations in Cameroon, sixteen in Chad, and ten in the Central African Republic.[30]

The genesis of indigenous Pentecostalism in Cameroon can be traced to a group of revivalists led by Samuel Obakar, a schoolteacher and son of a Presbyterian pastor. Commencing in 1959, Obakar and his cohort established several non-denominational Pentecostal groups in Edéa, Douala, and Yaoundé. Their non-denominational stance facilitated rapid proliferation and the emergence of charismatic leaders.[31]

The aforementioned Pentecostal churches predominantly represent the classical and indigenous groups, often associated with the "holiness"

---

26. Gifford, *African Christianity*, 289.
27. Gifford, *African Christianity*, 289.
28. Gifford, *African Christianity*, 289–90; Akoko, "Ask and You Shall Be Given," 68.
29. Gifford, *African Christianity*, 289–90; Akoko, "Ask and You Shall Be Given," 68.
30. Gifford, *African Christianity*, 289–90; Akoko, "Ask and You Shall Be Given," 290.
31. Matthews Ojo, "Nigerian Pentecostalism and Transnational Religious Networks in West African Coastal Regions," in Fourchard et al., *Entreprises Religieuses Transnationales*, 406.

tradition and tracing their direct or indirect origins to European missions.[32] They advocated for personal ethics closely mirroring biblical ideals, promoting the avoidance of worldly ways, and fostering personal behavior and modest dress codes. However, the Pentecostal landscape underwent a significant transformation during the 1990s, with the emergence of neo-Pentecostal movements. These movements challenged the traditional theological ideas, preaching prosperity, health, and wealth to their followers. Birgit Meyer eloquently articulates this transition from African indigenous "Spirit" churches or classical Pentecostal churches to neo-Pentecostal churches as a new empirical focus. Paraphrasing Ruth Marshall-Fratani's comment,[33] Meyer comments that:

> Nothing can best evoke what is at stake than the salience of the contrast between the familiar image of African prophets from Zionist, Nazarite or Aladura churches, dressed in white gowns, carrying crosses and going to pray in the bush, and the flamboyant leaders of new mega churches who dress in the latest (African) fashion, drive nothing less than a Mercedes Benz, participate in the global Pentecostal jet set, broadcast their messages through flashy TV and Radio programs and preach the prosperity gospel to their deprived and hitherto-hopeless born again followers at home and in the Diaspora.[34]

Perceptibly, Meyer highlights the stark contrast between traditional African religious practices and the contemporary, flamboyant practices of new megachurch leaders. She underscores the radical shift in the expression of religiosity, particularly within African Pentecostalism. The "familiar image of African prophets from Zionist, Nazarite or Aladura churches" evokes a traditional, humble, and devoutly spiritual approach to religion. These leaders are portrayed as austere and dedicated to their faith, as demonstrated by their white gowns, crosses, and prayer rituals in the bush. Their image is one of modesty and religious purity. In stark contrast, the leaders of new megachurches are portrayed as flashy, prosperous, and globally connected. Their attire is trendy and their mode of transportation extravagant, indicating a level of material wealth. Their participation in the "global Pentecostal jet set" suggests they are part of a worldwide network of influential religious leaders. They make use of modern broadcasting technologies for their sermons, emphasizing their

---

32. Kalu, *Introduction to Pentecostalism*.
33. Corten and Marshall-Fratani, *Between Babel and Pentecost*.
34. Meyer, "Christianity in Africa," 448.

adoption of contemporary methods for spreading their message. These leaders preach the "prosperity gospel," which argues that faith can lead to material wealth and success in this life, a deviation from the humble lifestyle of the traditional African religious figures. The reference to their "deprived and hitherto-hopeless born-again followers" suggests that these new religious leaders have amassed a significant following among those who have experienced hardship and are seeking not only spiritual salvation but also earthly prosperity. Here then is the transition from a humble, traditional form of religious practice to a more affluent, modern, and globally connected version, mirroring broader societal changes.

While it would be an oversimplification to posit that the neo-Pentecostal churches have unilaterally supplanted the older Spirit and classical Pentecostal churches, the proliferation of these contemporary movements indeed signals a pivotal turn in the African indigenization of Christianity, particularly in its Pentecostal manifestation. This development has profound implications in the sociology of religion and the understanding of world Christianity. Consequently, Robert Akoko[35] has described recent dynamics within the Full Gospel Mission, the Roman Catholic Church, and the Presbyterian Church in the Anglophone parts of Cameroon, underscoring the emergent trends within Pentecostal Christianity in Cameroon.[36] Akoko suggests that classical Pentecostal churches, such as the Full Gospel and Apostolic Missions, are undergoing a significant theological transformation. They are shifting from preaching a gospel grounded in asceticism to one promoting prosperity. This paradigm shift is partially motivated by the economic crisis that enveloped Cameroon in 1982, necessitating the formulation of innovative strategies by some classical Pentecostal churches to finance their operations and attract new members. By offering employment opportunities to jobless citizens and preaching a prosperity gospel in contrast to one of asceticism, Pentecostal churches have successfully drawn members from historic mission churches.[37] In response, the historic mission churches, such as the Roman Catholic Church and the Presbyterian Church in Cameroon, have accommodated or even promoted the Pentecostalization of their congregations to curtail member defections to Pentecostal churches.[38]

35. Akoko, "Ask and You Shall Be Given," 66–80.
36. Akoko, "Ask and You Shall Be Given," 69.
37. Akoko, "Ask and You Shall Be Given," 102–22.
38. Akoko, "Ask and You Shall Be Given," 143.

Further insights into the reasons behind the exponential proliferation of Pentecostal churches in Cameroon, especially in the 1990s, is provided by Paul Gifford. His study elucidates the significant role of transnational missionary actors. The renowned German Pentecostal evangelist Reinhardt Bonnke's impactful crusade ministry in 1989 and 1990, including "Fire Conferences," pastors' workshops, and sermons delivered in various stadiums in Kumba and Bamenda, shows how transnational Pentecostal preachers operate.[39] Gifford's assertion that around 250,000 people from over 65 churches from diverse countries attended the crusade in Bamenda[40] illustrates the successful outcomes of transnational missionary engagements in aligning with their mission objectives. It is hence unsurprising that there is a growing presence of Nigerian preachers who, over decades, have migrated to Cameroon for missionary purposes, leaving an indelible impact.

Nigerian Pentecostal Influence

Independent Pentecostal churches from Nigeria started to negotiate and occupy religious space within Cameroon in the 1990s, and they have substantially fostered religious change in the country.[41] The late Benson Idahosa[42] of Nigeria, for example, was one of the most famous Pentecostal leaders on the continent who popularized the prosperity-type Christianity in the African sub-region.[43] Through his institution, the Idahosa Bible College in Nigeria, he facilitated the education of many Pentecostal leaders from Cameroon, Ghana, and beyond, who later returned to their home countries to establish Pentecostal churches.[44] An example is Dun-

---

39. Akoko, *"Ask and You Shall Be Given,"* 143; Gifford, *African Christianity*, 290.

40. Gifford, *African Christianity*, 290–92.

41. Matthews Ojo, "Nigerian Pentecostalism and Transnational Religious Networks in West African Coastal Regions," in Fourchard et al., *Entreprises Religieuses Transnationales*, 407.

42. Idahosa epitomized the health and wealth prosperity gospel in Africa and exemplified it through his flamboyant lifestyle. This practice has become pervasive throughout the African continent in the twenty-first century, with some prominent church founders and owners such as Bishop Oyedepo flying up to four private jets.

43. Matthews Ojo, "Nigerian Pentecostalism and Transnational Religious Networks in West African Coastal Regions," in Fourchard et al., *Entreprises Religieuses Transnationales*, 168–77.

44. Matthews Ojo, "Nigerian Pentecostalism and Transnational Religious Networks in West African Coastal Regions," in Fourchard et al., *Entreprises Religieuses*

can Williams, an alumnus of Idahosa's All Nations for Christ Bible Institute, who subsequently founded the Christian Action Faith Ministries International (CAFM) in 1979, marking it as Ghana's first indigenous charismatic church.[45] Many other church founders and preachers, following their visit to Idahosa's "Miracle Centre" in Benin City, have professed to have been significantly empowered by this experience. Gifford is therefore justified in suggesting that "Idahosa was probably the best-known church leader the Pentecostal explosion has produced in Africa and who was frequently to be found on American platforms."[46]

Another influential preacher from Nigeria is Tunde Joda, the founder of Christ Chapel International Churches of Nigeria, which has several congregations in Cameroon. Joda's popularity in Cameroon was legitimized by his widely read publication *Prosperity Now*, which resonated greatly with the Pentecostal audience in Anglophone Cameroon.[47]

However, only one Cameroonian Pentecostal preacher has managed to attain a status of international recognition. The late Zacharias Fomum was initially a member of the Presbyterian Church in Cameroon (PCC), but he left for the Full Gospel Mission, eventually establishing the Christian Missionary Fellowship International (CMFI) in Yaoundé. As a highly accomplished university professor, Fomum's reputation as a spiritual authority among Pentecostals was widely acknowledged. He established congregations across Cameroon and some in Nigeria, before his demise in 2009.[48] Additionally, he ran the Christian Publishing House, which has a branch in Nigeria. Fomum was credited with the authorship of over eighty books, with the most renowned being *The Christian and the Money: Banking in Heaven Today*.[49]

Christianity in Cameroon represents a vast array of religious manifestations, encompassing imported mission churches from Europe or the United States, classical Pentecostal churches that were introduced from Nigeria by European missionaries, and the burgeoning neo-Pentecostal churches predominantly introduced through Nigerian transnational

---

Transnationales, 168–77.

45. Matthews Ojo, "Nigerian Pentecostalism and Transnational Religious Networks in West African Coastal Regions," in Fourchard et al., *Entreprises Religieuses Transnationales*,170.

46. Gifford, *African Christianity*, 290.

47. Gifford, *African Christianity*, 290.

48. Drønen, *Pentecostalism, Globalisation, and Islam*.

49. Drønen, *Pentecostalism, Globalisation, and Islam*.

missionary activities. The establishment of neo-Pentecostal churches across international borders has contributed to the self-portrayal of these movements as influential transnational entities. This phenomenon, in part, stems from a concerted effort to project an international image, especially given their expansion of missionary activities beyond Nigeria.[50] Consequently, Nigerian neo-Pentecostal churches operating in Cameroon have added new threads to the nation's religious fabric, but the next section will suggest that the movement has not been allowed to flourish in Cameroon, to the same extent as in other African countries.

Religious Freedom and Government Ambiguity

When compared with Ghana and Nigeria, the growth trajectory of Pentecostalism in Cameroon appears to be relatively sluggish.[51] This can be attributed, at least partially, to the stringent control exerted by the government on Pentecostal churches or the relative paucity of indigenous religious movements, such as the Aladura churches, which have historically acted as a springboard for the proliferation of Pentecostal movements elsewhere. The rise of neo-Pentecostal churches in most sub-Saharan African nations, such as Nigeria and Ghana, was precipitated by a long history of Christian missions where independent churches signaled indigenous initiative and local adaptations of the doctrines and traditions propagated by the missionaries.[52] Aladura, or independent African churches, have therefore been historically acclaimed for paving the way for later developments in Pentecostal Christianity.[53]

The relative absence of Aladura churches in the Christian culture of Cameroon, coupled with the state's strict control of evangelical churches,[54] might explain the slow growth of Pentecostalism in Cameroon.[55] The Cameroonian state's preoccupation with security has led to the creation of a political culture of subordination, adopted by dominant religious

50. Matthews Ojo, "Nigerian Pentecostalism and Transnational Religious Networks in West African Coastal Regions," in Fourchard et al., *Entreprises Religieuses Transnationales*, 167–79.
51. Akoko, *"Ask and You Shall Be Given."*
52. Meyer, "Christianity in Africa," 447–74.
53. Meyer, "Christianity in Africa," 44.
54. Gifford, *African Christianity*, 293.
55. Drønen, *Pentecostalism, Globalisation, and Islam*, 90, quoting Gifford, *African Christianity*.

communities and consequently stifling religious and cultural transformations.[56] The situation is exacerbated by power dynamics in which the historic mission churches, enjoying privileged positions, collude with the government against renewalist churches to forestall challenges from emerging competitive congregations.[57] For example, following a 2013 government shutdown of certain Pentecostal churches on allegations of illegal practices, the Roman Catholic bishops cautioned against the lure of Pentecostal churches.[58] Thus, it is conceivable that well-established historic mission churches are leveraging their advantageous positions to instigate the shutdown of Pentecostal churches when opportunities arise. Yet, in theory, religious groups should be shielded by religious freedom acts, notwithstanding the secular nature of the country.

The Cameroonian constitution and Law 90–93 (December 19, 1990), along with other laws and policies, collectively ensure religious freedom,[59] providing the right of individuals to choose, practice, and change their religion, and guarantees the right of citizens to sue the government for the violation of any constitutionally protected freedom.[60] Cameroon is one of several African states that have declared themselves secular in the sense that no one religion is privileged over the others.

The Cameroonian state, while proclaiming secularism, seems to exhibit a contradictory stance through actions like subsidizing religious festivals such as the annual Muslim pilgrimage. Asonzeh Ukah reports a similar situation in Nigeria, where the state interferes in religious matters by subsidizing pilgrimages, appointing Muslim leaders, and funding the construction of worship spaces.[61] Similar concerns have been raised in Ghana over plans to build a national cathedral. These instances collectively highlight the prevalent ambiguity in the relationship between religion and state in most of sub-Saharan Africa, whereby "religion is neither fully established nor totally disestablished and free from governmental interference."[62]

---

56. Gifford, *African Christianity*, 292.

57. Gifford, *African Christianity*, 292. Also see Akoko, "Ask and You Shall Be Given," 187.

58. BBC News, "Nigerian Pastors Spread into Cameroon."

59. Freedom House, *Freedom in the World 2016*.

60. Freedom House, *Freedom in the World 2016*.

61. Ukah, "Redeemed Christian Church of God," 4.

62. Ukah, "Redeemed Christian Church of God," 4.

In Cameroon, the constitution does not define in any detail the specific legal-political ramifications of the concepts of secularity, neutrality, or independence from state intervention in the way in which they are defined in some other constitutions. None of the thirty-six constitutional articles, ten of which explicitly deal with freedom of religion and worship and various facets of church-state relations, define any of these three constructs in detail.[63] This vagueness leads to frequent persecution and shutdown of emerging churches by the government, under the pretext that they are engaged in extortion or misleading Cameroonian citizens. An article by André Caballero titled "Pray or Prey? Cameroon's Pentecostal Churches Face Crackdown"[64] uses the argument of Issa Tchiroma Bakary, Cameroon's former minister of communication, as an exemplar of how government officials interpret the activities of some Pentecostal churches. Minister Bakary had claimed that revival churches were causing public disturbance with loud services, exploiting vulnerable individuals, and that some pastors were engaging in criminal activities such as extortion. Using these premises, the government resolved to shutter churches perceived to be detrimental to societal welfare.[65] Among those targeted was Winners' Chapel, Bamenda, which was closed down in 2013. Another church that shut down is the Ministry Faith Banner in Douala. The church's founder, Pastor George Nfor Asongyu, refuted the allegations, arguing that the church was accused of excessive prayer, causing disturbances, breaking up marriages, and exploiting homes. Asongyu unequivocally denied these allegations: "This is not true... Even if there are churches that do that, it is not me. I know what call God has given me for this nation."[66] The complexity and the challenges faced by emerging Pentecostal churches underscore the unique dynamics of religious development in Cameroon.

In examining the growth of Pentecostalism in Cameroon and its juxtaposition with countries like Ghana and Nigeria, several factors emerge: The stringent government controls, absence of certain indigenous religious movements like Aladura, and the conflicting relationship between the state and Pentecostal entities in Cameroon all play a part. There is also a clear discrepancy between the proclaimed religious freedom in the nation's constitution and the actual actions of the government. This

63. Fombad, "State, Religion and Law in Cameroon," 58.
64. Caballero, "Pray or Prey?"
65. Caballero, "Pray or Prey?"
66. Caballero, "Pray or Prey?," para. 9.

complex interplay has led to a more subdued proliferation of Pentecostalism in Cameroon when compared to its neighbors.

Yet, it is important to consider the bigger picture: African Pentecostalism as a force that is transcending borders and making waves in the religious global landscape. Tomas Drønen points out that while the influence of Nigerian Pentecostal churches in Cameroon is recognized, there is a gap in a comprehensive analysis of their transnational nature.[67] To understand the full spectrum and implications of this transnational religious dynamic, it is crucial to examine the literature and perceptions surrounding African Pentecostalism. As we turn to the next chapter, we will explore these shifting paradigms, focusing on how African Pentecostalism, especially from the Southern continent, is writing the global narrative.

---

67. Drønen, *Pentecostalism, Globalisation, and Islam*, 5–8.

Chapter Two

Shifting Paradigms in African Pentecostalism

DURING THE LAST FEW decades, there has been an unprecedented upsurge in scholarship on African Pentecostalism and religious transnationalism, possibly because of the multiplication of African Pentecostal movements in local and global contexts. This situation echoes earlier predictions of a new worldwide religious resurgence emanating from Africa. As long ago as 1970, David Barrett predicted that the rapid growth of Christianity in Africa was a sign that Christianity could become a non-Western religion in the near future.[1] Eighteen years later, Andrew Walls posited that African Christianity ought to be recognized as potentially representative of twenty-first-century Christianity. Walls argued that:

> The Christianity typical of the twenty-first century will be shaped by the events and processes that take place in the Southern continents, and above all by those that take place in Africa.... The things by which people recognize and judge what Christianity is will (for good or ill) increasingly be determined in Africa. The characteristic doctrines, liturgy, the ethical codes, the social

---

1. Barrett, "AD 2000: 350 Million Christians," 63.

applications of the faith will increasingly be those prominent in Africa. New agendas for theology will appear in Africa.[2]

Andrew Walls emphasized the growing influence of Africa in shaping the global narrative and practice of Christianity. Twenty-first-century Christianity, according to Walls, will be largely shaped by the developments and activities taking place in Africa. In the light of new religious movements in Africa, this comment indicates that these movements, which often fall under the umbrella of Pentecostal or Charismatic Christianity, are not merely localized phenomena but are increasingly shaping global Christian thought, theology, and practice. These new movements, with their emphasis on spiritual warfare, prosperity theology, and direct divine revelation, are introducing new ways of being Christian that are influencing not just African Christianity, but Christianity worldwide.

The surge of Christianity in Africa is a remarkable story of growth and change. It is not just about more people becoming Christians, but also about how Christianity is reshaping the African landscape. While in Europe and many parts of North America and Australasia, Christianity seems to be fading, Africa is experiencing a spiritual renaissance. People are converting to Christianity at a rapid pace, and new churches are popping up everywhere to meet the spiritual needs of these new believers. It is a stark contrast to the decline of organized religion in the Northern Hemisphere, where secularism is on the rise. Whereas in Europe, former churches have been converted to a variety of secular uses, in Africa, buildings that were once cinemas, nightclubs, or mosques are being transformed into churches, showing the incredible power of religious conversion on the continent.[3] But it is not just about the numbers; it is the dynamism of African Christianity that is truly remarkable. African Christians are passionate about spreading their faith, and they are on a mission to share the message of Christianity with the world. It is not about allegiance to a particular church; it is a universal message that transcends borders and identities. African Christians are driven by a deep commitment to evangelism, seeking to bring the truth of Christianity to every corner of the globe.[4]

There is significant evidence to suggest that African Pentecostal movements are making progress in both intra-African and inter-continental

2. Walls, "Africa in Christian History," 2.
3. Asamoah-Gyadu, *African Charismatics*, 10.
4. Marshall-Fratani, "Mediating the Global and the Local," 278.

diasporic contexts, fueled by their mission-driven orientation. While some scholars applaud this global religious resurgence from Africa as a determining force in the twenty-first-century landscape of world Christianity,[5] others voice scepticism concerning the character of this brand of Christianity and its actual capacity to address the multifaceted socio-political, and cultural quagmires that continue to litter the African landscape with the debris of "dysfunctional neo-colonial political systems."[6]

The twentieth century marked a significant shift of Christianity to the global South, a trend that has continued into the twenty-first century. From 1970 to 2020, the percentage of Christians from Africa, Asia, or Latin America rose from 41.3 percent to an expected 64.7 percent, indicating a robust growth of Christianity in these regions compared to the global North, where Christianity's share of the population is declining. This shift was underscored by the election of Cardinal Jorge Mario Bergoglio from Argentina as Pope Francis, the first Latin American head of the Roman Catholic Church, highlighting the global South's increasing influence on Christianity. In Africa, Christianity's growth is particularly striking, with its proportion of the continent's population growing from 38.7 percent in 1970 to an expected 49.3 percent by 2020. Conversely, Christianity is on the decline in Europe, Latin America, and Northern America as a percentage of the population, with Europe experiencing a significant move away from faith toward agnosticism and atheism, compounded by aging populations and low birth rates. Renewalists movements, encompassing Pentecostal and Charismatic churches, have seen exponential growth, from 62.7 million in 1970 to an expected 709.8 million by 2020. This growth not only signifies Renewalists becoming a larger share of the global Christian population but also shows the dynamic nature of Christianity in the global South, where these movements are growing most rapidly, especially in Africa, Latin America, and Asia.[7] Despite the impressive statistics including David Barrett's earlier impressive research findings, that 22,800 Africans embrace Pentecostalism daily, the debate gravitates toward the quality, role, and significance of this form of Christianity,[8] and how it resonates with broader perceptions of the African continent.

---

5. Sanneh, *Whose Religion Is Christianity?*
6. Gifford, "Trajectories in African Christianity," 275–76.
7. Centre for the Study of Global Christianity, *Christianity in Its Global Context*.
8. Gifford, "Trajectories in African Christianity," 275–76.

Redefining Africa: Beyond Stereotypes

The African continent has long been viewed by external observers as a locus of calamities. The initial depiction of Africa as the "dark continent" by Welsh journalist and colonial explorer Henry Morton Stanley stemmed from its mysterious landscapes and cultures, previously unknown to many outsiders until the late nineteenth century. The continent's predominant characterization in the Western consciousness remains tinged with images of primeval irrationality, tribal anarchy, civil war, political instability, endemic violence, flagrant corruption, managerial incompetence, and acute food insecurity. Africa is frequently associated with the spread of debilitating diseases, HIV/AIDS, and the Ebola virus. Strikingly, some Westerners perceive Africa as a single territorial and cultural unit, an error which has often led to misplaced assumptions and misinterpretations of the continent's vast and diverse nature. This means that the complexity of Africa is often lost in translation, with the continent's diversity frequently reduced to homogeneity in Western discourse.

Molefi Kete Asante highlights this conundrum, stating that Africa remains the most misunderstood continent, marred by stereotypical images shaped by imperial European ambitions.[9]

Indeed, during the outbreak of the COVID-19 pandemic in March 2020, there were widespread assumptions that Africa would bear the brunt of the crisis due to perceived poor healthcare systems and overpopulation. However, these prophecies were largely unfulfilled, with the West instead enduring the majority of the pandemic's effects. Providing further substantiation of these claims is a comprehensive study conducted in September 2021 by researchers from the distinguished Leverhulme Centre for Demographic Science at Oxford University. The team collated an unparalleled dataset encompassing mortality statistics from twenty-nine nations, inclusive of a significant portion of Europe, the United States, and Chile, for which official death registers for the year 2020 had been rendered accessible. Their findings revealed that life expectancy underwent a decline in twenty-seven out of the twenty-nine countries under investigation, a decline substantial enough to undo years of advancements made in terms of mortality rates.[10] This data strongly

---

9. Mengara, *Images of Africa*, XIII.
10. University of Oxford, "Covid-19 Continued to Hit."

suggests that the COVID-19 pandemic has precipitated the most substantial decrease in life expectancy within Europe since the cataclysm of World War II.

In stark contrast, the World Health Organization's (WHO) assessment report proffers a different perspective about Africa, highlighting an upward trajectory in the latter's healthy life expectancy. This metric has seen an average increase of ten years per individual between the years 2000 and 2019, a rate of improvement that surpasses all other global regions during the same time frame.[11] Even though the report notes that the upheaval caused by the COVID-19 pandemic could potentially destabilize these significant gains, it remains fair to posit that the West is presently encountering more severe struggles in this vital aspect of human life, given its current downward trajectory.

In his book *Africa: Altered States, Ordinary Miracles*,[12] the highly respected African journalist Richard Dowden presents a more balanced view on Africa, intertwining perspectives and voices from a multitude of sources. His portrayal of the continent blends an honest appraisal of its struggles with an appreciation of the resilience and vitality of African societies. Dowden underscores the importance of Africa's cultural heritage and unique worldview, characterized by an immediate and intense engagement with the fundamentals of human existence, which starkly contrasts with the Western lifestyles often marked by alienation and the erosion of human values.[13] Indeed, Dowden's work serves to challenge prevalent stereotypes, applaud the creativity and diversity of African cultures, and spotlight the knotty challenges and prospects that Africa faces in the twenty-first century. The sphere of religion is one such domain that exemplifies Africa's profound diversity and complexity.

Religion in Africa

Religion in Africa is characterized by a diversity of beliefs, practices, and traditions. Traditional religions, which predate the arrival of Christianity and Islam, are still practiced by many people, particularly in rural areas. These religions are typically polytheistic and involve the veneration of ancestors and spirits, as well as the use of ritual and sacrifice to

---

11. World Health Organization, "Healthy Life Expectancy in Africa."
12. Dowden, *Africa*.
13. Dowden, *Africa*, 1–2.

communicate with the spiritual world. Christianity and Islam were introduced to Africa through trade, conquest, and missionary activities, and have had a significant impact on African religious practices and beliefs.[14] Today, Christianity and Islam are the most widely practiced religions in Africa, with millions of followers across the continent.[15] In addition to these major religions, there are a number of syncretic and new religious movements that blend traditional African beliefs with Christianity, Islam, or other spiritual practices. The syncretistic predisposition of Islam, Christianity, and African Religion is exemplified in Corey Williams's study of "Multiple Religious Belonging and Identity among the Yorùbá of Ogbòmòsó, Nigeria."[16] These new religious movements often emphasize healing, prosperity, and the power of prayer.

Christianity in Africa may be divided into the historic Mission Churches, African Initiated Churches, and African Pentecostalism. African Pentecostalism may itself be categorized as three different but closely related groups:[17]

1. Classical Pentecostalism. This is the initial wave of Pentecostalism that arrived in Africa in the early twentieth century through the efforts of Western missionaries. This form of Pentecostalism is characterized by an emphasis on the "baptism of the Holy Spirit," the use of spiritual gifts such as speaking in tongues, and a strong belief in divine healing and deliverance. Classical Pentecostal churches tend to be organized hierarchically, with a centralized leadership structure.

2. Indigenous/Independent Pentecostalism, also known as African Initiated Churches (AICs), emerged in the mid-twentieth century as a response to the dominance of Western missions and the perceived inadequacy of their theology and practices. These churches are often led by African pastors and emphasize cultural practices and expressions of faith. Indigenous Pentecostal churches tended to be decentralized, with greater emphasis on lay leadership and community participation.

---

14. Aderigbe, "Religious Traditions in Africa," 7–29.

15. Aderigbe, "Religious Traditions in Africa," 7–29. Also see Mwangi and Mwakio, "African Traditional Religious Ontology," 21.

16. Williams, "Multiple Religious Belonging and Identity."

17. Kalu, *African Pentecostalism*. Also see Kollman, "Classifying African Christianities," 3–32.

3. The emergence of the newer Pentecostal churches, commonly referred to as Charismatic or neo-Pentecostal churches, in Africa during the late 1970s through the 1990s, marks a significant evolution in the landscape of modern Pentecostalism. These churches represent an intriguing divergence from the traditional framework of classical Pentecostalism. Characterized by a more fluid organizational structure, the neo-Pentecostal variants are particularly notable for their entrepreneurial approach to leadership. Central to the ethos of these newer Pentecostal churches is the concept of prosperity theology. This doctrine places a strong emphasis on the belief that spiritual faith is closely linked to material wealth and success, diverging from more traditional religious teachings. Furthermore, these churches have adeptly harnessed the power of modern media and technology, integrating these tools into their worship and evangelistic efforts with remarkable effect. This integration signifies a blending of secular elements with religious practice, reflecting a contemporary approach to faith expression. The term "charismatic" is often associated with those individuals within older Roman Catholic and Protestant denominations who engage in the practice of spiritual gifts. Within this context, Roman Catholic Charismatics constitute a significant majority. However, the neo-Charismatic movement extends beyond these traditional boundaries, encompassing a diverse array of independent churches. These independent entities, which form perhaps two-thirds of the total, bring fresh and varied perspective to the Charismatic movement, further enriching its tapestry and broadening its appeal in the modern religious landscape.[18]

The three forms of Pentecostalism reflect the diversity and complexity of the movement in Africa. However, each has its own strengths and weaknesses. Classical Pentecostalism has a strong emphasis on spiritual gifts and divine healing but can sometimes be overtly hierarchical and authoritarian. Indigenous Pentecostalism has a greater emphasis on African cultural expression and community participation but may struggle with theological coherence and leadership challenges. The newer Pentecostal churches are often innovative and dynamic but have been criticized for their focus on material prosperity and lack of accountability.

---

18. For an in-depth exploration of the varieties or classification of African Pentecostal churches also see Anderson Allan, "Varieties, Taxonomies, and Definitions," in Anderson et al., *Studying Global Pentecostalism*, 13–29.

However, the boundaries between the different forms of Pentecostalism have increasingly become blurred; for example, most of them espouse the prosperity gospel. Robert Akoko, in his book *"Ask and You Shall Be Given": Pentecostalism and the Economic Crisis in Cameroon*, examines the transition from "classical" to modern Pentecostalism and from a gospel of asceticism on the earth in anticipation of spiritual riches and blessing in the afterlife, to a gospel of accumulation and celebration of wealth in this world.[19]

The Rise of Prosperity Churches

As economic hardship gripped Africa, particularly due to the World Bank's restructuring decisions leading to job losses and societal disruption, a fresh wave of hope emerged in the form of new-age Pentecostal churches. The new churches, often spearheaded by well-educated religious elites, offered spiritual solutions to the growing secular problems of the people. At the heart of these churches is the classic evangelical belief in being "born again"—a spiritual transformation promising salvation. This transformation, often associated with speaking in tongues, sets members apart as uniquely chosen by God. Followers are encouraged to invest both spiritually and financially in the church, with promises of blessings, success, and healing. This concept, known as the prosperity gospel, suggests that financial success and well-being are divine entitlements for believers. Faith, positive confession, and generous donations are portrayed as avenues to secure divine favor, manifesting as material prosperity.[20]

A Brief Historical Context

The origins of the prosperity gospel can be traced back to the teachings of prominent North American evangelists such as T. L. Osborn, Kenneth Hagin, Kenneth Copeland, E. W. Kenyon, A. A. Allen, and Oral Roberts. Originating in the late nineteenth and early twentieth centuries, this doctrine emerged alongside the growing popularity of positive thinking and the belief in the human mind's power to influence reality. American and some British Pentecostal evangelists advocated that faith could be harnessed as a powerful force for securing divine blessings, including

---

19. Akoko, *"Ask and You Shall Be Given,"* 1.
20. Oyedepo, *Mandate*, 91.

financial prosperity and physical healing. This doctrine gained significant popularity within the United States during the economic boom of the 1960s and early 1970s. Pentecostal leaders capitalized on this era, using the prosperity gospel to fund evangelistic work, establish media networks, and build churches, thereby supporting their financial aspirations. As the leaders amassed substantial wealth and resources to fulfill their needs, it became imperative to further propagate this doctrine.[21]

African Connection

The introduction of the prosperity gospel to Africa closely ties with its connections to North American prosperity evangelists. Brian Stanley highlights the theological influence of Derek Prince, a prominent Pentecostal figure whose teachings significantly impacted Christian thought, particularly in Africa. Stanley notes how Prince's understanding of spiritual realities, influenced by platonic philosophy, informed his understanding of spiritual realities and their interplay with the physical world, particularly in matters of health and prosperity. Prince's teachings on demonology and ancestral curses affecting one's well-being found resonance with existing African cosmologies or spiritual beliefs, which often recognize the impact of spiritual forces on physical life. His focus on the spiritual roots of material conditions aligned well with the African worldview that visible, physical maladies often have invisible, spiritual causes. Consequently, Prince's teachings provided a theological framework that blended traditional African beliefs with Pentecostal Christianity. That is one reason why the prosperity gospel, emphasizing health, wealth, and spiritual victory through faith, found a receptive audience in Africa.[22]

Training and Expansion

Numerous African pastors sought education through programs and correspondence courses offered by American prosperity gospel preachers. A notable example is Benson Idahosa, a student at Kenneth Hagin's Rhema Bible College, Oklahoma. Although Idahosa did not complete his course due to a perceived divine calling to return to Nigeria and continue his

---

21. Gifford, *Ghana's New Christianity*, 39.

22. Brian Stanley, "From Plato to Pentecostalism: Sickness and Deliverance in the Theology of Derek Prince," in Methuen and Spicer, *Church in Sickness*, 394–414.

mission, he founded his own Bible school in Benin City. This institution provided theological training to a significant number of Africans. Graduates from his school, including figures like Bishop Oyedepo, went on to establish their own churches and proliferated the prosperity gospel message across most of Africa.[23] Nigeria emerged as one of the earliest adopters of the prosperity gospel, and it has since played a substantial role in promoting and influencing Pentecostal Christianity across the African continent.

The "Nigerianization" of African Christianity

The "Nigerianization" of African Christianity signifies the burgeoning influence and supremacy of Nigerian Christians and Christianity, specifically Pentecostals, across the African continent. Nigeria is endowed with the largest population in Africa. It has a vibrant Christian community, and a thriving economy. These and many other advantages have positioned Nigeria as the principal exporter of Christian missionaries, preachers, and religious resources to other African nations. As previously observed in chapter 1, Nigerian Pentecostal pastors were instrumental in pioneering the brand of prosperity-driven Pentecostal Christianity in Africa, and they continue to dominate the movement across the continent. The ascendency of Nigerian Pentecostalism is often attributed to its emphasis on prosperity, miracles, and spiritual warfare. These aspects also visible in Ghanaian Pentecostalism resonate with followers of the movement in other African nations, who perceive it as offering solutions to poverty, illness, and societal dilemmas. Nigerian churches such as the Redeemed Christian Church of God, the Winners' Chapel, and Christ Embassy have, thus, established numerous branches throughout Africa.

The process of "Nigerianization" has been further expedited by the strategic employment of media and technology. Nigerian leaders have leveraged social media, satellite television, and other platforms to spread their message across the continent. This has led to the emergence of a digital Pentecostalism that transcends national and linguistic boundaries and creates a shared African Christian identity. Their transnational evangelization and mission goals have also been actualized through the training of pastors and missionaries, the exportation of founders' and

---

23. Matthews Ojo, "Nigerian Pentecostalism and Transnational Religious Networks in West African Coastal Regions," in Fourchard et al., *Entreprises Religieuses Transnationales*, 168–77.

leaders' books, multimedia materials, and the establishment of foreign branches led by Nigerian missionaries.

While the Nigerian and Ghanaian Christian influence has catalyzed a dynamic Christian culture across much of the continent, concerns regarding the preponderance of Nigerian perspectives in African Christian discourse have also surfaced. Additional apprehension has arisen over potential exploitations of local populations and cultures by Nigerian pastors and churches. In other words, the proliferation of Nigerian Pentecostalism could potentially trigger tensions with other Christian groups, including historic mission churches and indigenous Pentecostal movements, which perceive Nigerian Pentecostalism as authoritative, overly materialistic, and lacking in theological profundity. These developments warrant broader inquiries into the nature of African Pentecostalism and its impact on the African continent.

Paradoxes in African Christianity

In 2018, Agbonkhianmeghe E. Orobator published an insightful account of his spiritual journey and the interplay between faith and religion in the African context. A significant portion of the book involves an analytical re-examination of the exponential proliferation of Christianity in sub-Saharan Africa. He also tries to reconcile the growth patterns of Christianity in Africa with the experiential realities of the people despite the prosperity claims of Pentecostal churches. In a section referred to as "Pathological Performance and Prophetic Practice,"[24] Orobator investigates the multifaceted nature of religious affiliations within African religion, exploring what faith and religion signify for Africans, and how these elements operate, are utilized, and are potentially exploited.[25] Eccentric illustrations of Christian belief affiliated with certain African Pentecostal churches pervade the narrative. These include depictions of pastors or prophets asserting to communicate directly with God via cell phones; healers or spirit mediums claiming to extract diesel fuel from a rock in an apparent emulation of the biblical Moses drawing water from a rock as a demonstration of spiritual potency; prophets purportedly curing diseases with insecticides; or a pastor exhorting his congregation to consume live

---

24. Orobator, *Religion and Faith in Africa*, 77–79.
25. Orobator, *Religion and Faith in Africa*, 77–79.

snakes.[26] These peculiar practices underscore the complexities and some of the distinguishing characteristics of African Pentecostalism.

A BBC newspaper published in November 2016 validated accounts of a South African Pentecostal prophet enacting a healing ritual involving the spraying of insecticide on his congregants.[27] Further anomalous episodes include a preacher compelling his congregation to consume petrol under the pretense of it being transformed into pineapple juice, and yet another advocating for his followers to eat grass, flowers, and snakes. These grotesque illustrations represent practices currently extant within certain emergent neo-Pentecostal churches in Africa.

A recent case from Kenya, where a pastor encouraged his congregation to starve themselves to death in order to expedite their meeting with Jesus, is another poignant illustration. This pastor, Paul Nthenge Mackenzi, is a former taxi driver turned televangelist who led a Christian doomsday cult. Declaring the imminent end of the world, he promoted Shakahola as a safe haven for his followers from the purported approaching apocalypse.[28] The calamitous fate that befell numerous innocent individuals, combined with the brutal circumstances of their demise, can only be classified as a heinous crime of extreme deviance.

A distinguishing characteristic of African Pentecostalism lies in its association with spiritual warfare, involving the application of prayer and spiritual discipline to combat evil spirits and demons. This practice is frequently tied to beliefs in witchcraft and fears of spiritual attacks, which are perceived as ubiquitous threats in many African societies. It is critical to note that the Bible often serves as a strategic instrument in the hands of believers and church leaders, employed to combat these malevolent forces.

"The Materialization of Spiritual Grace and Power"

In African Pentecostalism, the concept of "materialization of spiritual grace and power" refers to the utilization of physical objects as conduits for divine intervention, closely paralleling the pre-Vatican II Catholic veneration of relics. This is particularly evident in the Pentecostal practice of imbuing objects like Bibles with the capacity to confer spiritual and material prosperity, as well as healing and social transformation. The

26. Orobator, *Religion and Faith in Africa*, 77–79.
27. BBC News, "South Africa's 'Prophet of Doom.'"
28. Wangira, "Kenya Starvation Cult."

Bible itself is revered not just as sacred scripture but as a repository of divine power. The manifestation of this materialization in African Pentecostalism can be delineated into three predominant methods:

Firstly, the prosperity gospel is a prevalent teaching that interprets the Bible as promising material wealth and health in exchange for faith and obedience. Scriptures such as Mal 3:10; Deut 28:1–14; and Matt 6:33 are frequently quoted to support the claim that financial giving, particularly tithing, is directly linked to receiving God's blessings.

Secondly, there is an emphasis on spiritual warfare, with the belief that the Bible equips believers with the knowledge and power to combat demonic influences. Biblical verses from Eph 6:10–18; 2 Cor 10:3–5; Ps 91:16; Col 2:15; and Jas 4:7 and others are used to validate this practice.

Thirdly, the emphasis on prophetic and charismatic gifts such as speaking in tongues and prophecy is seen as evidence of the Holy Spirit's presence. The Bible is used as a guiding force to authenticate and encourage these gifts.

An example of the materialization of spiritual grace is the innovation of "the mantle" by Bishop Oyedepo. He promotes the belief that materials like handkerchiefs, once in contact with him or his appointed representatives, are endowed with divine "unction." This practice is supported by recontextualizing biblical narratives such as those of Elijah, David, the woman with the issue of blood, and the apostle Paul to validate the idea that such materials can carry divine power.[29] Bishop Oyedepo claims that God endowed him with "the mantle" ministry for the liberation of humankind, and he outlines the manner in which the mantle should be administered within his congregations: the anointed fabric (typically a handkerchief) must originate from the prophet, that is, Oyedepo himself or his appointed representative. This anointed material is then entrusted to the designated steward of the congregation, who circulates the mantle row by row for individual members to make physical contact as directed.[30]

Bishop Oyedepo's mantle ministry claims to address a multitude of needs, with reported miracles like resurrection, healing of mental illness, restoration of fertility, and enhancement of academic performance.[31] The efficacy of the mantle is believed to stem from its origin with Bishop Oyedepo, which is reminiscent of the Catholic understanding of relics connected to saints.

29. Oyedepo, *Mandate*, 149.
30. Oyedepo, *Mandate*, 150.
31. Oyedepo, *Walking in Dominion*, 18, 215, 233.

In the perceptive understanding of Bishop Oyedepo's followers, the efficacy of the mantle resides not in its physical existence but in the transformative capabilities it embodies, such as healing and dispensation of supernatural blessings. However, the power vested in the mantle is perceived to be dependent on its origin, that is, it must come from Bishop Oyedepo. A mantle that does not share this pedigree is deemed powerless. In essence, it is the transference of spiritual prowess into physical objects like handkerchiefs, aimed at catalyzing affirmative, potent, and supernatural outcomes in the lives of individuals, that must be comprehended in this context.

This approach to spirituality in African Pentecostalism draws clear parallels with traditional Catholic beliefs concerning the sacredness of material objects associated with holy figures. Both traditions invest objects with spiritual authority, suggesting a transferable and tangible aspect of divine grace. Similarly, in both neo-Pentecostal and Catholic contexts, spiritual authority and apostolic lineage are pivotal, with the belief that certain individuals are especially anointed to serve as channels of divine power. The use of the "mantle" in Pentecostal practices underscores a movement toward a sacramental understanding of material objects as bearers of grace. This reflects a synthesis of faith and culture, where the spiritual and material are intertwined, much like the Catholic emphasis on the physicality of grace before Vatican II.[32]

The power of Bishop Oyedepo's mantle and its understanding among Winners' Chapel followers seems to underscore the propensity for faith-based practices to veer into the realm of magical thinking, blurring the line between faith in divine intervention and faith in a spiritual talisman. Therefore, it is important to critically analyze these practices and beliefs in the context of wider Christian theology and Pentecostal tradition. On the one hand, the faith-based actions of Oyedepo's followers can be seen as an expression of deep faith and trust in God's healing power, a theme common in many Christian communities as I have earlier illustrated with the Catholic church. On the other hand, these practices raise significant theological and ethical questions. The claims made by Oyedepo about the power of "the mantle" can be perceived as a personalization and monopolization of divine power and grace, which may potentially lead to the manipulation and displacement of faith from God to a human intermediary. As such, a discerning exploration of these practices in the light of the broader Christian tradition and ethical standards is necessary.

32. Bouyer, *Church of God*.

The "materialization of spiritual grace and power" in African Pentecostalism reflects the stratagems employed to leverage the faith of Pentecostal adherents in navigating the exigencies of their daily lives. By underscoring the transformative capacity of the Bible to reshape lives and bring forth material and spiritual prosperity, African Pentecostals have fashioned a unique form of Christianity, one deeply entwined with local cultures and traditions.

Scholars generally agree that religion in Africa is largely preoccupied with elucidating, forecasting, and modulating worldly events, and that African Pentecostalism, via the prosperity gospel and adept interpretations of biblical verses, is aimed at fulfilling these needs. However, concerns abound regarding the ramifications of the prosperity gospel's dominance in African Pentecostalism, particularly teachings centered on demonology, exorcism, health, and wealth. The critical question that emerges is whether these teachings, despite their widespread acceptance and propagation, have the potential to engender substantial transformations within the African demographic.

Pentecostalism and Development

Paul Gifford has consistently interrogated the correlation between the prosperity gospel and development in Africa. Gifford speaks of the "enchanted" religious imagination represented by African Pentecostalism, as opposed to a "disenchanted" form of Christianity embodied by Roman Catholicism, which, he argues, is more directly associated with developmental undertakings such as the construction of schools and hospitals, the establishment of micro-finance institutions, the monitoring of elections, conflict resolution, and human rights advocacy.[33] Gifford's critique insinuates that the "enchanted" Pentecostal emphasis on spiritual and miraculous interventions undermines tangible developmental efforts. However, this perspective has been met with dissent.

Contending with Pentecostalism

Paul Gifford's persistent underestimation of African Pentecostal churches' role in addressing Africa's socio-political exigencies has incited vehement criticism from scholars who perceive his claims as somewhat

---

33. Bouyer, *Church of God*, 73.

skewed and not entirely reflective of the churches' authentic motivations. This critique is encapsulated in Ogbu Kalu's intriguingly titled commentary "Yabbing the Pentecostals: Paul Gifford's Image of Ghana's New Christianity."[34] In this discourse, Kalu calls into question Gifford's pessimistic standpoint and critique of the movement's missionary endeavors. Using Ghana as a representative microcosm of the African continent, Gifford advanced the notion that Africa's ailments stem from self-interest among those in power, a glaring absence of good governance, and the obstinate tenacity of African leaders to maintain their grip on power. Within this Afro-pessimistic analysis of the continent, Gifford posits that the Pentecostal churches' message of prosperity, status, and success is ineffectual in mobilizing social capital and invigorating the political economy, thus leaving Ghana stranded on the periphery of the world's modern economic system.[35]

While acknowledging the depth and insight of Gifford's research, Kalu counters this argument, asserting that Gifford's evidence for African Pentecostalism's inadequacy in propelling the continent into the global sphere relies heavily on a single source—the media—and hence presents a myopic view. According to Kalu, the true measure of a church lies in its embodiment, proclamation, and enactment of God's reign in communities. Therefore, these three facets warrant a comprehensive, holistic study.[36] Kalu laments that social scientists confine their research to the content and mode of transmission of Pentecostal churches' messages, emphasizing their reliance on modern media technology and, by implication, their dependency on the West, or what Kalu terms "ecclesiastical externality."[37] In doing so, they inadvertently overlook the grassroots initiatives and active participation of adherents within the African Pentecostal movements. Hence, a more nuanced and holistic perspective is necessary to fully appreciate the dynamic and transformative potential of these movements.

---

34. Kalu et al., *Collected Essays of Ogbu Kalu*, 148–62.

35. Gifford, *Ghana's New Christianity*, quoted in Kalu et al., *Collected Essays of Ogbu Kalu*, 156.

36. Gifford, *Ghana's New Christianity*, quoted in Kalu et al., *Collected Essays of Ogbu Kalu*, 148–62.

37. Gifford, *Ghana's New Christianity*, quoted in Kalu et al., *Collected Essays of Ogbu Kalu*, 148–62

"Development from Below"

In his 2016 analysis of "African Christianities and the Politics of Development from Below,"[38] Afe Adogame critiques Paul Gifford's view on Christianity's role in African development. He argues that Gifford's perspectives are overly simplistic, ignoring the intricate layers and nuances of African Christianity. Adogame suggests that understanding the true essence of African Christianity requires tapping into local narratives, rather than just focusing on formal declarations and media reports.

This argument is of paramount importance, because it underscores the need for scholars to extend their methodological and analytical purview beyond authoritative sources and engage with the lived realities of adherents. The critical commentary presents a refreshing perspective, one that champions a more holistic and contextually sensitive approach to understanding the role of African Christianities in development. However, it raises questions about the ways Adogame's call for an appreciation of local narratives can be pragmatically integrated into broader research methodologies in the study of African Christianities and development.

The preceding arguments encapsulate methodological concerns concerning how researchers should approach studies in religion and world Christianity, especially in Africa, but they also question the actual relevance of Pentecostal churches in Africa, where socioeconomic and political challenges remain unabated. Intriguingly, it appears there is a presumption that African Pentecostal churches ought to act as catalysts for development within their nation-states.

One of the main questions arising from these comments is: Should Pentecostal churches be responsible for socio-political and economic development? To what extent should the church, or the Pentecostal church, be responsible for the socio-political and economic development in any society, besides its responsibility of providing spiritual nurture? Is economic development not principally the responsibility of the secular state, which has governance over a plural and multi-religious population? In other words, is it justifiable to assess a Pentecostal church's involvement in the socioeconomic life of a nation, using the same evaluative criteria applied to a secular government? The nuance here seems to be the conflating of responsibilities of the church with that of the state. Both entities operate within distinct realms, brandishing different types of power, dictated by their respective access to power and resources. We cannot

38. Adogame, "African Christianities."

assume that Pentecostal churches have the same power as nation-states to provide development.

However, while the primary obligation of Pentecostal churches centers on the provision of spiritual nourishment to their congregations, they have increasingly become involved in developmental initiatives. Many have instituted schools, hospitals, and an array of social programmes to confront challenges relating to poverty, health, education, and gender inequality. Nonetheless, it is crucial to acknowledge that these developmental initiatives should not be perceived as substitutes for government-led efforts. Rather, they ought to complement the work of the government and other developmental actors. Furthermore, Pentecostal churches should ascertain that their developmental initiatives are firmly anchored in the specific needs and contexts of the communities they aim to serve and should refrain from superimposing their own agendas on these communities. These communities should also maintain transparency in their resource utilization and ensure that their efforts do not inadvertently contribute to the further marginalization or exclusion of vulnerable groups.

Jehu Hanciles posits that African Christianity is innately equipped to adapt to fluctuating socio-political contexts by perpetually remodelling its religious maps, thereby bridging the gap between physical realities and spiritual needs in situations characterized by hopelessness and, often, destitution. He situates the emergence of Pentecostal churches in Africa within the backdrop of burgeoning cities, rife with socioeconomic dilemmas, providing fertile grounds for evangelistic crusades and the propagation of the prosperity gospel. Yet, he critiques the irrationality of constructing megachurches at astronomical costs, while the individuals they seek to reach remain in the throes of abject poverty.[39] As the role of Pentecostal churches in Africa continues to evolve, Jehu Hanciles points out an important dynamic in the religious landscape: the emergence of megachurches. Hanciles observes that as African cities expand and face a myriad of socioeconomic challenges, they become ripe grounds for the growth of Pentecostalism, particularly the prosperity gospel. However, a major critique arises when we consider the establishment of sprawling megachurches with towering costs in areas where most people are grappling with economic hardship. Such grand establishments stand in stark contrast to the poverty that surrounds them.

39. Jehu Hanciles, "Interpreting Contemporary Christianity: Global Processes and Local Identities," in Kalu and Low, *Interpreting Contemporary Christianity*, 84.

African Megachurches: A Double-Edged Sword?

The phenomenon of African megachurches presents an intriguing paradox that is hard to ignore. On the one hand, these churches serve as centers of hope and community in fast-evolving urban environments. Yet, the scale of their infrastructure and the opulence they exude raise questions about their alignment with the socioeconomic realities of their congregants.

Recent studies, like Wanjiru M. Gitau's exploration of megachurches, examine their role in the modern era. Gitau specifically highlights Mavuno Church in Kenya to show how megachurches often rise in regions undergoing significant socio-cultural shifts, offering guidance to the youth amid these changes.[40] Nonetheless, Gitau's analysis stops short of reconciling how the ostentatious wealth manifested in the construction of African megachurches aligns with the stark realities of poverty and deprivation experienced daily within these same communities. This critique underscores the necessity for a more nuanced and contextually sensitive understanding of the role of megachurches in African societies, especially in light of the paradoxical juxtaposition of abundant wealth and pervasive poverty. It raises critical questions about the socioeconomic responsibilities of religious institutions in addressing inequality and fostering sustainable development in the communities they serve.

Nigeria's Dual Reality: Prosperity Pulpits and Pervasive Poverty

In 2015, Bishop Oyedepo unveiled an ambitious vision: "The Ark," formerly known as the "Faith Theatre." Envisioned as a massive church auditorium, this project, with an inaugural budget of N45 billion (approximately $50.8), is poised to host up to one hundred thousand worshipers. Nestled on a vast, one thousand-hectare land, it boasts plans for a twenty-four–story mission tower, dedicated prayer spaces, a baptismal pool, shopping venues, and even a unique rotating altar. For Oyedepo, "The Ark" symbolizes a haven akin to Noah's sanctuary during the great flood. He assured his followers that this grand venture would progress without soliciting their donations.[41]

---

40. Gitau, *Megachurch Christianity Reconsidered*.
41. Sahara Reporters, "Oyedepo's Church, Living Faith."

This megachurch initiative mirrors the insights from Asamoah-Gyadu's work "God Is Big in Africa."[42] Gyadu identifies the trend among Pentecostal leaders of envisioning expansive projects as manifestations of the prosperity gospel. Such endeavors—monumental auditoriums, modern worship styles, and expansive media outlets—symbolize success and power. These megachurches, in their vastness, promise followers not just spiritual but also material prosperity.[43] However, in a country like Nigeria, where Bishop Oyedepo's grand visions are becoming a reality, the World Bank paints a different, more sobering picture. While these massive church projects soar, a significant chunk of the Nigerian population grapples with poverty.

On March 22, 2022, the World Bank called for urgent reforms in Nigeria, highlighting that despite its vast potential, over one hundred million Nigerians languish below the poverty line. Based on comprehensive surveys, the report detailed the underlying challenges: stunted economic growth, limited access to basic necessities, and weak labor markets. Most alarmingly, Nigeria stands out as a major contributor to poverty in sub-Saharan Africa, with nearly one in five impoverished individuals in the region residing in Nigeria.[44] This duality between the meteoric rise of the prosperity gospel and deepening poverty is perplexing. One Nigerian took to YouTube, urging Bishop Oyedepo to divert his resources from building churches to creating industries.[45]

Pentecostal churches, particularly in Nigeria, have surged in prominence and wealth. Their leaders offer a potent blend of divine intervention and material prosperity, a formula that resonates deeply with the hopes and needs of their followers. These adherents seek prosperity within a nation infamous for the highest global incidence of extreme poverty and corruption. Nonetheless, the allure of affluence, embodied by charismatic leaders, grandiose churches, successful businesses helmed by church founders, and hefty bank balances, continues to captivate even the most impoverished. This tantalizing vision of potential prosperity maintains their loyalty to these churches, fueled by the hope that they may eventually emulate their esteemed pastors' success.

Critics, however, castigate these practices as exploitation of faith and accuse church leaders of fostering unfounded optimism. While

---

42. Asamoah-Gyadu, "God Is Big in Africa," 390–92.
43. Asamoah-Gyadu, "God Is Big in Africa," 390–92.
44. World Bank, "Deep Structural Reforms."
45. Chinedu, "Nigerian Man Beg Bishop Oyedepo."

the allure of the prosperity gospel is evident, it is crucial to scrutinize its tangible impact on socioeconomic conditions. Despite its burgeoning popularity, the lack of a direct correlation between the prosperity gospel and reduced poverty highlights the need for a more comprehensive approach to socioeconomic development that extends beyond the sphere of religious institutions. Such approach could involve government intervention, public policy reforms, and strategic investments in sectors such as education, health, and infrastructure, which have a more direct impact on human development outcomes. However, it is important to acknowledge that, notwithstanding its ineffectiveness in directly ameliorating poverty among the indigent, there is empirical evidence to suggest that the prosperity gospel may facilitate upward mobility for individuals situated at the lower echelons of the middle class. This phenomenon can be attributed to the gospel's emphasis on prudent financial management, renunciation of profligate expenditure deemed spiritually deleterious.

The Prosperity Gospel Conundrum

In the light of rigorous analysis and wider discourses, it would be overly simplistic to suggest that African Pentecostal churches, exemplified by the Winners' Chapel, are solely concerned on erecting vast edifices to accommodate burgeoning congregations, with scant regard for alternative forms of human developmental initiatives. Empirical evidence suggests that numerous Pentecostal congregations are deeply involved in socio-economic pursuits.

Bishop Oyedepo, for instance, has established over a hundred educational institutions across Nigeria, each rooted in Christian principles. These establishments, ranging from primary to tertiary educational stages, are intended to empower the younger generation, foster human capacity, and augment the Nigerian educational system. The church proudly claims ownership of two universities, namely Covenant University and Landmark University, founded in 2002 and 2011, respectively. Inaugurated in 2002 under the visionary leadership of Bishop Oyedepo and in alignment with the principles of the Living Faith Church Worldwide, Covenant University has emerged as a vanguard in the realm of higher education. As a venerated member of illustrious academic consortia, including the Association of Commonwealth Universities, the Association of African Universities, and the National Universities Commission,

Covenant University epitomizes academic rigor and innovation. In a commendable feat, the Times Higher Education acknowledged Covenant University in the prestigious 401–500 echelon of global universities in 2019. A testament to its exceptional standards and expedited growth, CU proudly holds the distinction of receiving the swiftest operational license approval ever conferred by the National Universities Commission. Landmark University, established in 2011 through the foresight and dedication of Bishop Oyedepo, stands as a trailblazing private university in Nigeria, with a special emphasis on agricultural sciences. Born from the ethos of the Living Faith Church Worldwide, Landmark University is driven by a mission to catalyze an agrarian revolution, with the lofty goal of propelling Africa toward self-reliance in food security through the power of education. The university is at the forefront of nurturing graduates who are not only academically proficient but also imbued with the character and skill set necessary to address the continent's burgeoning food requirements. This progressive educational institution is fast becoming a crucible for future leaders and innovators in the agricultural domain, poised to make significant contributions to the continent's sustenance and prosperity.[46] The provision of quality education and job opportunities within these institutions underscores the church's relevance within civic society and its contributions to the development of Nigeria.

However, this positive narrative is not without contestations. There have been concerns regarding the affordability of these elite institutions, particularly considering the exorbitant tuition fees, for the average Nigerian or African with modest income. The paradox of the prosperity gospel coexisting with escalating poverty and surging insecurity, particularly in nations like Nigeria, amid the construction of opulent megachurches funded by substantial financial investments, seems to challenge the equilibrium between structural development and human development indices, despite the prosperity claims propounded by new Pentecostal churches.

This scenario encapsulates the inherent ambiguity pervading the discourse of African Pentecostal missionary work, particularly with respect to its dominant prosperity gospel. The preaching of this gospel, often buttressed with the promises of wealth and health, frequently appears utopian, considering that a significant number of Africans, including many adherents to this form of Christianity, continue to live in conditions of poverty and are susceptible to disease and other adversities.

---

46. Moor, "Revealed: 8 Incredible Businesses."

The raison d'être of these movements seem to elude our grasp, despite their avowed antagonism to the secularism prevalent elsewhere. Consequently, this serves as a salient reminder to scholars of world Christianity on the necessity for ongoing re-evaluation of the relationship between the prosperity gospel and the actual manifestation of prosperity within Pentecostal imagination and context.

Shifts in Understanding the Prosperity Gospel

Naomi Haynes has identified a discernible shift in understanding the prosperity gospel in African Pentecostalism. In her exploration of Pentecostalism in Zambia's Copperbelt, Haynes observed that when prosperity gospel adherents failed to attain the frequently espoused affluence from prosperity preachers, religious leaders proposed an alternative conceptualization of prosperity. This revised interpretation is marked not by uniform, individualistic wealth, but by progression along a gradient of material gain, facilitated through relationships spanning divergent economic statuses. This reformulated understanding serves to incorporate Pentecostals into broader discourses on prosperity within Pentecostal spheres, accommodating material inequality and advocating for wealth proliferation.[47]

The majority of Pentecostal churches acknowledge the disparities among their congregants in terms of income distribution, wealth accumulation, educational attainment, health status, autonomy, prestige, and political power, among other desired social attributes, across groups defined by social classes, occupations, age groups, and sexual orientation. Prosperity teachings often encapsulate and endorse wealth distribution among church members, stimulating the more established individuals to aid and provide opportunities for their less privileged counterparts.

For example, Oluyemi Oluleke Osinbajo, the former vice president of Nigeria from 2015 to 2023, also serving as a pastor of the Redeemed Christian Church of God, wielded political influence due to his elite government position, as well as religious power within the church. Under the concept of material inequality and wealth promotion, the vice president was expected to use his political power to empower fellow church members, aiding them in securing employment or accessing privileges not typically available to those outside their religious affiliation.

---

47. Haynes, "Pentecostalism and the Morality of Money," 1.

Most Pentecostal churches have evolved into extended family structures where assistance is provided during periods of illness or financial hardship. Greater involvement in the church often equips individuals with skills beneficial in both their personal lives and professional spaces. This dynamic illustrates how Pentecostal churches instigate social change both within their immediate contexts and beyond. However, my example of the Nigerian vice president wielding both religious and political power for the benefit of his fellow church members and potentially other Christian groups invites inquiries into the intersection between politics and religion, and the resulting emergence of a new elite class in Africa.

Theocratic Political Elitism

Academic discourse in the areas of political science, religious studies, and sociology is increasingly engaged with the phenomenon of a burgeoning theocratic political elite in Africa, involving the relationship between religion and politics. In *Worlds of Power: Religious Thought and Political Practice in Africa*,[48] Stephen Ellis and Gerrie ter Haar examine the dynamics of theocratic political elitism on the African continent. They suggest that the foundational structure of such political systems is deeply entrenched in religious ideologies, with a pronounced emphasis on Pentecostalism. This religious framework serves as a tool for political figures to authenticate their authority and to consolidate support among the populace.[49]

In nations marked by a high degree of religious fervor, such as Nigeria, the interweaving of political discourse with religious narrative and symbolism is a strategic move employed by political leaders to resonate with, and rally, their constituents. The interdependency between the religious and the political spheres is further exemplified by the alliances some politicians forge with Pentecostal pastors, and the reverse is true. Such alliances are often tactical, ensuring that political figures receive the backing of the pastors' congregations and the pastors receive the backing of the politicians, thereby weaving their political aspirations with the spiritual expectations of the people. The architecture of theocratic politics within the African context leans heavily on religious ideologies, predominantly Pentecostalism, as mechanisms to validate the power of politicians and garner support. In theocratic political elitism, individuals

---

48. Ellis and Haar, *Worlds of Power*.
49. Ellis and Haar, *Worlds of Power*.

in positions of political power, who possess significant religious influence, often draw upon religious doctrines to justify their governance. By framing their political agenda within a religious context, they aim to provide a divine justification for their policies, effectively dampening dissent and criticism by attributing their leadership to a higher, ostensibly unimpeachable, spiritual mandate.

Examples of theocratic political elites in Africa include President Yoweri Museveni of Uganda, who has been in power since 1986. President Museveni arguably exploits religious convictions to fortify his political legitimacy. He has endorsed the proliferation of Pentecostalism in Uganda and has appointed numerous Pentecostal leaders to government offices.[50] Similarly, in Kenya, Pentecostalism has amassed considerable influence, with many religious figures wielding political power and using their religious authority to affect governmental policies. Churches in Nairobi's bustling streets are not just places of worship; they have become arenas of political mobilization, with pastors and bishops frequently commenting on, and sometimes directing, the nation's political discourse. From the late twentieth and early twenty-first century, Kenya has significantly witnessed an intertwining of the pulpit and the political podium, with Pentecostal leaders transitioning from spiritual shepherding to political leadership.

In Cameroon, manifestations of theocratic political elitism are particularly evident, with the late self-styled prophet Frankline Ndifor of Kingship International Pentecostal Church, Bonaberi. In April 2020, self-proclaimed prophet Ndifor orchestrated a symbolic campaign against the COVID-19 pandemic, extending donations of vital sanitation supplies to both the inhabitants of Douala and the Littoral Regional Delegation of Public Health. Notably, Prophet Ndifor had not only established himself as a religious luminary but also ventured into the political sphere. In 2018, he sought the presidential office under the aegis of the National Citizens Movement Party (NCMP). His candidature was emblematic of a departure from traditional politics, which he critically evaluated as a failing system. Despite his non-conformist stance, Ndifor was aspirational, envisioning a transformative leadership for Cameroon through the ethos of the NCMP. Nonetheless, his electoral journey culminated in his acquisition of a lowly seventh position among nine contenders, securing only 0.67 percent of the total votes. The unexpected demise of Prophet Ndifor in 2020, attributed to the COVID-19 pandemic, sparked a maelstrom of

---

50. PPU, "You Will Do Miracles."

conjectures. Some followers and close associates suggested that his death was not merely an unfortunate health-related incident but a calculated assassination by government officials threatened by his rising political influence. A close spiritual associate of the prophet detailed an account in which the prophet's sudden ailment after a high-level meeting in Yaoundé was indicative of a potential poisoning.[51]

The convergence of theocratic pursuits with political aspirations, as illustrated by late Prophet Ndifor's life, underscores the complexities arising from the amalgamation of religion and statecraft. When intertwined, the domains of religion and politics can be fertile ground for conjectures, especially in the face of unforeseen adversities. This complexity is further articulated by a sympathizer, who remarked that "this is a pastor that has been laying hands on the sick and claiming that he cures COVID-19. If you, the person that claims that you are curing COVID-19, are dead, what about those you laid hands upon? Now that he is no more, the fate of those he claimed to heal remains uncertain."[52] This poignant observation underscores the dilemmas and questions arising from such theocratic-political intersections.

In Nigeria, several Pentecostal leaders possess substantial political sway and have been observed manipulating their religious authority to shape governmental policies and decision-making. A notable incident happened in March 2016, when Governor Nasir El-Rufai of Kaduna State proposed a bill to regulate religious preaching across the state. The new bill was aimed at replacing the Kaduna State religious preaching law of 1984, and it generated significant controversy, particularly within Nigeria's Pentecostal community known for its exuberant religious activities. Apostle Johnson Suleman of the Omega Fire Ministries International, one of Nigeria's most prominent and controversial Pentecostal leaders, offered a bold rebuttal.

In a widely circulated video, Suleman cautioned against challenging Nigeria's constitutional right to freedom of worship and asserted a willingness to test the power of his faith against the state's authority:

> I am not against sanitizing a state, but you say people should get license for practicing, it is not applicable in Nigeria. Even a herbalist does not get a licence for practicing herbalism. When you say license for preaching you are standing against the

---

51. Blair, "Pastor Dies from Coronavirus."
52. Blair, "Pastor Dies from Coronavirus," para. 4.

constitution of Nigeria, which says freedom of worship. I have no problem! We can test powers now! Listen! There are certain laws that cannot happen in this country; Not when Nigeria is under God. If need be, over this matter, heaven will intervene. I am saying this to the Executive Governor of Kaduna state, "Revoke this law or die."[53]

Apostle Suleman's provocative reaction and threats toward a state governor's leadership brings to question the hierarchical relationship between the state and the church. His assertion that he and the governor could "test powers," alluding to the powers of state law and divine intervention, exposes his interpretation of national politics, where at least two forms of power exist in opposition to each other, with divine power reigning supreme.

Such remarks by the apostle call to mind the concept of Pentecostal nationalism or a political theology of alternative state formation. This notion, rooted in the colonial and mainstream church's control of political and ecclesiastical order in Nigeria and other parts of Africa, suggests that religious leaders, particularly those who hold significant sway within their religious communities, might erode the secular principles of governance when they lend their support to specific religious or ideological causes.[54] The point seems to be that the post-independence Nigerian Pentecostal churches have also become dissatisfied with the ways various governments are administering the country and many Pentecostal pastors are now meddling in political affairs.

Theocratically oriented politics can incite a conflict between secular ideals intrinsic to modern democracy and religious values that underscore African societies. A prime example of this tension is the recent passage of the Anti-Homosexuality Act by the Ugandan parliament, which has incited international backlash and led to a suspension of aid from several affluent countries. The potential erosion of secularism and the risk of religious discrimination and persecution highlight the critical need to balance religious values with the principles of democratic governance and human rights.

Religion can be a powerful force for social change and political engagement, but it is important to recognize the diverse and often competing interests that exist within religious communities, as well as the need to balance religious values with principles of democratic governance and

---

53. Ekwere, "'El Rufai, Either You Revoke.'"

54. Allan H. Anderson, "'Stretching out Hands to God': Origins and Development of Pentecostalism in Africa," in Lindhardt, *Pentecostalism in Africa*, 54–74.

human rights. It is also important to ensure that religious movements and individuals involved in politics do not undermine the fundamental principles of democracy and that they promote an inclusive vision of society that recognizes the diversity of religious and cultural traditions. Theocratic politics can provide a moral compass and promote social justice, but it can result in religious discrimination, the erosion of democratic values, and the concentration of power in the hands of a few individuals, not least, in the context of the prosperity preaching.

The prosperity gospel in African Pentecostalism focuses on the values of social justice, community building, and holistic well-being. Instead of emphasizing individual wealth and success, it might be helpful for Pentecostal churches to increase their focus on empowering communities to work together to address issues of power, inequality, and social injustice. This approach will create a holistic, inclusive, and socially just Christian culture that is more in line with the teachings of Jesus Christ. It will also justify Pentecostal transnationalization on grounds of spiritually and socially empowering neighboring countries.

Intra-African Pentecostalism

Literature on transnationalism predominantly examines the tangible circulation of individuals, services, and information across territorial boundaries, often propelled by transnational institutions and macro-trends within the global political economy. Typically, these movements occur from one nation to another or across continental expanses. However, the concept of intra-African Pentecostalism deviates from this paradigm. It denotes the internal engagements of Pentecostal churches within the African continent, where religiously motivated migrations and interactions are occurring.

One of the aims of this book is to analyze evidence concerning the modalities through which religious communities in Nigeria forge connections with their counterparts in Cameroon. This analysis takes into consideration the motivations underpinning these cross-border missionary movements. In the following sections, I will examine the reasons advanced by African Pentecostal churches for their cross-border missionary activities in Africa.

The Failure of European Christianity

When Christianity was introduced to Africa by Europe and North American missionaries, local beliefs, cultures, and traditions were often sidelined. Instead of embracing Africa's rich cultural diversity, missionaries imposed a Europeanized version of Christianity that did not resonate with African traditions and spiritual needs. This Westernized Christianity is viewed by some commentators as a negative outcome of missionary efforts. Research on missionary activities reveal their struggles in Africa, including hunger, isolation and disease, all against the backdrop of Africa's internal tumultuous slave trade. A key debate is whether missionary Christianity truly met the spiritual needs of Africans and drew them away from their indigenous beliefs. Converts who returned to their traditional religious practices were labeled as having "backslidden." This topic is significant because some older Christian denominations stress the importance of converts completely letting go of past religious practices. However, many converts often continue to honor ancestral and local deities alongside their new Christian beliefs.

Within the Presbyterian Church in Cameroon, for instance, candidates for confirmation of their baptism are required to publicly renounce certain practices before the congregation. Some of the questions include: "Do you renounce Satan and all his evil works, such as witchcraft, magic, fortune telling? Do you renounce idolatry in all its forms such as invoking the dead, ancestral sacrifices, the use of charms and every other type of worship which is in opposition to God and his Christ, and does not offer him true honor?" The candidate is expected to respond, "I renounce them." In this way, all baptized and confirmed adult Christians are expected to "make a complete break with their past"—sinful, and idolatrous ways. But despite these declarations, it remains challenging to evaluate whether these Christians genuinely sever their ties with past practices following their public declarations in the church. Evidence suggests that many church-going Christians continue to consult diviners and pay homage to supernatural powers outside the Christian faith.

During one of my annual leaves to Cameroon in 2019, I reconnected with a former secondary school classmate in Buea, now an academic and adherent of Winners' Chapel. Intrigued by his transition from Roman Catholicism, a faith shared by his family and uniformly observed during our youth, I engaged him in a discussion that would later enrich this book project. What unfolded was a compelling exploration of the resilience of indigenous belief systems amid the encroachment of Western religious orthodoxy. My friend invited me to his house to explain the rationale behind his religious realignment. After a warm welcome by his wife, whom I was meeting for the first time, I was ushered into their living room where he presented an eclectic collection of religious texts and artifacts: prominently, a Bible, the foundational *Mandate* of Winners' Chapel by Bishop Oyedepo, a Qur'an, issues of the Watchtower from Jehovah's Witnesses, a yoga manual acquired in China during one of his professional trips, and a rosary retained from his Catholic upbringing. He revealed a narrative of existential uncertainty and spiritual pragmatism. In a world besieged by unpredictability, he admitted to an eclectic approach to spirituality, one that ostensibly hedged against the spiritual risks of exclusive doctrinal commitment. His syncretic spiritual toolkit included frequent consultations with a diviner from Esu, a village in Menchum Division of the North West region of Cameroon, notorious for its dark magical practices, to secure protection against malevolent forces beleaguering his family.[55]

This poignant anecdote epitomizes the profound religious pluralism pervasive in Africa today. It underscores not only the failure of European Christianity to fully supplant indigenous spiritual practices but also highlights the African recourse to a multiplicity of religious beliefs as a bulwark against life's capricious adversities. This phenomenon reflects a broader, more complex dialogue between traditional African religious identities and the monotheistic imports of colonial and post-colonial missionaries. Such narratives are crucial in understanding the dynamic landscape of contemporary African spirituality, where the past and present coalesce in unique expressions of religious identity.

In response to perceived inadequacies of historical Western missionary efforts, African Pentecostal churches and charismatic prophets have risen, asserting that they offer the solutions to issues left unaddressed by established Christian missions. Prominent among these is Pastor Olukoya's Mountain of Fire and Miracles Ministries (MFM), which presents itself as a vanguard of contemporary Pentecostalism, particularly in its dedication to the revival of apostolic miracles and an ethos of stringent holiness as the bedrock for salvation. MFM is distinctive in its martial spirituality—believers are schooled in the art of spiritual warfare, engaging in ceaseless prayer as a means to counter both corporeal

---

55. Personal interview with Terence Mbo (pseudonym) in Buea (Nov. 10, 2019).

temptations and demonic forces. The relentless and perpetual prayer sessions at MFM "Prayer City" signify an institutional embodiment, rendering MFM a sanctuary for those seeking deliverance from spiritual malaise.[56] Throughout Africa, Pentecostal church founders and leaders like Olukoya claim to be helping people confront challenges they believe arise from demonic influences.[57]

The deliverance ministry of MFM is not simply an accessory to the church's function; it is its quintessence. MFM's unequivocal message is that deliverance from demonic influence is a non-negotiable element of the Christian journey. The church's aim to "purify the Pentecostal dirtiness of this age" points to a self-assigned role of rectification within the Pentecostal movement, asserting a purest return to a form of Christianity that it perceives as corrupted by worldly compromises.[58]

Researchers have also observed that the Winners' Chapel and the Redeemed Christian Church of God have expanded their reach across borders because of the perceived inability of early missionary Christianity to address Africa's spiritual needs and the lack of influential religious figures beyond Nigeria. Ogbu Kalu believed that this missionary push aimed to fill a spiritual void in Africa and reclaim the continent for Christ. He suggested that while early missionary efforts introduced Christianity, many followers blended it with local beliefs, potentially diluting its message. This made it challenging to address the negative spiritual influences that plagued many Africans. To combat this, Pentecostal churches employ dynamic evangelism, modern media, and effective management techniques to foster a deep personal faith in Jesus Christ and the Holy Spirit.[59] Kirsty Rowan, in her article "Who Are You in This Body?," sheds light on how Pentecostal churches, both in Africa and globally, are actively addressing the spiritual well-being of their members.[60]

The perceived failure of mission Christianity to combat evil forces in Africa has contributed to the dramatic growth of African Pentecostalism since the 1990s, with its emphasis on overcoming spiritual and physical problems. The catalyst for this growth has been a combination of spiritual drought in Africa, the desire to claim the continent for Christ,

---

56. Mountain of Fire and Miracles Ministries, "Welcome."
57. Gifford, *Christianity, Development and Modernity*, 18–29.
58. Mountain of Fire and Miracles Ministries, "Welcome."
59. Kalu, *African Pentecostalism*, 88.
60. Rowan, "'Who Are You?,'" 247–70.

and the aspiration to liberate Africa from the remnants of colonialism.[61] For example, Reuben Ezemadu, the leader of the Christian Mission Foundation, declared in 1977 that Nigerian Christians would strive to bring the gospel to the darkest places in Africa. This was intended to challenge prevailing perceptions of Africa as the "dark continent," and to counteract the opposition and resentment toward white missionaries in Africa.[62] The intercessors for Africa, as some of them were later called, networked throughout the continent to present a better image of Africa.[63]

Notably, the impetus for a pan-African ideology has also played a significant role in promoting the spread of Christianity across Africa. The propagation of Christianity throughout the continent of Africa sought to reshape Africa's image positively. Thus, the intersection of Pentecostalism and pan-African ideology has fostered an alternative religious narrative, shaping a unique African Christian identity independent of Western influences.

Christian Pan-Africanism

In recent years, a growing cognizance has dawned among African Christians, not only about their shared historical and cultural lineage but also their distinctive potential in molding Africa's destiny. This awakening has led to the emergence of Christian Pan-Africanist movements across Christian denominations.

The roots of Christian Pan-Africanism highlight a crucial historical intersection between religion and the socio-political ideology that sought to unite African people both on the continent and in the diaspora against colonial oppression and racial discrimination. Edward Wilmot Blyden, Joseph Ephraim Casely Hayford, and Tiyo Soga were among the early pan-African thinkers who used their Christian beliefs to frame their arguments for African unity, dignity, and self-determination. Their Christian faith, which often emphasized values such as equality, justice, and communal support, provided a moral and ethical foundation for their activism and intellectual work.

The emergence of Pentecostalism in the twenty-first-century pan-African context can be seen as a continuation of this legacy, albeit in a

---

61. Kalu, *African Pentecostalism*, 123.
62. Kalu, *African Pentecostalism*, 124.
63. Kalu, *African Pentecostalism*, 124.

more contemporary and dynamic fashion. Pentecostal, Christian Pan-Africanism is a burgeoning force, striving to unite African Christians across national and denominational lines. Their ultimate pursuit? To foster the growth of the African church and craft solutions to the myriad socio-political challenges faced by the continent. The dynamism of the Pentecostal movement, with its characteristic emphasis on spiritual gifts, and societal outreach, has been pivotal in sculpting this Pan-Africanist narrative in Africa. These Pentecostal churches assert their vanguard position in tackling societal plagues like poverty, corruption, and iniquity. Moreover, they are the torchbearers igniting a sense of African unity and camaraderie among Christians. A hallmark of this Christian Pan-Africanism is its emphasis on the empowerment of African Christians. This vision manifests in nurturing indigenous leadership and seamlessly integrating African languages and cultural nuances into worship.

One cannot discuss this phenomenon without mentioning the Zimbabwe Assemblies of God Africa (henceforth ZAOGA). David Maxwell heralds ZAOGA as the epitome of African transnationalism and Pan-Africanism.[64] He masterfully weaves the spiritual and pan-African motives of this movement, highlighting its trajectory of expansion since the 1990s. These churches, through an interconnected system of mutual support, ensure a harmonious equilibrium that augments growth. "Small cottage meetings became Home Groups, then 'Cells,' and their spread across townships became the 'chain of multiplication.'"[65] For instance, the Assemblies of God in Manicaland would support sister assemblies in Mozambique in monthly and bi-monthly Sunday meetings, while members in Bulawayo would take care of those in Botswana.[66] The creation of these intricate networks of mutual assistance have characterized the creation of new ZAOGA church branches and their spread across the continent of Africa and beyond.

The ethos of ZAOGA's Pan-Africanism is tethered to Maxwell's concept of "post-colonial redefinition of mission."[67] ZAOGA's archbishop juxtaposes Africa's vibrant church initiatives with the diminishing spiritual essence in the West, emphasizing that the true church's heart now beats in Africa. Africans are encouraged to cherish and propagate the genuine gospel rather than imitating a Western world seemingly drifting

64. Maxwell, *African Gifts of the Spirit*, 163–83.
65. Maxwell, *African Gifts of the Spirit*, 166.
66. Maxwell, *African Gifts of the Spirit*, 169.
67. Maxwell, *African Gifts of the Spirit*, 170.

into spiritual decline. "I believe this is our time. It is time for black people and their churches to rise up. Don't go to Europe and learn their ungodly things. Learn what they used to do before. . . . It is time for Africans to bless Western nations with the true gospel."[68]

Central to ZAOGA's mission strategy is a focus on grassroots. They champion the belief that the path to a thriving church lies in fostering small, localized groups committed to discipleship and evangelism.[69] In essence, this aligns with the broader theme of contextualizing the gospel. The essence is that local nuances and community-driven initiatives are invaluable in interpreting the teachings of Jesus Christ and ensuring that religion harmoniously coexists with cultural and societal processes.

The reciprocity between religion and social processes is well articulated in the literature. André Droogers underlines the mutual influence between religion and surrounding cultures or society. Several questions posed by Droogers are essential for transnational studies, including queries about the autonomy of cultures in relation to their interaction, the degree of cultural homogeneity, and the connection between universal human nature and culture.[70] The basic questions raised by Droogers, and those that are crucial for our purposes, include: How does the autonomy of cultures relate to contact between them? Does culture make people (a culturalist view), or do people make culture (a constructivist view)? To what degree is a national or ethnic culture homogeneous? How are the universal human and the cultural related? Finally, and most importantly, when Pentecostalism spreads to other cultures, how does its specific character relate to that of those other cultures and to human nature in general, and how does this relate to the internal organization of that religion?[71] These questions are instrumental in comprehending the character of intra-African Pentecostalism and other aspects of mobilization that ensure the establishment of the church in new "mission fields."

---

68. Maxwell, *African Gifts of the Spirit*, 163.

69. Maxwell, *African Gifts of the Spirit*.

70. André Droogers, "Globalisation and Pentecostal Success," in Corten and Marshall-Fratani, *Between Babel and Pentecost*, 42.

71. André Droogers, "Globalisation and Pentecostal Success," in Corten and Marshall-Fratani, *Between Babel and Pentecost*, 42.

Theorizing Intra-African Pentecostalism

African neo-Pentecostal churches, in their transcendent nature, extend beyond local boundaries, networking and spreading as far as they possibly can. While their transnational characteristic has been increasingly underscored in the academic literature, these examinations typically focus on their movement from one locale to another, neglecting other power-related dynamics resulting from their encounters in new host territories.

In attempting to conceptualize intra-African Pentecostalism within contexts of power I propose a broadening of the scope to include other modalities through which transnational group practices extend from their origins to new spaces. As Michael Peter Smith et al. argue, studies in transnationalism should fundamentally be guided by an interest in understanding how the process of transnationalism "affects power relations, cultural constructions, economic interactions, and, more generally, social organizations at the level of the locality."[72] In migration studies, concepts such as transnationalism, globalization, and diaspora are conflated to comprehend migrant and refugee practices and the long-term, long-distance connections maintained between family members, communities and states across international borders.[73]

The definition of transnationalism has to be expansive enough to capture the movement of groups from one nation to another while acknowledging possible contestations between transnational groups and receiving nations. However, it should also recognize the power structures inherent in the operations of transnational groups across borders. Transnational Pentecostal churches frequently operate within a continuum of existing structures in new host contexts. This necessitates an investigation into the networks, loyalties, tensions, and resistance emerging from multidimensional engagements of transnational churches in new host territories.

A few questions may clarify my argument. What are the current motivational and strategic dynamics of transnational religious movements such as Winners' Chapel in other countries? What are the various networks, exchanges, and contestations that characterize their interactions in new "mission fields"? There is substantial evidence indicating that new circumstances and contextual factors in new host cultural contexts often provoke migrants or organizations to reconfigure their religion

---

72. Smith and Guarnizo, *Transnationalism from Below*, 8.
73. Schiller et al., "From Immigrant to Transmigrant," 48–63.

and operations to resonate with the conditions of their new homes.[74] If indeed transnational religious movements reconfigure their missionary perspectives to adequately capture the reality of their receiving countries, what could be the possible outcome of relationships between representative transnational groups and members of the group in the receiving countries? Moreover, what are the benefits of replicating the values and practices of transnational movements across international boundaries? Roger Waldinger and David Fitzgerald argue that "migration networks generate a multiplicity of 'imagined communities organized along different, often conflicting principles.'"[75]

For these reasons, I would define transnationalism as the network of exchanges linking individuals and groups across countries and the fluidity and diversity of these exchanges in new geo-cultural host spaces. Such exchanges could be tripartite, involving intricate networks of loyalty, contestation, and resistance among members of the transnational group, existing similar groups, and state authorities of host nation states. My definition is relevant because the current salience of religious transnationalism within anthropology and the social sciences necessitates that scholars consider both the movement and establishment of religious groups in new contexts and investigate the various exchanges that occur between transnational religious actors. Only in this way will scholars be able to provide evidence for the existence of the phenomenon being studied and the reasonableness of the group in terms of representation.

Portes et al. have helpfully cautioned that it is useless attempting to explain a phenomenon whose existence has not been proved—a common fallacy within the social sciences where explanations have been offered for processes whose reality remains controversial.[76] Moreover, it is disingenuous to examine transnational movements without considering power relations in their operations. That explains why in her article "Transnational Social Fields and Imperialism," Nina Glick Schiller bemoaned the fact that transnational studies turn to focus on transnational communities or diasporas only and obscure important relations of power.[77] Thus, I suggest that relations of power within transnational groups and their new contexts need to be examined critically.

74. Adogame, "Transnational Migration and Pentecostalism in Europe," 56.
75. Waldinger and Fitzgerald, "Transnationalism in Question," 1177.
76. Portes et al., "Study of Transnationalism," 218.
77. Schiller, "Transnational Social Fields and Imperialism," 439–61.

The complex interplay between cross-border movements and power dynamics within African Pentecostal churches underscores the importance of deeply understanding their interactions, both within their community and in the new regions they establish themselves. To truly grasp this, our study of international movements need to consider a wide range of influences and power shifts. With this foundation in place, we now turn to chapter 3 and try to explore the experiential aspects of power within African Pentecostalism.

Chapter Three

The Phenomenology of Pentecostal Power

AFRICAN PENTECOSTALISM IS RICH in spiritual fervor. It is not merely a set of beliefs confined to the walls of the church; instead, it weaves together an intricate fabric of deep-rooted spiritual experiences, community testimonies, and individual transformations. At its core, Pentecostalism is anchored in belief in the supernatural power of the Holy Spirit, an entity that blesses its followers with various transformative experiences, from speaking in tongues to physical healing. These experiences are not just internal; they become public testimonies, sharing the wonder of spiritual transformations with the wider community. Such testimonies serve not only as a form of spiritual affirmation but also as a conduit for social influence.

The embodiment of Pentecostal power can often be observed in the charismatic presence of its leaders—pastors who are perceived to be endowed with divine anointing, enabling them to perform miracles and offer spiritual guidance. Bishop Oyedepo, for example, presents himself as a figure chosen by the Holy Spirit to disseminate new spiritual insights, reinforcing his authority through tales of miraculous healings and divine interventions. However, the narrative of Pentecostal power is multi-layered. Beyond overt displays of spiritual prowess, the more subtle nuances lie in the dynamics of power. As Pentecostalism spreads across borders, it intersects with local cultural and political terrains, raising questions about the transfer, negotiation, and sometimes the resistance of power. This is evident when considering the relationship dynamics between mother churches, such as those in Nigeria, and their international branches. Moreover, the exercise of power in Pentecostalism does not solely rest on overt spiritual displays or charismatic leadership. The "soft power" approach, which I employ in this book, drawing parallels with international relations theories,[1] sheds light on how influential religious figures persuade their followers through a combination of attraction, shared values, and cultural ties. This non-coercive form of power, intertwined with the more direct, charismatic power, creates a multifaceted tapestry of influence within the Pentecostal landscape. However, where there is power, there is also the potential for powerlessness. In such influential structures, there is an inherent risk of disempowerment for those on the periphery. It raises essential questions: How do individuals navigate this dynamic? Do they feel oppressed, or do they find empowerment in their spiritual journey?

Using the intellectual frameworks proposed by Michel Foucault[2] and Max Weber,[3] this chapter endeavors to unravel the layers of Pentecostal power structures. Another facet this chapter examines is the role of the media in the Pentecostal narrative. As religious movements increasingly adopt digital channels, one must ponder: How do these platforms reshape and amplify the religious doctrine? How do socioeconomic dynamics in regions like Africa shape the reception and interpretation of this digital religious content? This chapter sets out to examine the thoughts raised, offering initial insights into the fascinating interplay of power, spirituality, media, and individual agency in transnational African Pentecostalism, aspects that will form the main argument of this book concerning the Winners' Chapel.

Manifestations of Pentecostal Power

At the heart of Pentecostalism lies the important concept of power or charisma, which symbolizes a strong belief in the supernatural power of

1. Nye, "Public Diplomacy and Soft Power," 94–109.
2. Foucault, *Power*.
3. Weber, *Theory of Social and Economic Organization*.

the Holy Spirit. This belief encompasses a spectrum of transformative experiences, each with its unique nuances and significance.

1. **Direct Encounter:** Central to Pentecostal power is the idea of deep personal experience of connecting directly with the Holy Spirit. This deep spiritual communion often manifests in various forms: from speaking in tongues and prophesying to physical sensations like trembling or even collapsing.

2. **The Power of Testimony:** Sharing personal encounters with the Holy Spirit serves as a pivotal aspect of Pentecostalism. Through testimonies, individuals narrate their transformative spiritual journey, shedding light on their newfound strength and enlightenment. These heartfelt stories find expression in diverse arenas—from church pulpits to the digital corridors of social media.

3. **Healing, Physical and Spiritual:** Pentecostalism places emphasis on the healing power of the Holy Spirit. Under the guidance of spiritually anointed leaders, individuals seek respite from their physical or emotional ailments.

4. **Transformational Awakening:** An authentic encounter with the Holy Spirit can pivotally shift an individual's worldview. Such a transformation rejuvenates one's ethical and moral compass, fostering a renewed dedication to personal piety, prayer, and the overarching desire to share these enlightened experiences with others.

5. **Spiritual Authority of Pastors:** Perhaps the most significant facet of Pentecostal power is the revered stature of pastors. These are individuals believed to be specially anointed by the Holy Spirit, entrusted with the divine capability to perform miracles, heal the ailing, and champion spiritual battles.

In essence, Pentecostal power is a rich mosaic of experiences, blending stories of faith, healing, and transformation, all deeply rooted in the perceived strength of the Holy Spirit. But key to these experiences is the charismatic power of the Pentecostal leader.

Charismatic Power

Charismatic power in neo-Pentecostal contexts is often interpreted as a special type of influence held by prominent religious figures, whereas in historic Pentecostalism the emphasis fell more on the spirit falling on all flesh, that is on spiritual egalitarianism. This unique power stems from their perceived divine "anointing," which grants them access to the much-needed resources of power within and beyond their churches. In their understanding, such power can positively impact believers' lives, offering relief from poverty and illness or even granting unexpected prosperity, like securing prestigious jobs without traditional qualifications. Bishop Oyedepo aptly captures the essence of charismatic power by referring to his mandate of liberation:

> The Holy Ghost has sent me to open a new chapter to this generation. He has sent me with the powerful Word of Faith and has also delivered into my hands mysterious instruments that have been used over the years to raise the dead, destroy HIV/AIDS, dissolve cancers, establish liberty, provoke success, and command favour, all for the uplift of Zion! We are grateful to God for counting us privileged to know these things which hitherto had been hidden, but which are now revealed to us by His Spirit. God has delivered into our hands divine instruments for victory. Through their use, the lame have walked, withered limbs have been cured, the mad have been restored back to sanity, and the barren have become joyful mothers of children. It's been signs and wonders galore! [These] biblical instruments of power ... were delivered [to me] purely by revelation.[4]

The quotation from Oyedepo relates to a divine mission and the instruments of faith given by God to enable its accomplishment. Remarkably, he suggests that the Holy Spirit has chosen him to introduce these new spiritual insights to the world. He has also been entrusted with the influential "Word of Faith" and unique tools that have performed miracles over time: reviving the lifeless, healing severe illnesses like HIV/AIDS and cancer, inspiring success, and granting favor to many people. All these actions are aimed at elevating his faith communities. He also believes that he has been granted knowledge of truths that were hitherto hidden from people. These divine tools have brought about miracles, enabling the paralyzed to walk, healing the sick, restoring the mentally challenged, and turning infertile couples into joyful parents.

Many Pentecostal leaders, harnessing their spiritual gifts, have also spearheaded projects like establishing schools and hospitals. Their influence extends to grand international events, displays of wealth, luxury

---

4. Oyedepo, *Signs and Wonders*, 58.

lifestyles, and political engagements. It is critical to note that on the one hand, Pentecostal leaders emphasize their direct connection with the divine and their ability to channel the Charismata, resulting in miraculous healing and breakthroughs. On the other hand, the establishment of hospitals by the same leaders suggests an acknowledgment of the efficacy and necessity of medical science and healthcare. This juxtaposition raises questions about the compatibility of spiritual and medical approaches to healing within Pentecostalism. One could argue that the act of founding hospitals while also proclaiming the power of spiritual healing reflects a complex understanding of health and wellness, one that is not necessarily mutually exclusive but rather complementary. This duality may also be a practical recognition of the varying needs and beliefs of their followers, accommodating both those who favor a spiritual remedy and those who seek conventional medical intervention. However, one critical aspect of this seeming conundrum pertains to the financial aspect of these hospitals. If the spiritual services are portrayed as a divinely empowered and presumably altruistic aspect of the leaders' ministries, the commercial nature of hospital care, requiring significant payment for services, may appear contradictory. This could lead to skepticism, particularly if the financial burden on the sick is high or if it seems that the religious rhetoric around healing is being used to funnel individuals toward paid services. The existence of both spiritual and medical services within one religious organization may also invite scrutiny over the motives of the leadership and the overall message being communicated to adherents. Is the leadership genuinely providing a range of options to cater to diverse needs, or is there an underlying profit motive that complicates the ostensibly spiritual nature of their mission?

However, Pentecostal leaders act as intermediaries between their followers, who seek solutions to their problems and the divine source of these solutions. The importance of such pastors is undeniable. Oyedepo, for example, believes that every Christian can access God's covenant for problem-solving. Yet, in practice, his presence is often seen as essential for positive changes in his followers' lives. He has claimed that with just a touch from him, businesses can thrive and the ailing can heal. He recalls an instance where a man with a seventeen-year-old spinal injury was cured just by touching Oyedepo's garment.[5]

---

5. Oyedepo, *Walking in Dominion*, 91.

In Pentecostal transnationalism, power dynamics evolve creatively due to the interconnectedness of diverse groups within the church. For example, Nigerians participating in a Nigerian church located in Cameroon interact differently than do native Cameroonians in the same church. It is crucial to understand how power functions within these relationships and how it is used by church members and leaders alike. A central question is whether spiritual power from the originating church is universally embraced or, at times, challenged within its international branches. Moreover, how do these power dynamics benefit members of the host religious communities? This question mirrors Nelson Polsby's exploration into community politics, where he emphasizes understanding participation, benefits, losses, and decision-making influences. He suggests that studies of power need to capture the essence of "who participates, who gains and loses, and who prevails in decision-making."[6] That is why, when discussing the concept of power in transnational Pentecostalism, it is essential to distinguish between the leaders and the more peripheral members.[7]

Typically, power is held by a select few leaders who possess significant authority, leveraging their charisma, talents, and the capacity to rally both people and resources toward specific goals. In essence, true leadership within this context is about galvanizing others toward collective objectives, ensuring actions taken are in the best interest of the community.[8] The evidence suggests that in African Transnational Pentecostalism, a church's power can be traced back to its original location and the influence of its founding leader. This influence radiates from the church's origin to its new mission locations and its people due to the links created from the mother to the daughter church.

This book uncovers a new understanding about those who hold power in the global outreach of transnational Pentecostal churches in Africa, and the tools they employ to exert authority. Taking the Winners' Chapel as its central case study, its leader Bishop Oyedepo selects missionaries as his representatives. These envoys not only represent him but also champion the church's objectives across the world. Their primary task is to preserve and promote the core teachings and practices of the Living Faith Church Worldwide.[9] Essentially, these missionaries are seen as apostles, legitimizing the founder's authority in new locations, given his pivotal role

---

6. Polsby, *Community Power and Political Theory*, 55.
7. Tettey, "Pentecostalism and Empowerment," 65.
8. Rosen, "Leadership Systems in World Cultures," 39.
9. Oyedepo, *Mandate*, 235.

and spiritual anointing in guiding the church's global mission. However, within Pentecostalism, there is an apparent relationship between traditional leadership in the past and more modern leadership dynamics.

Traditional Authority in Modern Pentecostalism

When Peter Blau wrote of authority that is legitimated by the sanctity of tradition, he was referring to what Max Weber called "traditional authority" in which a "social order is viewed as sacred eternal, and inviolable . . . and where the dominant person . . . is thought to have been preordained to rule over the rest."[10]

Bishop Oyedepo exemplifies this model. Even from Nigeria he extends his spiritual leadership to Cameroon and other regions through his missionaries, cementing his position as a revered spiritual leader. This interconnected web of influence and shared beliefs keeps Oyedepo as a central figure among his followers both in Cameroon and globally. Blau described this bond as followers tied to their leader through a blend of loyalty, personal dependence, and cultural beliefs, such as the age-old notion of "divine kings."[11] Pentecostal leaders transmit this spiritual authority to ensure a robust connection with their followers. However, a looming question remains: Can such concentrated power ever risk leading the followers toward a sense of powerlessness?

Powerlessness

Powerlessness arises when individuals or groups feel their actions cannot influence outcomes in life. Blau identified at least two types: "Real powerlessness" and "Surplus powerlessness."[12] The former relates to oppressive control by systems or individuals, while the latter is an internal belief that change is unattainable, leading to apathy. In surplus powerlessness, individuals often feel destined to remain defeated, isolated, and feel they won't be taken seriously regardless of their efforts.[13]

---

10. Blau, "Critical Remarks," 308.

11. Blau, "Critical Remarks," 308. For a more relevant application of this theme to global religious history see Strathern, *Unearthly Powers*, chapter 3.

12. Tettey, "Pentecostalism and Empowerment," 64–67.

13. Blau, "Critical Remarks," 308.

The remaining chapters of this book examine these power dynamics within the context of Winners' Chapel in Cameroon, particularly the tension between the powerful and the powerless. A critical concern is how the powerless either conform to or resist the dominating forces. Notably, when indications suggest that people within a transnational religious movement feel oppressed, it sparks questions of resistance. However, in some cases we find acquiescence instead of resistance, and this mirrors John Gaventa's question: Why do communities that seem prime for revolt instead appear passive?[14] While Gaventa's inquiry was rooted in political theory, it is pivotal for our discussions because it highlights potential tensions between influential transnational figures and their less powerful counterparts.

The two concepts of power and powerlessness are important in interpreting religious phenomena of groups such as Pentecostal churches whose conception of power forms their ideological basis. For example, the Holy Spirit is always associated with physical, moral, and spiritual power. The Holy Spirit is regarded as the all-embracing, pervading power of God.[15] But apart from the Holy Spirit who is believed to be transmitted by powerful religious leaders to combat evil spiritual forces that threaten people's lives, Pentecostal church leaders also exercise authoritative control to maintain and promote the transmission of their power. The appropriation of power is particularly important in intra-African Pentecostalism where the constitution of a transnational church's work force often involves participants that could too easily be categorized as "insiders" (those who own the church or come from its place of origin as missionaries) and "outsiders" (those who have joined them for work purposes in new mission fields).

This tension raises questions about the missionary strategy of sending out missionaries from mother to daughter churches. The idea is not new. Take, for example, the RCCG, which pioneered the transnationalization of Pentecostal churches in Africa by extending to Ghana in 1981 before moving to other West African countries. Its growth was facilitated by the appointment and sending of missionaries from Nigeria to other countries to serve as coordinators and representatives of the leadership in Nigeria.[16] In this way, a relationship between the Nigerian headquar-

14. Gaventa, *Power and Powerlessness*, 1.
15. Anderson, "Pentecostal Pneumatology," 73.
16. Llufunke A. Adeboye, "Transnational Pentecostalism in Africa, the Redeemed Christian Church of God, Nigeria," in Fourchard et al., *Entreprises Religieuses*

ters and other branches became a major feature of the church. These missionaries served as the link between the leadership in Nigeria and the churches in foreign countries. Another relationship is between Nigerian missionaries and indigenes of the receiving country serving as pastors or other staff of the church. Within such relationships, contestations of power and loyalty are bound to emerge, when missionaries try to implement the policies of the church, as directed from Nigeria. That is why it is important for transnational Pentecostal churches to develop complex strategies that can consolidate the presence and influence of the church in foreign territories.

The Nexus between Charismatic and "Soft Power"

In the previous section, we noted that one dimension of charismatic power in African Pentecostalism is the influence and authority that a religious leader or figure wields over their followers through their perceived spiritual gifts, such as healing, prophecy, or speaking in tongues. This power is often tied to the leader's ability to connect with their followers emotionally, create a sense of community, and inspire devotion. The public display of spiritual gifts by neo-Pentecostal leaders can be highly performative, involving emotionally charged services, dramatic faith healings, and prophetic declarations that are designed to create an atmosphere of spiritual intensity. On the other hand, Joseph Nye's concept of "soft power" explains the ways in which dominant groups situate themselves on certain vantage points to persuade others to succumb to their leadership or to admire what they do, enjoy it, and aspire to be like them. According to Nye, a country's "soft power" rests on its resources of culture, values, and policies.[17] With "soft power," powerful institutions and organizations or individuals use persuasion rather than coercion to make others yield to their leadership.

While the context and manifestation of these two concepts of power are different, they both emphasize the importance of influence and attraction in achieving desired outcomes. Charismatic power in African Pentecostalism and soft power in international relations share the idea that power can be exercised through non-coercive means, and that these means can be just as effective as more traditional forms of power. In this

---

Transnationales, 453.

17. Nye, "Public Diplomacy and Soft Power," 94–109.

sense, both concepts highlight the importance of building relationships and creating a sense of community to achieve influence and power.

The arguments in this book will reveal that Winners' Chapel uses the concept of "soft power" to maintain its authority and control in Cameroon and that the Cameroonian daughter church yields to the power of the Nigerian mother church but also resists it in some cases. So, it is important to ask: What is the goal that shapes the exercise of power? How do temporal power through the missionaries and the charismatic power of Bishop Oyedepo relate to each other? And what forms of resistance are being perpetrated by the Cameroonian daughter church? These questions are important, not least because Max Weber placed power within a trajectory where power brokers continue to wield their power and influence despite resistance. According to Weber, power is "the probability that one actor within a social relationship will be in a position to carry out his own will despite resistance."[18] The understanding is that power is negotiated between two or more actors and is based on the ability of the powerful to effectively use material and nonmaterial resources effectively in a specific context, to get others to do something they would not otherwise do and enforce outcomes suiting the preferences of the one with power.[19]

In his insightful research, Ezekiel Oladapo investigates the intricate web of Pentecostal transnationalism, revealing how the flow of ideas, people, and finances weave together the West African branches with their Nigerian headquarters. These connections, Oladapo suggests, are the lifeblood of the church, comprising both tangible and intangible elements—ideas, individuals, and monetary support.[20]

Chapters 4, 5, and 6 of this book takes a closer look at Winners' Chapel by focusing on its outreach to Cameroon. The chapters explore the various tangible and intangible assets exported from Nigeria to Cameroon, assets that play a pivotal role in reinforcing the spiritual and societal influence of the Nigerian church in its Cameroonian counterpart. Interestingly, the dynamics of power and influence are seen in contrasting lights. While the host community in Cameroon may perceive these interactions as a form of dominance, the Nigerian church views them as an empowering exchange. This exchange is not limited to spiritual growth alone but extends into the realm of social capital, enhancing the interconnectedness and strength of transnational communities. Through

18. Weber, *Theory of Social and Economic Organization*, 70.
19. Pustovitovskij and Kremer, *Structural Power and International Relations*, 3.
20. Ajani, "Leadership Roles in the Transnationalisation," 23.

Pentecostalism and Empowerment

The study of Pentecostalism and empowerment and/or disempowerment is crucial to the discourse of religion and development and religion as social capital.[21] We can identify the following forms of empowerment in the Pentecostal religious worldview: Spiritual empowerment through healing and deliverance; economic and financial empowerment through prosperity and success messages and outcomes; family empowerment, relating to God's power in the family, as a divine creation and institution; and personal and collective empowerment. We can also weave concepts of power and powerlessness as key categories that are useful for understanding empowerment in Pentecostalism.[22]

The empowerment that is most acclaimed by Pentecostals refers to the influence of the Holy Spirit in the lives of Pentecostal adherents. However, Christian pneumatology affirms that the power of the Holy Spirit transcends "spiritual" significance to dignity, authority, and power over all types of oppression because people who are faced with injustices that undermine their personal dignity lack power as well.[23] Anderson's comments were originally made in reference to "Black Power" of the liberationists in South Africa.[24] However, they significantly affirm that elements of power, authority, and oppression are concomitant with discourses of Holy Spirit power, and that the holistic African worldview recognizes people's physical, social, political, and economic needs as inseparable from their spiritual needs.[25]

The holistic proclamation of the word of God, which involves the physical, social, and economic, as well as spiritual needs of people, unravels the relationship between religion and development or religion and empowerment. This is important because development economics often

---

21. See for example Tettey, "Pentecostalism and Empowerment," 64–67.
22. Tettey, "Pentecostalism and Empowerment," 64–67.
23. Anderson, "African Initiated Churches," 178–86.
24. Anderson, "African Initiated Churches," 178–86.
25. Anderson, "African Initiated Churches," 178.

ignores the importance of religion in African societies.[26] Paul Gifford's enchanted African religious imagination[27] concludes that contemporary African Christianity is not capable of providing meaningful economic development in the continent. But other scholars have argued that religious and spiritual resources can produce knowledge that is relevant to development.[28] It is therefore important for researchers to rethink earlier assumptions concerning the relationship between religion and development in the broadest sense. A superficial view of the importance of religion to development in tangible terms must be dismissed and a consideration that transcends spiritual understanding to actual socioeconomic relevance considered. This is referred to as human development. The United Nations Development Programme describes this as an environment enabling people to harness their full potential, harmonizing their needs and interests.[29]

For comprehensive development to be promoted in underprivileged nations, it is indispensable to harness all resources, including religious experiences, which have demonstrated significance in sectors like governance, economy, health, and education.[30] Yet, two crucial pieces of this puzzle remain: the exchange of both tangible and intangible resources between transnational churches and their new domains, and the question of pastoral power within transnational dynamics involving Nigerian mother and Cameroonian daughter churches.

Pastoral Power

As noted earlier, power dynamics within Pentecostalism, especially related to the church leaders, is crucial because Pentecostal Christians perceive their leaders as the epitome of power. This extends beyond the spiritual into financial and political spheres.[31] Pentecostal leaders are seen as possessing a heightened level of charisma, making them uniquely positioned to guide their congregations. A key belief is the "anointing of

---

26. Haar and Ellis, "Role of Religion in Development," 351–67.
27. Gifford, *Christianity, Development and Modernity*.
28. Haar and Ellis, "Role of Religion in Development," 351–67.
29. United Nations Development Programme, "2023 Global Multidimensional Poverty Index."
30. Haar and Ellis, "Role of Religion in Development," 355.
31. Tettey, "Pentecostalism and Empowerment," 67.

the man of God," suggesting that the leader's power can be transferred to the followers, anchoring them in reliance for spiritual empowerment.[32]

The concept of anointing occupies a place of significant importance, often sparking the question: Is the sacred anointing a transferable endowment? Historically, the anointing of a king as the chosen vessel of the Lord's will carried with it an aura of singular authority, a divine mandate that was typically seen as untransferable, its cessation only imaginable upon the monarch's demise. However, a more nuanced examination of scriptural precedents, both in the Old and New Testament, reveals a different narrative—one where the mantle of God-appointed leadership can indeed be passed down, as suggested by certain scriptural narratives, including those found in the book of Numbers. The narrative invites contemplation on the fluidity of divine empowerment within sacred texts, challenging the notion that spiritual authority, once conferred, is locked within the confines of a single individual's lifetime. It suggests a dynamism in divine favor, a possibility that the sacred oil which once anointed a leader could, under divine directive, grace another chosen by God. Thus, in the realm of neo-Pentecostal belief and practice, anointing emerges not merely as a symbol of consecration but as a potential vessel for the continuity of spiritual leadership and legacy.[33]

However, the transfer and preservation of spiritual power in transnational Pentecostalism hinges more upon maintaining certain control structures. This is where missionaries in intra-African Pentecostalism come into play, symbolizing these temporal power structures that uphold and protect the central spiritual authority. Their role is to ensure that the spiritual power of the founder/leader is transmitted and remains untainted and authentic.

This practice draws parallels from biblical traditions. For instance, the Bible speaks of Moses, imbued with the Holy Spirit's power, transferring this divine energy to Israel's seventy elders through the act of laying hands.[34] Contemporary Pentecostal churches embrace this tradition, believing that their leaders can transfer the Holy Spirit's blessings to them using similar ritualistic gestures.[35] In this way, founder-leaders of Pentecostal churches have been revered as the primary bearers of spiritual power, exerting significant influence over their followers.

32. Asamoah-Gyadu, "Anointing through the Screen," 9–28.
33. See Strathern, *Unearthly Powers*, chapter 3.
34. Num 11:17–25.
35. Anderson, "African Initiated Churches," 180–81.

This dynamic resonates with Michel Foucault's concept of "pastoral power," which he defines as a unique form of authority. Furthermore, it evokes Max Weber's discussions on charisma and leadership, emphasizing the relationship between leaders and their followers in religious contexts.[36] Foucault's interpretation of "Pastor" underscores the distinct nature of this power, suggesting a deep-rooted, symbolic bond between religious leaders and their congregations. He characterizes pastoral power as follows:

1. It is a form of power whose ultimate aim is to assure individual salvation in the next world.

2. Pastoral power is not merely a form of power that commands; it must also be prepared to sacrifice itself for the life and salvation of the flock. Therefore, it is different from royal power, which demands from its subjects to save the throne.

3. It is the form of power that looks after not just the whole community but each individual in particular, during his entire life.

4. Finally, this form of power cannot be exercised without knowing the inside of people's minds, without exploring their souls, without making them reveal their innermost secrets. It implies a knowledge of the conscience and an ability to direct it.[37]

Foucault saw pastoral power as selfless and sacrificial, the main goal being both individual and communal care and an assurance of individual salvation in the next world. He suggests that the vantage ground for pastoral power is an understanding of the psychological and spiritual needs of the people. In essence, Foucault's interpretation of pastoral power presents a detailed framework for understanding the depth and dimensions of spiritual leadership. It showcases pastoral power as a unique blend of eschatological concern, altruistic leadership, holistic care, and profound spiritual intimacy, positioning the pastor as a pivotal figure in the spiritual landscape of their followers.

However, Max Weber's theory of charismatic leadership was significantly different. Weber characterized charismatic leadership as the desire to wield power over others, provide leadership through certain ideologies that motivate their followers to enjoy their power, and create a sense of

36. Foucault, *Power*, 79–80.
37. Foucault, *Power*, 79–80.

common identity. Weber's view on charismatic leadership is less about deep spiritual connections and more about the dynamics of influence and power. He suggests that charismatic leaders harness their unique qualities to exert power, guide followers through specific ideologies, and foster a shared identity. To better understand Weber's view, we turn to six defining traits of charismatic leadership that he proposes:

1. Having a strong desire to influence others.
2. Being a role model for the beliefs and values leaders want their followers to adopt.
3. Articulating ideological goals with moral overtones.
4. Communicating high expectations and showing confidence in followers' abilities to meet these expectations, which then increases their self-efficacy and sense of competence; this in turn increases their performance.
5. Arousing task-relevant motivation by tapping followers' needs for esteem, power, and/or affiliation.
6. Linking the identity of followers to the collective identity of the organization.[38]

Charismatic leadership as suggested in those six characteristics revolves around the power of influence, mentorship, and the creation of a shared vision. Later chapters of this book will unravel the fascinating interplay between Foucault's concept of "pastoral power" and Weber's notions of charismatic leadership within the framework of the Winners' Chapel in Cameroon.

At this point in the argument, we need to understand the power hierarchies in African Pentecostalism, using Winners' Chapel as our reference. This will illuminate the distinct power structures within the church's Cameroonian branch.

The Hierarchization of Pentecostal Churches

In his book *The African Christian Diaspora*, Afe Adogame has written about the "Phenomenology of African Christian Communities," dealing with the organizational intricacies of Pentecostal churches. What he uncovers is a tapestry of varied structures, from churches with flexible, almost free-form structures to those with close administrative systems.

38. Weber, *Theory of Social and Economic Organization*, 700–701.

Some churches are sinuously shaped by the vision and influence of the leader, alongside their family and close associates. His thesis examines three distinctive African churches: The Celestial Church of Christ (an African Initiated Church); the Redeemed Christian Church of God (a classical Pentecostal church), both headquartered in Nigeria, and the Christian Church Outreach, a neo-Pentecostal movement, with headquarters in Hamburg, Germany. These churches, despite their geographical and doctrinal differences, all demonstrate one constant: Leadership at the helm negotiates an intricate web of relationships. These connections span across borders, facilitated by shared events, exchange visits, innovative use of new media, and grassroots initiatives.[39] But beyond just connection, there is an embedded hierarchy of values in these power structures, emphasizing their global nature and interconnections. This intricate dance between local practices and global ties paints a fascinating picture of Pentecostalism's reach and depth in the modern world.

The hierarchical structure of any organization is important for the distribution of duties among groups of people according to ability and status and for the proper functioning of the organization. As we have seen, in neo-Pentecostal churches, it is the configurations of charismatic power and channel of vision that characterizes hierarchy and power.[40] Hierarchization of power within large-scale transnational religious movements which operate a central system of control enables the leaders to keep in check branches of the church that are established beyond the originating base of the movement. For example, David Maxwell shows how leaders and structures of power in ZAOGA are stationed at the church's headquarters in Harare from where external branches such as those in Mozambique, South Africa, and England are controlled.[41] However, the questions and forms of resistance that have resulted from some of the peripheral branches of the church relating to a centralized ideology of authoritarian leadership,[42] needs further consideration as an important aspect of transnational religious studies.

---

39. Adogame, *African Christian Diaspora*, 84.
40. Ukah, "Redeemed Christian Church," 107.
41. Maxwell, *African Gifts of the Spirit*, 218.
42. Maxwell, *African Gifts of the Spirit*, 218.

The Structure of Power in Winners' Chapel

The Winners' Chapel International is a genre of neo-Pentecostal churches with its distinct hierarchical structure. Central to its operations is Bishop Oyedepo, the founder-leader. Revered as "the visioner," he is perceived as a conduit for divine inspiration, directing the entire church's vision and mission.[43]

From a structural perspective, the church operates through a series of councils, each with its unique role. Topping this structure is the board of trustees (henceforth BoTs). Legally, the trustees manage the church's finances and property, but in practice, Bishop Oyedepo handpicks members, and they remain loyal solely to him. The Executive Council (EC) then follows, managing the day-to-day affairs, yet still influenced significantly by Oyedepo's direction. There is also a series of other councils, like the Council of Bishops and National Council, all furthering the church's mission in various regions and capacities.

The principal officers of the Winners' Chapel include the president, Bishop Oyedepo, who is the highest officer, and founding bishop of the church. He is also the chairman of the BoTs and the chief executive officer of the LFCW. As president, he exercises absolute control over the affairs of DOMI conglomerate as well as the LFCW. He is also referred to as the "visioner," embodying the pre-eminent source of divine ideas and pronouncements which support the functioning of the LFCW.[44] He is also regarded as the liaison between members of his church and God. For this reason, his decisions are laws and must be implemented as such. He appoints and consecrates all LFCW bishops and delegates authority when and where necessary. He is the principal signatory to all LFCW official documents and the chief accountant as well as the custodian of the seal of the organization. In theory, the executive council is the policymaking and monitoring body of the LFCW; in practice, the concentration of power and authority in the person and office of the president makes the function of the executive council peripheral.[45] As the president, Oyedepo appoints all the members of the council and has the power to remove them from office. The president is also the presiding officer at the Council of Bishops of LFCW.[46] Oyedepo himself reckons that "the office of the

---

43. Kuponu, "Living Faith Church," 39.
44. Kuponu, "Living Faith Church," 45.
45. Kuponu, "Living Faith Church," 45.
46. Kuponu, "Living Faith Church," 45–47.

President shall be the highest spiritual and administrative office of the church worldwide, and the presidency shall be resident with the founder all through his lifetime."[47]

The executive vice president is next in command. He is variously called the "chief missioner," and the disseminator of the LFCW's missionary and expansionary zeal. In addition to this, he may be delegated by the president to perform any functions deemed necessary. However, since the creation of this office, the only occupier has in fact been the president and founding bishop of LFCW, David Oyedepo.[48] According to Oyedepo, he needs to be directed by God to select a capable candidate for the office. Since God has not yet directed him on who to appoint, Oyedepo occupies the position himself in the meantime.[49]

The executive secretary comes after the vice president and has direct oversight of the physical development, finance, and human resource management of the organization.[50] The secretary keeps all records pertaining to the church in both national and international matters, monitors and supervises all church organizations and activities which do not fall directly within the domain of the president/vice president of the LFCW, and reports directly to the president. Until recently, Faith Oyedepo, the wife of the president of LFCW, was the sole occupier of this office. Her knowledge in economics and her position as wife of the church founder might have informed her suitability for this powerful office.[51] In addition to being the executive secretary, she has been (and still is) a member of the LFCW's BoTs and the executive council. It is possible that Faith Oyedepo is the most powerful woman in the LFCW in her position as executive secretary because the position is next to that of the vice president.[52]

Following in the structure of power are diocesan bishops. The LFCW is grouped into regional dioceses, and a bishop is the spiritual head of a diocese. Oyedepo, as the president and founding bishop, has the sole responsibility and power to appoint a local bishop. Bishops function as executive chairmen as well as the chief accounting officers of their dioceses. To be a bishop in the LFCW, one must have served the church for fourteen years without warning letters, reprimands, or exit.

47. Oyedepo, *Mandate*, 227.
48. Kuponu, "Living Faith Church," 47.
49. Kuponu, "Living Faith Church," 47.
50. Oyedepo, *Mandate*, 232.
51. Kuponu, "Living Faith Church," 47–50.
52. Kuponu, "Living Faith Church," 50.

Bishops ensure that the spiritual and socioeconomic welfare of members of their dioceses are achieved. They, however, report all the activities of their dioceses to the founding bishop from time to time. In the year 2000 the LFCW had a total number of nine bishops including the founding bishop. As mentioned earlier, two of these bishops left the church in 2004 and 2005. Pastors who now bear the title "diocesan heads" rather than "bishops" have filled their positions.[53]

Associate bishops or senior pastors are next in the ladder of leadership. These are ordained, full-time employed pastors assisting the diocesan bishop in each diocese. They have the same status as district pastors. The district pastors represent the bishop in particular areas carved out of a diocese. Among this category of pastors are directors of national projects, finance, missions, and social services. They operate in the diocese and report directly to the executive secretary of LFCW. The wives of bishops are pastors and are rated in this category. Other officers of the church include the following in order of importance: pastors, assistant pastors, deacon/deaconess, and elders.

The power structure of the Winners' Chapel shows that at the very top of the administrative bloc is the national church, which is the umbrella body worldwide. It is in Nigeria and further divided into dioceses. The next administrative bloc are regions which are constituted by a group of countries in the foreign mission. For example, Cameroon, the Democratic Republic of Congo, Equatorial Guinea, and the Central African Republic make up the Central African Region of Winners' Chapel. Provinces are individual nations. For example, Cameroon is a province. Within a province there are Districts, Zones, Areas, and the Local Assemblies. These different blocs of power ensure that there is a proper transmission of the ideas and spiritual power of Bishop Oyedepo through the various officers, from Nigeria down to the local assemblies in the provinces that are in foreign territories. Oyedepo has thus commented that the various officers in the hierarchy of the church "serve as vital spiritual props for the office of the President to enhance his visionary responsibilities in leading the church into the future."[54] This is even clearer in the roles that Oyedepo occupies in his organization as earlier mentioned.

The way Winners' Chapel is led and governed reveals a structure of power and authority that resides with Bishop Oyedepo, the founder

---

53. Kuponu, "Living Faith Church," 50.
54. Oyedepo, *Mandate*, 228.

and leader of the church. This is understandable because, as the church founder, Oyedepo believes and affirms that he is the one who received the message from God and is the only one who understands the mission for which God called him. He is therefore the most pivotal person to fulfill that mission or what he calls the "Mandate." This explains why Winners' Chapel Christians in Cameroon constantly refer to the "Mandate."[55] This unique revelatory act of divine guidance is a cornerstone belief among the church's followers in Cameroon, reinforcing the idea that all church activities are divinely inspired and passed down from God to Bishop Oyedepo, and then to the congregation.

Oyedepo has crafted a system of governance that, while including others in roles of leadership and administration, ensures his central authority remains intact. His involvement in key decision-making processes, including appointments and dismissals, highlights his hands-on leadership style. Furthermore, his tendency to retain his multiple leadership roles or delegate them within his family cements his influential and enduring hold over the church. Bishop Oyedepo has candidly asserted that Winners' Chapel is rooted in apostolic traditions, implying lifelong leadership. Therefore, the role of presidency within the church is not transient; it is envisioned as a lifetime commitment.[56]

Examining the dynamics of power in the context of religious leadership, one can draw parallels with Peter Blau's insights into the underpinnings of charismatic power. Reflecting on Weber's theory, Blau succinctly captures the essence of Charismatic leadership, noting that:

> Charismatic authority defines a leader and his mission as being inspired by divine or supernatural powers . . . there is a sense of being "called" to spread the new gospel . . . and devotion to the leader and the conviction that his pronouncements embody the spirit and ideals of the movement are the source of the group's willing obedience to his commands.[57]

According to Blau, charismatic authority is about more than leadership skills; it is about a leader who is perceived as divinely or supernaturally inspired. Such leaders often feel a profound sense of destiny or a "calling" to propagate their message. The fervent dedication of followers to such a leader is not just out of respect, but a deep-rooted belief that the leader's

55. Oyedepo, *Mandate*, 259.
56. Oyedepo, *Mandate*.
57. Blau, "Critical Remarks," 308.

words and actions are the very essence of the movement. This unwavering trust prompts willing compliance to the leader's directives.

Blau's understanding resonates with the structure and dynamics of many African Pentecostal churches. The RCCG, for example, showcases a hierarchy of power with its pinnacle being the general overseer. Notably, this leader is not just a figurehead; he shoulders the responsibilities of both the national and international domains, exemplified by his dual roles in Lagos and Loburo, Ogun State, Nigeria.[58] This centralization of authority in one individual echoes Blau's characterization of a charismatic leader, further highlighting the influence such leaders can have over their congregations. The power dynamics within institutions like Winners' Chapel and RCCG primarily center around the roles of their founders or lead figures. These structures illuminate how authority is wielded to ensure stability, maintain the church's integrity, and guarantee its continued existence. This is perhaps why the Nigerian Pentecostal pastor Enoch Adeboye famously asserted that "God is not a Democrat."[59]

In a significant address during the second biennial meeting of the Pentecostal Fellowship of Nigeria (PFN) in 1993, of which he was then the president, Pastor Adeboye emphasized the imperative of unwavering allegiance to the leading authority. He asserted that everyone must heed the instructions of the commander in chief. There is no room for disputes or discussion.[60] He dreamed of a PFN that would act as a transformative force, striving against Nigeria's socio-political and spiritual impasses—challenges that even political leaders struggled to address. Drawing upon his tenure as leader of RCCG, Pastor Adeboye highlighted his views on leadership and the exercise of authority. He suggested that his fellow leaders should adopt a similar understanding of power dynamics within their respective institutions, explaining that upon his assumption as the general overseer of the RCCG, there was a noticeable autonomy, with many workers acting based on personal convictions. When directives were given, responses ranged from seeking divine clarity through prayers to outright resignations, sometimes even leading to division within the church. However, a transformative shift occurred, one that he ardently hoped for within the broader Pentecostal community. After a pivotal meeting, the PFN pastors collectively decided that the directives from the general overseer would be regarded as final. Subsequently, the pastors

58. Marshall-Fratani, *Political Spiritualities*, 308.
59. Marshall-Fratani, *Political Spiritualities*, 202.
60. Marshall-Fratani, *Political Spiritualities*, 202.

pledged their commitment to ensuring the implementation of such directives. Here are Adeboye's own words:

> When I became the General overseer of the RCCG, everybody was doing what he thinks is right in his own sight. Ask someone to go on transfer, they will tell you, "Let me go and pray about it," or they may even resign, or take the church away. Then all of a sudden, the Holy Spirit moved. He did something that I am praying He will do among the Pentecostals. All of a sudden, we held a meeting, we reached an agreement that from now on, once the General overseer has spoken, the pastors will see to it that it comes to pass.[61]

From Adeboye's discourse, several key insights emerge: Firstly, it underscores the belief in God's miraculous intervention, illustrating his ability to influence the daily political dynamics of nations, particularly through fervent prayers and guidance of his chosen leaders. Furthermore, it highlights the global reach of the Pentecostal community and acknowledges the crucial role of institutions such as the Pentecostal Fellowship of Nigeria. This body is not only significant for Nigeria's religious trajectory but is also integral to shaping the political futures of several African nations. Additionally, the discourse introduces the concept of a supreme authority within the movement, which governs the behaviors and actions of its members.[62]

This power structure, as the analysis suggests, establishes a complex political spirituality. While it sometimes veers toward a more negative political theology, it simultaneously indicates potential pathways to realize their objectives. These paths, at times, might involve strategies of dominance, exploitation, and even exclusionary or retaliatory politics.[63] The overarching takeaway from these analyses is the distinctive power dynamics present within Pentecostal leadership. These leaders wield distinct authority, crafted to effectively steer the church's global operations effectively. This, in turn, facilitates the transfer of their spiritual might to followers, irrespective of geographical boundaries.

In chapter 5 of this book, we examine the power dynamics within Winners' Chapel Cameroon. This exploration will highlight the mirroring of power structures from Nigeria in its Cameroonian counterpart, offering

---

61. Enoch Adeboye, "Who Is on the Lord's Side," PFN Biennial Conference, Lagos, February 13, 1993, cited in Marshall-Fratani, *Political Spiritualities*, 201–4.
62. Marshall-Fratani, *Political Spiritualities*, 204.
63. Marshall-Fratani, *Political Spiritualities*, 204.

insights into the nuances of intra-African Pentecostalism. As posited by Michael Peter Smith et al., examining the practices of a particular group across diverse localities, be it a migrant group or a constituent of a transnational social movement, can be instrumental.[64] Such comparative analyses not only show the influence of different environments but significantly shed light on the missionary ambitions and tactics employed by global religious entities. However, it is important to examine some of the motivational dynamics that drive the mission agendas of Pentecostal churches.

Missionary Motivations of Winners' Chapel

Winners' Chapel chronicles its missionary mandate on its website in a bid to justify its missionary endeavors, thus:

> Our Mandate speaks of liberation in all facets of human existence; we focus mainly on destinies that have been afflicted, battered, beaten, tattered, deformed and subsequently in groaning and agonies, as a result of pains, pangs and crying . . . . The hour has come to liberate the world from all oppressions of the Devil through the preaching of the word of faith, and I am sending you to undertake this task.[65]

The manifesto lucidly maps out the church's missionary vision and objectives of the church and specifically of its leader ("I am sending you . . ."). It positions its mission as a rejuvenating force for individuals plagued by myriad trials, both tangible and spiritual. This edict is deeply intertwined with the appointment of the church's venerated leader, Bishop Oyedepo, entrusted with the sacred duty of orchestrating this global liberation. The scope of this divine charge is vast, aiming to free every corner of the world from oppression, thereby enabling individuals to reclaim their preordained destinies.

Tomas Drønen has defined Bishop David Oyedepo as a paradigmatic figure of a pastor who has achieved global recognition, marked by the vast international reach of his ministry and his transformative spiritual journey.[66] Drønen, however, interrogates Oyedepo's divine commissioning and missionary mandate, seeking clarity on the essentiality of Bishop Oyedepo's spiritual rebirth, from a pastor within the Cherubim and Seraphim

---

64. Smith and Guarnizo, *Transnationalism from Below*, 28.
65. Winners' Chapel International, "Our Mandate."
66. Drønen, *Pentecostalism, Globalisation, and Islam*, 72.

church[67] to the founder of a prosperity driven church. This intriguing evolution, from an "otherworldly" spiritual stance to a doctrine that accentuates material prosperity and worldly success, demands contemplation.[68] The doctrinal philosophy of Winners' Chapel is visibly expressed in slogans such as "I am a winner," "I am smelling success," "Be a winner in Jesus Christ," "Winning ways," "I am on the winning side."[69] For the adherents of Winners' Chapel and analogous modern Pentecostal movements, success becomes synonymous with devout Christian life, while its absence is viewed as an aberration that demands a spiritual explanation.[70]

The missionary ethos of Winners' Chapel can be explained through a thoughtful examination of its emblematic logotype: a globe adorned with five ascending flames.[71] The flames, symbolic of tongues of fire, are indicative of the multifaceted ministries under the Living Faith Church Worldwide (LFCW) umbrella, each striving to make an important global impact.[72] The globe itself encapsulates the church's envisioned realm of influence. This design signifies not merely the church's aspiration to be an influential force within both Nigeria and the wider world but also its intent to leave an indelible mark within the broader public spheres, both locally and internationally.[73] This initiative is facilitated by a missionary organization called The Living Faith World Outreach Centre (LFWOC), whose primary objective is defined as "the general development and upliftment of mankind by stirring up the God given potentials embedded in people of all races and nations through the propagation of the gospel of Jesus Christ."[74] By awakening the intrinsic, divine potentials within individuals across racial and national divides, LFWOC ardently propagates the gospel of Jesus Christ, aiming to uplift souls worldwide.

The use of the metaphor of fire in Winners' Chapel logo, presumably symbolizing the Holy Spirit, is pivotal in the discourse of Pentecostal missionary activities. This symbolism harks back to early missionary engagements ignited by "tongues of fire," most notably associated with

---

67. Drønen, *Pentecostalism, Globalisation, and Islam*, 72.
68. Drønen, *Pentecostalism, Globalisation, and Islam*, 72.
69. Kuponu, "Living Faith Church," 2.
70. Gifford, "Trajectories in African Christianity," 283.
71. Such slogans are fairly typical of Neo-Pentecostalism in West Africa. See Kuponu, "Living Faith Church," 1; and Gifford, *Ghana's New Christianity*.
72. See Kuponu, "Living Faith Church," 1; and Gifford, *Ghana's New Christianity*.
73. See Kuponu, "Living Faith Church," 1; and Gifford, *Ghana's New Christianity*.
74. Winners' Chapel International, "Our Mandate."

the disciples of Jesus, as chronicled in the Acts of the Apostles. Such representations underscore the emphasis many Pentecostal movements place on the baptism or the influence of the Holy Spirit as central to their missionary objectives.

Daniel Walker's doctoral work, "The Pentecost Fire Is Burning: Models of Mission Activities in the Church of Pentecost,"[75] argues that the Church of Pentecost's (CoP) growth and outreach, stretching from Ghana to other parts of Africa and beyond, can be attributed to the guiding hand of the Holy Spirit. Walker demonstrates how individuals, upon receiving the Holy Spirit's baptism within the Church of Pentecost, promptly embark on evangelistic pursuits, leading to further conversions. This ripple effect of conversions substantially contributes to the church's rapid global expansion.[76]

J. Kwabena Asamoah-Gyadu supports Walker's spiritual affirmation by suggesting that the resurgence of Pentecostalism and the reinvigoration of Christianity in Africa and other regions bear the hallmarks of the Holy Spirit's transformative influence, often likened to a prevailing wind.[77] Citing the Gospel of John, particularly Jesus' dialogue with Nicodemus, Asamoah-Gyadu interprets Nicodemus's Pharisaic stance as emblematic of an old, entrenched religious order, juxtaposed against the Spirit's dynamic and transformative nature—a wind that "blows wherever it pleases."[78]

While the power of the Holy Spirit is deemed paramount in Pentecostal mission strategies, it alone is not sufficient to steer the expansive missionary efforts of the Christian church. This might explain why Winners' Chapel also employs the services of the LFWOC to delineate and drive its missionary practices.[79] The church also uses other media outlets for its purposes.

A Strategic Endeavor: The Dominion Publishing House

The Winners' Chapel has strategically integrated the Dominion Publishing House (DPH) into its missionary framework. As the dedicated publishing division of the David Oyedepo Ministries International (DOMI),

---

75. Walker, "Pentecost Fire Is Burning."
76. Walker, "Pentecost Fire Is Burning."
77. Asamoah-Gyadu, *Contemporary Pentecostal Christianity*, 1.
78. Asamoah-Gyadu, *Contemporary Pentecostal Christianity*, 1.
79. Faith Tabernacle Canaanland, OTA, "Dominion Publishing House."

DPH's core mission revolves around knowledge dissemination via print media. Bishop Oyedepo, the driving force behind the institution, contends that the magnitude of truth one grasps directly impacts one's level of liberation. Consequently, DPH seeks to saturate the market with insightful, affordable literature accessible to a broad readership.[80]

The significance of DPH was underscored when Pastor Dr. E. A. Adeboye, general overseer of the RCCG, was invited officially to inaugurate the publishing arm on December 5, 1992, at the National Arts Theatre in Lagos.[81] This occasion not only showcased the church's adeptness in harnessing media for evangelistic purposes but was also a platform for launching six of Bishop Oyedepo's insightful works. Titles like *Releasing the Supernatural, Understanding Vision, Excellency of Wisdom,* and *Covenant Wealth* encapsulate the spirit of his writings.

It is essential to understand Bishop Oyedepo's perspective on these publications. Contrary to a profit-oriented outlook, he envisions these writings as tools of enlightenment to alleviate spiritual despondency. He asserts: "we owe people education, and this is what we are doing with the 'Word of Faith' in print, it is a ministry of illumination by literature."[82] Reflecting on the broader influence of DPH, Bishop Oyedepo emphasized during its inauguration that printed words, be it books, tracts, or newsletters, possess a transcendent reach, accessing realms often inaccessible to individuals.[83] The bishop's thoughts raise questions about the link between media and religion. However, it is important to note that from the Reformation onward, Protestants have emphasized the strategic role of printed books, pamphlets, and newsletters in propagating the gospel and educating the faithful. What seems to be new or more recent from the mid-twentieth century onward is the use of electronic media—radio, TV, film, cassettes, and now social media—for such purposes.

The Interplay between Media and Religion

Contemporary studies in religion and Christian mission reveal an increasingly intricate relationship between media and religious practices. This linkage is gaining paramount significance as numerous religious

---

80. Faith Tabernacle Canaanland, OTA, "Dominion Publishing House."
81. Faith Tabernacle Canaanland, OTA, "Dominion Publishing House."
82. Faith Tabernacle Canaanland, OTA, "Dominion Publishing House."
83. Faith Tabernacle Canaanland, OTA, "Dominion Publishing House."

movements are embracing the concept of "mediatization of religion" and, concurrently, "religionization of the media" within their ambit of outreach endeavors. It is within this domain that we encounter various forms of media, including individual church websites, television channels, radio programs, and publications authored by church founders and leaders. These media serve a dual purpose: to showcase the vibrancy and visibility of religious establishments and to effectively facilitate their missionary initiatives. Thus, recent scholarly work on religious media has foregrounded the potential for this central category of analysis in the study of religion to provide fresh perspectives on many of the core concepts in the social sciences.[84] Such concepts include power, representation, transformation, citizenship, authority, diaspora, and agency.[85]

An example of such academic explorations is the work of Innocent Chiluwa, who employs a sociolinguistic-based discourse analytical approach to the negotiation and practice of African-Christian activities on the internet. His study shows that worshipers perceive Christian media as a sanctified space reserved exclusively for spiritual pursuits, distinct from platforms for sharing social or individual emotions and concerns.[86] In a similar vein, Larsen observes that the internet has undergone a process of "spiritualization" where worshipers employ conventional discourses in digital spaces or popular media for religious intents.[87] Rosalind Hackett offers a comprehensive framework for understanding these perspectives within the context of transnational discourses. She posits that the use of the media not only functions as a tool for expansion and a reflection of globalizing aspirations but is also an intentional effort to transform and infuse popular culture with Christian values, rendering it palatable for consumption by "born-again" Christians.[88]

The relationship between religion and media in the contemporary world is one that invites rigorous scrutiny. The assertion that the media holds the power to surpass local and national barriers, potentially attracting individuals to Christianity through print literature, is both enlightening and contentious. While such arguments highlight the growing influence of media on religious narratives, a critical appraisal suggests a

84. Hackett et al., "Interview: Rosalind Hackett Reflects," 68.

85. Hackett et al., "Interview: Rosalind Hackett Reflects," 68.

86. Chiluwa, "Community and Social Interaction," 1–2.

87. E. Larsen, "Cyberfaith: How Americans Pursue Religion Online," in Dawson and Cowan, *Religion Online*, 17–20.

88. Hackett, "Charismatic/Pentecostal Appropriation," 258.

potential oversight in considering the broader socioeconomic landscape, particularly in Africa. The primary concern lies in quantifying the reach of these religious media forms. How widespread is the readership of these books, particularly in remote African regions where day-to-day survival and manual labor dominate people's lives? A significant number of these populations return home exhausted from farm work, often without access to basic amenities such as electricity—a prerequisite for reading in the dark or utilizing other forms of media like television or the internet.

However, these concerns collocate against a stereotype that alleges an inherent disinterest or apathy among Africans toward print literature, encapsulated in the old adage "if you want to hide something from blacks, you put it in books." The burgeoning consumption of Christian publications by Africans challenges this assumption, rendering it outdated and arguably invalid. The rise in literacy rates across the continent not only signifies a thirst for education but also underlines the pivotal role print media plays in the proliferation of Christianity.[89] Historical antecedents underscore the significant influence of print in advancing Christian narratives.[90] Given this backdrop, it is hardly surprising that religious establishments, such as the LFCW, leverage print media as a strategic tool to expand their global footprint and disseminate their foundational values.

---

89. Coppedge, *African Literacies and Western Oralities?*
90. Granberg-Michaelson, *From Times Square to Timbuktu*, 2.

Chapter Four

The Strategic Rise of Winners' Chapel in Cameroon

IN 1996, CAMEROON WITNESSED the establishment of Winners' Chapel, an initiative spearheaded by two dedicated missionaries from Nigeria. These individuals were representing the African Gospel Invasion Programme, an extension of the World Mission Agency of Winners' Chapel, conceived by Bishop Oyedepo on May 8, 1994. This entity was passionately committed to spreading the gospel of Jesus Christ across Africa. The inaugural mission took place on January 15, 1995, targeting seven African nations. Initial efforts included establishing Bible schools to impart teachings on faith and prosperity. By the end of 1995, Winners' Chapel had established its presence in nations such as Ethiopia, Kenya, Zaire, Uganda, Brazzaville (Republic of Congo), Monrovia (Liberia), and Freetown (Sierra Leon).[1] Cameroon joined the fold in March 1996, along with other nations like Togo, the Republic of Benin, Burkina Faso, Chad, Ghana, Côte d'Ivoire, and Senegal.[2] Traversing through Mamfe, the two

1. Matthews Ojo, "Nigerian Pentecostalism and Transnational Religious Networks in West African Coastal Regions," in Fourchard et al., *Entreprises Religieuses Transnationales*, 170.

2. Matthews Ojo, "Nigerian Pentecostalism and Transnational Religious Networks in West African Coastal Regions," in Fourchard et al., *Entreprises Religieuses Transnationales*, 170.

Nigerian missionaries eventually reached the coastal city of Limbe in Cameroon's South West region. However, their efforts in Limbe were met with limited success. Seeking a more favorable location, they shifted their focus to Douala, Cameroon's economic epicenter, by April 1996.

Douala's appeal to the missionaries was not merely coincidental. Not only is Douala recognized as the economic heartbeat of Cameroon, but it also boasts a burgeoning population, conservatively estimated at 4,203,000 in 2024. The city is adorned with a diverse tapestry of cultures, significantly influenced by substantial Nigerian and French communities. As the wealthiest metropolis in Central Africa, Douala emanates a cosmopolitan aura, further accentuated by its bustling international airport.[3] Its strategic importance could not be overlooked. While the city's economic vitality undoubtedly enticed the Winners' Chapel missionaries, one could posit that Douala's selection was intrinsically aligned with Bishop Oyedepo's overarching vision for his church. Insights from a member of the Douala church further corroborate this perspective.

> I was not even a member of Winners' Chapel when the church spread to Cameroon but according to Bishop Oyedepo's vision and what he told us in most of our meetings since I joined, Cameroon was one of the countries that God showed him in that vision. He told us that God directed him to start the church in Douala and that is why missionaries from Winners' Chapel Nigeria first established themselves in Douala.[4]

This testimony from an individual who joined Winners' Chapel after its establishment in Cameroon reflects the foundational principles and inspirations behind the church's expansion to Cameroon, as communicated by Bishop Oyedepo. According to the bishop, the decision to branch out to Cameroon, specifically Douala, was divinely inspired. In his vision, God showed him Cameroon as a focal point for the church's growth. The divine directive specifically emphasized Douala as the starting point, leading the missionaries from Winners' Chapel Nigeria to begin their endeavors in this city. The individual's recollection underscores the belief that the church's establishment in Douala was not arbitrary but rather a direct result of divine guidance and the bishop's visionary leadership.

At another level of explanation, it is noteworthy that neo-Pentecostal church leaders frequently choose urban centers for establishing their

---

3. Gale, *World Encyclopaedia of Nations*.
4. Personal interview, Pastor Paul Menyole (pseudonym), in Douala (Feb. 4, 2016).

congregations, targeting the affluent and upwardly mobile segments of society. Consequently, neo-Pentecostalism is often characterized as an urban-centric movement. Lovemore Togarasei's study of the Family of God Church in Zimbabwe exemplifies this trend, noting the church's focus on urban locales that predominantly house the society's middle and upper classes.[5] Factors such as population density, economic potential, cultural diversity, and modern infrastructure further contribute to the urban preference of Pentecostal Charismatic churches.

In the case of Winners' Chapel, the initial area of operation for the missionaries in Douala was Bonaberi, a region primarily inhabited by Anglophone Cameroonians. This choice aimed to ensure seamless communication, sidestepping potential language barriers. To integrate themselves within the community and introduce their mission, the missionaries initially approached established Pentecostal churches during Sunday services. Presenting themselves as envoys from Winners' Chapel, Nigeria, they clarified their goal: not to plant new churches, but to spiritually reinforce existing ones. They sought partnerships to bolster spiritual strength and kindle the fervor of the Holy Spirit within these congregations. Such intentions echoed earlier statements made by Bishop Oyedepo during the nascent phases of his ministry:

> When the Mandate was delivered in 1981, I saw it mainly as an outreach, because at that time, church planting was not considered relevant. We were more concerned about believing God for revival in the existing churches. Also, when the Mandate was delivered, church wasn't particularly mentioned. I thought it was going to be an outreach ministry. My stand was that there were enough churches already, so we didn't need another one.[6]

Oyedepo's comments reflect his initial perceptions and priorities concerning his spiritual mission or "Mandate" received in 1981. At that juncture, the focus was not establishing new churches, but rather on invigorating the spiritual vitality of existing ones. He saw the Mandate primarily as a call to outreach, likely meaning a mission to extend spiritual help and teachings outside the confines of the traditional church setting. The absence of explicit mention of "church" in the Mandate further strengthens his perspective. Oyedepo's sentiment that there were already

---

5. Togarasei, "Modern Pentecostalism as an Urban Phenomenon," 349–75. Also see Parsitau and Mwaura, "God in the City," 95–112.

6. Oyedepo, *Mandate*, 20.

an ample number of churches suggests a desire to enhance the quality and depth of existing spiritual communities rather than proliferate more institutions. In essence, the emphasis was on spiritual rejuvenation and revival, not expansion.

The idea of spiritual reformation, rather than foundation, is central. Oyedepo's mission appears to position Nigeria, or more specifically his church, within a narrative of chosen entities tasked with spiritual reformation in Africa. Given the already vast number of churches, Oyedepo felt it nonessential to add to their number. Thus, the missionaries' initial strategy in Cameroon was to collaborate with existing churches, offering training and empowerment. Their aim was a spiritual resurgence, a revitalization of the authentic presence and power of God with the Cameroonian religious landscape. Among the churches they collaborated with were the Full Gospel Mission Cameroon, the Apostolic Church, and the Bible Pentecostal Church.

In June 1996, the Winners' Chapel missionaries visited the Faith Bible Church.[7] They were warmly welcomed by its founder and senior pastor, Rev. Zach Njafuh, at the Bonaberi branch. Presented with the opportunity to address the congregation, the missionaries shared their mission's objectives, emphasizing the spiritual enlightenment they hoped to impart through their Bible school. Njafuh, deeply moved by their message, anticipated immense spiritual benefits for his church from this collaboration. He was quick to extend an invitation for the missionaries to deliver a sermon the following Sunday.

The subsequent session conducted by the missionaries profoundly impacted the members of the Faith Bible Church. A testament to the depth of this influence was a member who graciously offered to house the missionaries. This same individual later introduced the missionaries to their first Cameroonian staff member. Initially serving as a secretary, introducing and documenting the missionaries' endeavors, this individual has since advanced to become one of the church's accountants and an assistant pastor at a local Winners' Chapel congregation.

---

7. According to the website of the Faith Bible Church, "Who We Are," "Faith Bible Church was founded on the 21st of August 1994 by Rev. Zach Njafuh, Senior Pastor. He is said to be commissioned by God to minister to the whole man (soul, spirit and body). God gave him a mandate to minister the uncompromised Word of God and to demonstrate His healing power to this generation. FBC (the headquarters) is a church of about 1000 members presently. She started her expansion in 1999 and now has 8 branch churches around the nation."

Following the impactful ministration by the missionaries at the Faith Bible Church, they announced the commencement of a Bible school the following day. In July 1996, the Bible school was founded at "Centre Caisse in Bonaberi" with an initial enrollment of eleven. Classes were scheduled for Mondays, Tuesdays, Thursdays, and Saturdays, focusing primarily on prosperity, health, and wealth, which are central tenets of Oyedepo's theological doctrine. Initially, attendees were encouraged by the missionaries to continue attending their respective churches on Sunday mornings, reserving the Bible school sessions for specific weekdays. By August 1996, the attendance at the Bible school had swelled from eleven to over fifty, showing no signs of abating. The venue at Centre Caisse Bonaberi soon became too small to accommodate the growing numbers. Consequently, the group decided to relocate to the Douala city center, hoping to secure a larger facility. They eventually found a rental property adjacent to Akwa, specifically at Rue Bebey Eyidi, and formally established the Word of Faith Bible Institute (WOFBI) in November 1996.

As the Bible school sessions began to whet the spiritual appetite of its attendees, they increasingly yearned for regular worship services on Sunday mornings. They sought an environment that would allow them to fully experience this new variant of Pentecostalism that had taken root in Cameroon. The teachings revolving around health, wealth, and success resonated deeply with the prevailing socioeconomic challenges faced by Cameroon, mirroring the struggles of many African nations during this period of economic turmoil. Furthermore, for adherents of classical Pentecostal churches such as the Full Gospel Mission International, the teachings of the missionaries offered a distinct perspective. It did not censure the pursuit of material prosperity like the older Pentecostal churches but instead promoted it. This emerging gospel was forward-looking, charismatic, and life-affirming. Interpretations of scriptural passages in a manner that celebrated worldly materialism in its temporal and spatial dimensions instilled hope and assurance in many individuals grappling with the difficulties of earthly existence. For a significant number of attendees, this was their initial exposure to teachings that presented prosperity, health, and wealth in such a compelling manner, firmly grounded in scriptural foundations. The distinctiveness of these novel teachings, coupled with the experience of witnessing signs and wonders among the Christian community, led to an ever-increasing thirst for spiritual nourishment. Eventually, this hunger culminated in a demand for the establishment of a new church. One of the pioneering attendees of WOFBI shares his personal experience:

> I had been a Christian from birth and had attended the Roman Catholic Church before joining the Apostolic Church. But the day I attended the Word of Faith Bible Institute, everything was different. I had never been so touched by the word of God the way I felt. Those men could preach the word of God . . . . What I really enjoyed was the way they were encouraging us to become rich, to make money, to be wealthy, to prosper. And they were using the Bible to support all the things they were telling us. The Apostolic Church was only telling us that our riches are in heaven. But I learned from these Nigerians that we should seek riches here on earth. What I have discovered with Winners' Chapel is their ability to transform man because their teachings are so practical, and they give people the opportunity to develop their skills using the Bible. That is how I fell in love with the Winners' Chapel family. Through their teachings, I am a prosperous man today.[8]

This quotation reflects the transformative experience that ensued upon attending the Word of Faith Bible Institute. Having been raised in the Christian faith and having attended more traditional Christian denominations, the commentator found that the teachings at the Institute represented a marked departure from what he had previously known. The primary difference that stood out was the Institute's empowering approach to interpreting the Bible. Instead of emphasizing asceticism or the belief that one's riches lie in the afterlife (as they had learned in previous denominations), the teachings at the Institute focused on the idea that believers can and should seek prosperity in their earthly lives. This prosperity was not just about wealth, but also about personal development, skill enhancement, and living a fulfilled life. The Institute used scriptural references to back up these teachings, which was novel and impactful for the individuals.

The emphasis on prosperity, both in terms of wealth and personal development, greatly resonated with the individual. It offered a more pragmatic and tangible approach to spirituality, suggesting that one's faith could be a guiding force for success and prosperity in the present world, not just the hereafter. The teachings at the Institute were not just

---

8. Personal interview with Sam Loco (pseudonym) in Bonaberi-Douala (Oct. 6, 2016).

theoretical; they were actionable, giving attendees tools and perspectives to practically apply in their lives.

This distinct approach to scripture instilled a sense of exceptionality and resonance among the listeners. Consequently, many were drawn toward the idea of departing from their traditional religious affiliations to embrace a new, independent Pentecostal community. This new congregation would consistently champion the triumphant essence of the gospel and provide an environment to practice the principles of prosperity as taught by their new mentors. However, despite this mounting enthusiasm, the missionaries remained reluctant to establish a standalone church. This hesitancy persisted until a fresh initiative within the Bible school faced scrutiny, intensifying the congregation's desire for a dedicated place of worship.

"Manna from Heaven"

In early 1997, the missionaries started what they called "Manna from Heaven." This program was held every Sunday evening from 4:00 to 6:00 p.m. It was primarily a session of worship and scriptural proclamation, rather than a traditional church service. The intention was to cater to those Bible school attendees who had not affiliated with any church. Conversely, those already affiliated to existing churches were encouraged to remain steadfast in their original congregations. However, this innovative approach did not sit well with established Pentecostal denominations. They expressed concerns over the missionaries' dual engagements: running a Bible school and conducting Sunday evening services. This was problematic enough for the missionaries but what further exacerbated tensions was the critique and skepticism faced by attendees of the "Manna from Heaven" sessions, especially those from other churches. Their peers questioned the new teaching that accentuated prospects of material prosperity.

Critics argued that this approach, which emphasized material blessings as an avenue to salvation and undermined the spiritual significance of suffering, was at odds with traditional biblical teachings. They believed that the central theme of these teachings, focusing on acquiring wealth and perceiving giving as a means to attain material benefits, was fundamentally misaligned with the essence of biblical salvation, the role of adversity in Christian life, and the genuine spirit of generosity. The naysayers posited that such teachings seemed more attuned to generating revenue rather than genuinely propagating God's word. This skepticism was palpable, with followers occasionally being portrayed as misguided souls on the path to damnation. This sentiment is vividly captured in the words of an elder from the Full Gospel Church, recounted by a former member who faced reproach:

> What are you doing there? They don't talk about holiness in their teachings but only about prosperity! Have those your preachers ever looked at what Jesus meant in the New Testament when he asked: "what would it profit a man if he gains the whole world and loses his soul? All they talk about is money, houses, cars, comfort, and nothing else! I pity those of you who are following such misleading teachings in the name of the gospel." However, "I" [respondent] told the elder that all what is being preached in the Winners' Chapel is in the Bible; it is just that the other churches don't want to teach the truth to their Christians. But I had to make up my mind completely to be attending *Manna from Heaven* and after the elder spoke to me like that I decided to leave my former church and join the Winners' Chapel, when they started their own branches in Cameroon. I was not happy with the way he spoke to me about something that I was really enjoying and knew it was the best and right thing.[9]

Such dismissive and challenging remarks became catalysts, prompting many attendees of the WOFBI to advocate for the inception of a dedicated Winners' Chapel congregation in Cameroon. They sought an environment where they would feel not just secure and welcomed but spiritually invigorated, especially as their former affiliations seemed less accommodating. These newly transformed believers aspired to be in a setting that resonated with their newfound comprehension of biblical teachings. As they immersed themselves into these new teachings, they encountered interpretations of familiar scriptures that were refreshingly insightful, leading some to exclaim, "what is this new thing that we are hearing, let's go and see."[10]

In discussing the expansion of Winners' Chapel in Africa, Matthews Ojo has suggested that the emphasis on success and prosperity by missionaries seemed to align seamlessly with the ambitions of an emerging

---

9. Personal interview with Sam Loco (pseudonym) in Bonaberi-Douala (Oct. 6, 2016).

10. Personal interview with Sam Loco (pseudonym) in Bonaberi-Douala (Oct. 6, 2016).

class of young, educated individuals navigating the currents of modernization.[11] Ruth Marshall-Fratani distinguishes between the traditional manifestations of Pentecostalism, exemplified by churches like the Full Gospel Mission, and the more contemporary expressions like Winners' Chapel. The former often accentuated a "holiness" doctrine and a leaning toward anti-materialism, while the latter positions itself more robustly within worldly aspirations.[12] For adherents of these newer Pentecostal churches, the reward of a devout Christian life encompasses both spiritual and material blessings.[13] While it may be an overgeneralization to state that one Pentecostal subset is solely dedicated to the principles of holiness and the other exclusively to material prosperity,[14] the paradigm shift from a primary "holiness" doctrine to a prevailing "prosperity" orientation arguably propelled the WOFBI devotees to establish a church that fully embodies these modern tenets.

The Emergence of Winners' Chapel Congregations in Cameroon

In the latter part of 1997, Winners' Chapel Cameroon made its official debut in a leased hall at "Bus Du Travail," Douala, starting with an initial congregation of eighty.[15] To mitigate criticisms and showcase their benign intentions, the missionaries implemented a unique policy. New members were asked to produce a letter from their previous churches, confirming they had departed on amicable terms. This was a strategic attempt to demonstrate that individuals were gravitating toward Winners' Chapel out of genuine spiritual resonance rather than compulsion.[16] However, this policy has since been phased out. The contemporary focus seems to have shifted toward fostering growth and expansion; larger

---

11. Matthews Ojo, "Nigerian Pentecostalism and Transnational Religious Networks in West African Coastal Regions," in Fourchard et al., *Entreprises Religieuses Transnationales*, 170.

12. Marshall-Fratani, "Mediating the Global and Local," 282.

13. Marshall-Fratani, "Mediating the Global and Local," 285.

14. The theological boundaries between classical Pentecostal and Pentecostal/Charismatic churches have become increasingly fluid in recent years.

15. Pastors Peter Toh and Victor Bong, various interviews in Douala.

16. Pastors Peter Toh and Victor Bong, various interviews in Douala.

congregations symbolize success and can potentially lead to elevated roles and responsibilities for pastors.[17]

The gradual expansion of the church in Douala, with rapid growth from about 150 members in early 2001 to over 500 by 2006, underscored the need for a more expansive, permanent location. Answering this need, the church secured a property at Carrefour Zachmann in Ndogbong, Douala, in 2006, with significant financial backing from its international headquarters based in Nigeria. Now serving as the Cameroonian national headquarters of Winners' Chapel, the Ndogbong facility houses the administrative nerve center, orchestrating nationwide operations and liaising with the Nigerian base. In 2021 it welcomed over 4,400 attendees across its two Sunday services.

The Growth of Winners' Chapel Cameroon

An analysis spanning over two decades (1996–2022) paints a vivid portrait of the remarkable expansion of Winners' Chapel within Cameroon. Data sourced from Douala in 2019 catalogues a commendable proliferation of congregations, numbering at over 135. Dissecting this further, the Francophone regions hosted 74, while the Anglophone regions were home to 61 congregations. An interesting observation is the establishment of 8 branches in the Northern regions, predominantly Francophone yet significantly influenced by Muslim culture. Beyond the borders of Cameroon, yet under its provincial purview as per the global church mapping of Winners' Chapel, 8 more churches were operational. They were situated in diverse locations such as Malabo (Equatorial Guinea), Ndjamena, Doba, Moundou, Abeche, Bongor (all in Chad), and extending to Guadalupe-Sao Tome and Trinidad in Sao Tome. A visual representation of these congregations across the province of Cameroon is provided in the ensuing chart from 2019.

---

17. Pastor Paul Menyole, interview, Douala (Feb. 4, 2016).

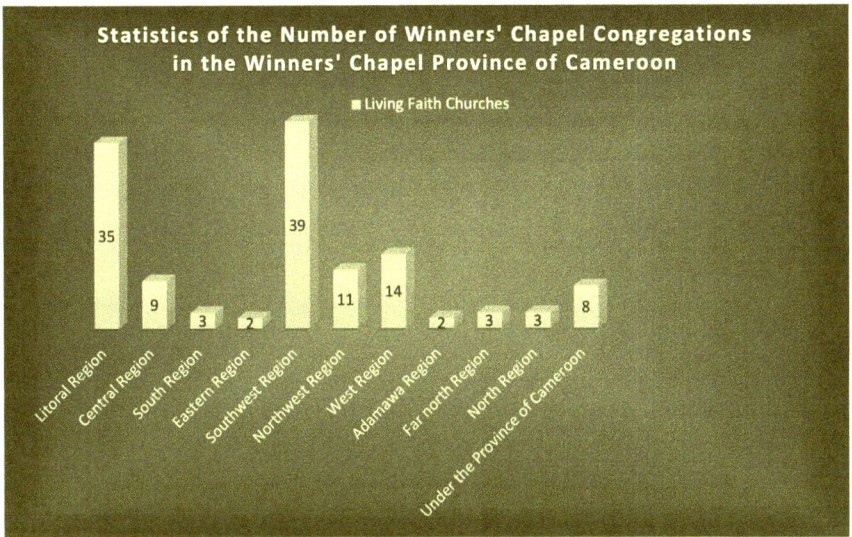

Figure 1: Statistics of Winners' Chapel congregations in the province of Cameroon in 2019.[18]

The spatial distribution of Winners' Chapel congregations across Cameroon exhibits a remarkable intersection of religious and linguistic geographies. Within the ten administrative regions of Cameroon, Winners' Chapel has established a total of over 135 congregations that punctuate the national landscape, extending its ecclesiastical network to eight additional congregations within neighboring territories—territories that collectively fall under the administrative oversight of the Winners' Chapel province of Cameroon.[19]

The diffusion of these congregations is not uniform; rather, it reflects a significant degree of linguistic and cultural integration. In the Francophone urban agglomerates of Douala, Yaoundé, Ebolowa, Bertoua, and Bafoussam, which are anchored in the southern belt of the nation, there is a pronounced presence of Winners' Chapel assemblies. This is indicative of the church's penetration into regions characterized by a dominant French linguistic influence. In stark contrast, the northern regions,

18. This chart and table have been created from a document entitled "Winners Chapel Locations in the Region, 2015 statistics." Document obtained in Douala, Feb. 5, 2016, and in the possession of the author.

19. All nations where Winners' Chapel has extended and is spreading are known as provinces, which fall under a region. Cameroon is a province under the Central African region of the Winners' Chapel.

encapsulated by Ngaoundere, Maroua, and Garoua—also Francophone but with a pronounced Islamic cultural influence—present a different pattern of Winners' Chapel congregation distribution.

In the Anglophone sphere, Buea and Bamenda emerge as emblematic of the English-speaking regions, situated within the southern corridor of the nation. Here, the South West region, distinguished by its coastal identity, is identified as having the most substantial concentration of Winners' Chapel churches within the Anglophone geographic confines. This preponderance in the Anglophone regions could suggest a strategic or organic affiliation with the linguistic and cultural ethos of the community. Conversely, in the Littoral region—Francophone in character—there is a noteworthy density of Winners' Chapel congregations, underscoring the church's robust presence even within the French-speaking areas of the country. The sparsest distribution of Winners' Chapel congregations is observed within the Adamawa and Eastern regions. The lesser congregation density in these areas could be reflective of a multitude of factors ranging from demographic to cultural and socioeconomic dimensions that may influence religious affiliation and church establishment.

The evidence suggests that the actual number of congregations may have exceeded 135, as not all branches were mentioned in the official records. Particularly, congregations in semi-urban and rural areas were often overlooked. An example is the Winners' Chapel branch in Wum, a semi-urban region, conspicuously missing from official records. Such omissions may stem from the church's tendency to prioritize urban, affluent congregations. Illustrating this urban-centric approach is the fact that no Nigerian national pastors from Douala had visited the Wum branch in its more than two-decade history in Cameroon. Furthermore, it is intriguing to note that the Wum church was headed by a Cameroonian woman, a departure from the church's conventional leadership patterns, as female heads are seldom observed within the broader Winners' Chapel community.[20]

This distributional analysis of Winners' Chapel in Cameroon not only underlines the church's comprehensive national reach but also raises intriguing questions about the interaction between religious movements and the complex socio-linguistic tapestry within which they operate. The variegated presence across different regions, with varying degrees of concentration, suggests a nuanced pattern of religious engagement

---

20. "Winners Chapel Locations in the Region, 2015 statistics." Document obtained in Douala, Feb. 5, 2016.

and propagation that intertwines with the diverse cultural and linguistic landscape of Cameroon. It also reveals a well-defined structure that guarantees the effective mission of the church.

Power Structures of Winners' Chapel in Cameroon

As mentioned earlier, a structured hierarchy exists within Winners' Chapel, meticulously organizing the flow of power and authority from the national echelon down to the grassroots level. This intricate network is centered on the Nation (Nigeria) as its apex body, bearing resemblance to the historical significance of the nation of Israel in biblical contexts. This equivalence implies that Nigerians occupy a pivotal role, potentially portraying them as the divinely chosen, or, at the very least, a favored demographic where spiritual luminaries within the movement reside. Consequently, Christianity's influence and fortunes extend outward from this epicenter to encompass other regions and populations.

The Nation is overseen by a National Council, the chairman of which is Bishop Oyedepo. Subsequently, there are Regions, each encompassing several countries. For instance, the Central African Region incorporates countries within Central Africa, with Congo Kinshasa serving as its hub. Further below are Provinces, which are the constituent countries forming a Region, in this context, Cameroon functions as a Province. Within a Province, the organizational structure comprises Districts, Zones, Areas, and Local Assemblies. Each of these administrative entities is overseen by its respective council, charged with both spiritual and administrative responsibilities, efficiently managing the vast ecclesiastical network under their purview. Figure 2 shows the administrative structure of the Winners' Chapel in the province of Cameroon and their representative leaders.

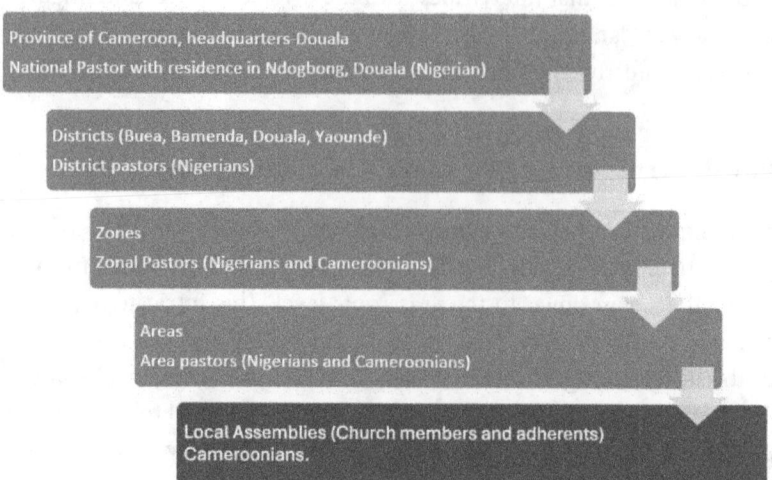

Figure 2: The administrative structure of Winners' Chapel in Cameroon in order of hierarchy from top down.[21]

The province of Cameroon is made up of all Winners' Chapel congregations in Cameroon including eight congregations in Equatorial Guinea, Chad, and Sao Tome, as shown in figure 1.[22] There are four Districts in the province (Buea, Bamenda, Douala, and Yaoundé), led by Nigerian missionaries. There are nine Zones in the province, also led by Nigerian missionaries and some Cameroonians.[23] There are twenty Winners' Chapel Areas in Cameroon. The province, districts, zones and areas are managed by councils led by chairpersons who are all pastors with direct connections to the leadership in Nigeria. There were more than twenty Nigerian Winners' Chapel missionaries in Cameroon in 2019.[24]

The hierarchical architecture of Winners' Chapel, as delineated in figure 1, underscores the prominence of Nigerian missionaries. This prominence is attributable to their pivotal links with Nigeria and direct affiliations with the bishop. The systematic chain of communication, extending from area pastors to zonal and district pastors, eventually

---

21. This smart chart has been adapted from the National Church Structure of the Winners Chapel as outlined in Oyedepo, *Mandate*, 275.

22. See figure 1 for details of the total number of congregations in the province of Cameroon.

23. Telephone conversation with Pastor Peter Toh (pseudonym) (Feb. 17 2019).

24. Telephone conversation with Pastor Peter Toh (pseudonym) (Feb. 17 2019).

culminates with the national pastor. The latter then liaises with the regional pastor in Congo Kinshasa before ultimately relaying information to David Oyedepo in Nigeria. This meticulously crafted structure not only ensures accountability toward the church's visionary leader but also facilitates the dissemination of Bishop Oyedepo's spiritual and charismatic influence from Nigeria to his followers in Cameroon and throughout the province.

Strategies for Establishing Winners' Chapel Branches

Winners' Chapel adopts a systematic approach when establishing new branches in Cameroon. Initially, a city is pinpointed based on recommendations from current church members residing in the prospective location. Subsequently, promotional handbills, emphasizing the church's core philosophies such as success, wealth, healing, and miracles, are crafted. These materials also announce a designated date for an upcoming church conference. Once these handbills are disseminated throughout the city, a conference is convened on the specific date. High-ranking church officials explain the fundamental tenets of Winners' Chapel and urge attendees to embrace Christ. These new members are then organized into smaller "Satellite Churches," which are advised to convene biweekly. The culmination of this process sees the assignment of a pastor from the Douala headquarters to unite these satellite groups in a leased venue. Although the national headquarters in Douala initially shoulders the rent, the local assembly eventually assumes this responsibility, as well as covering the pastor's salary and remitting a portion of their earnings back to Douala. An assembly's inability to generate adequate funds and fulfill these obligations may result in its closure due to underperformance. This strategy has facilitated the widespread presence of Winners' Chapel across all ten regions of Cameroon.[25]

In one of his analyses, Afe Adogame references Clifford Hill to contrast the dwindling influence of traditional Christianity in Britain against the burgeoning presence of black Christian movements. Adogame draws attention to the trajectory of the Celestial Churches of God in Europe as a testament to how Pentecostal movements can both expand transnationally and flourish domestically.[26] While Adogame's observation about

25. Personal interview with Pastor Peter Siegnie (pseudonym), Douala (Feb. 2, 2016).
26. Adogame, "Home away from Home," 141–60.

the waning influence of traditional Christianity in Great Britain may not entirely apply to Cameroon, where such traditions remain robust, his insight about the spread of Pentecostal religious movements is resonant. This is evident in the proliferation of Winners' Chapel in Cameroon and the growth of similar African Pentecostal movements across various regions. The Nigerian-based RCCG, much like Winners' Chapel, made a foray into Cameroon in the late 1990s and has since also established its presence across all ten regions of the country.[27] This has largely been engineered by the ability of transnational Pentecostal churches to modify their missionary strategies, to be flexible and responsive to new situations, challenges, or environments, ensuring that goals can still be met even if the original plans need to change.

Strategic Adaptability

The emergence of Winners' Chapel in Cameroon appears to be a blend of deliberate strategy and situational adaptation. The initial phase seemed meticulously orchestrated, as evidenced by the Nigerian missionaries who arrived with a clear blueprint for evangelizing within this fresh missionary, or spiritually malnourished, territory—Cameroon. Their primary objective, as portrayed, was to instill the faith gospel through education and to empower Cameroonians to rejuvenate existing churches. Interestingly, the missionaries had initially indicated no inclination toward establishing distinct Winners' Chapel congregations within the nation.

However, three pivotal factors influenced the birth of Winners' Chapel in Cameroon. Firstly, the teachings of the missionaries deeply resonated with the spiritual yearnings of the local populations. Secondly, the perceived marginalization and judgment faced by adherents from their original church communities fostered feelings of alienation. Lastly, the Sunday evening sessions, titled "Manna from Heaven," began to attract a diverse set of attendees, both affiliated and unaffiliated with other churches. These compelling developments led to the transformation of the Bible school into a fully fledged church.

In retrospect, while the emergence of Winners' Chapel in Cameroon might seem serendipitous, it also hints at a strategic foresight by the missionaries. Their initial reluctance to set up individual congregations might have been a calculated move to integrate seamlessly into existing

---

27. Adogame, "Home away from Home," 141–60.

Cameroonian congregations, thereby creating a foundational base for their own church. This strategic intent becomes perceptible when considering a statement by Bishop Oyedepo:

> One early morning . . . God showed me something else from Luke chapter 1: For as much as many have taken in hand to set forth in order a declaration of those things which are most surely believed among us, even as they delivered them unto us, which from the beginning were eyewitnesses, and ministers of the word; it seemed good to me also . . . Luke 1:1–3. God was telling me, "there are many churches, yes; but I am giving you a portion of the church ministry." I also . . . became the marching order for our Church Ministry. That is "others have written it, but you have a part of it to write."[28]

This quotation contrasts two separate claims or visions that Oyedepo reportedly received from God. The first vision emphasized the revival of existing churches, while the subsequent vision from 1982 allegedly directed Oyedepo to start new churches. The chronological sequence, with missionaries going to Cameroon in 1996, years after the second vision, raises questions about the missionaries' true intentions. One can refer to this dynamic as pragmatic opportunism, suggesting that the missionaries might have been concealing or adjusting their real objectives to adapt to their surroundings, possibly in a strategic attempt to penetrate the existing churches before establishing their own. This balance between adaptability and commitment to core principles is brought into question.

It is evident that there are inconsistencies between Oyedepo's initial and subsequent revelations. This inconsistency raises significant questions about the actual intentions behind the missionary work in Cameroon. If the second vision was truly received in 1982, why was there a delay until 1996 to act upon it, and why wasn't this vision the clear direction from the outset of the missionary journey? What might have been the underlying motivations? Was the initial claim of solely providing Bible training a more accessible entry point into Cameroon's religious landscape, with the larger intent of establishing new churches only revealed once a foothold was secured? Such strategic manoeuvring, if true, could be seen as manipulative and not genuinely in alignment with divinely inspired motives. The oscillation between these visions might be

---

28. Oyedepo, *Mandate*, 21.

indicative of a larger tension between the authentic spiritual mission and the practicalities and politics of expanding a religious institution.

In 2007, Selome Kuponu studied the origins of Winners' Chapel in Lagos and found striking similarities to its foundation in Cameroon. David Oyedepo initiated monthly seminars titled "breakthrough" at the Ikeja Airport Hotel, Lagos. His endeavors received significant endorsement from fellow Pentecostal leaders, who encouraged their congregations to participate. As the attendees gradually absorbed and enjoyed the teachings centered on faith and prosperity, there arose a collective call for the establishment of a new church. Surprisingly, despite previous assertions to the contrary, Oyedepo unveiled plans for a special service, marking the beginning of the Winners' Chapel in Lagos at New Road, Iyana-Lagos.[29]

The strategic model adopted by Winners' Chapel seems to be that Bible training serves as a conduit to infiltrate new territories and attract members from pre-existing congregations. This method not only facilitates the growth of new church branches but also allows Oyedepo to craft a unique narrative within the Christian domain. Given this strategic prowess, the global reach and impact of Winners' Chapel is unsurprising. In Cameroon, for instance, over 90 percent of its members switched from other denominations, including both Pentecostal and historically established churches, to join Winners' Chapel.

Julie and Wonsuk Ma noted that many Pentecostal churches see their main mission as winning souls and therefore to spread Christianity worldwide (Matt 24:14), a belief rooted in many strands of the evangelical tradition including the North American Holiness movement. They believe that all church activities, like Bible schools or charity work, should lead to expanding the church.[30] This proposition hinges on the winning of souls of people who have not yet come to Christ. But for Winners' Chapel, their mission goes beyond just reaching those unfamiliar with Christ. They believe even those already in churches can still face physical and spiritual challenges. Their idea is that if everyone joined Winners' Chapel, the world would be free from suffering and hardship. Paul Gifford observed that, in 2006, every Winners' Chapel service he attended for research included a moment where everyone recited a special promise from Oyedepo, ending with a collective "Amen":

29. Kuponu, "Living Faith Church," 36.
30. Ma and Ma, *Mission in the Spirit*, 5; Anderson, *Introduction to Pentecostalism*.

> In 2006: Everything that shall make your laughter complete, and total shall be added unto you. The desire of everyone's heart shall be delivered. Every trial shall be turned to testimonies. Every struggle shall be turned to miracles. Every form of bareness shall be turned to fruitfulness. Every frustration shall be turned to celebration. Every humiliation shall be turned into honour. Every shame shall be turned to glory. And every curse shall be turned into blessings.[31]

Oyedepo's promise paints a hopeful and optimistic future for adherents of his church, drawing on the idea that hardships and adversities will be transformed into blessings. It embodies the essence of positive outcomes, derived from faith, resilience, and divine providence. The promise that every negative aspect of life, be it trials, struggles, or humiliations, will eventually pave the way for positive outcomes and celebrations, underlines a deeply comforting message often found in Oyedepo's teachings and messages of new-Pentecostal churches.

However, while the quotation offers solace and hope, it raises pertinent questions about passive reliance on divine intervention versus active human agency. While the assurance of every adversity turning into a blessing provides psychological comfort, it may also inadvertently encourage complacency. In real-world situations, while faith can be a pillar of strength, active efforts, perseverance, and resilience are equally important and should be promoted the more. When prosperity promises are not always fulfilled, it might lead to disillusionment and the "revolving door" syndrome in which seekers wander from one prosperity church to another in search of the elusive "golden ticket."[32] A statement that promotes the prosperity gospel can often create unrealistic expectations among followers, making them potentially vulnerable to disillusionment if positive transformations don't manifest as anticipated.

Birgit Meyer pointed out that Pentecostal churches have become well-known for their "prosperity gospel," which suggests that faith can lead to material wealth and health. These churches also have a global vision. You can see it in their names! For example, Winners' Chapel International or the "Mountain of Fire and Miracle Ministries International" show that these churches want to reach people worldwide. They are not just focusing on Africa; they want to be known and influential everywhere.[33] If Birgit

---

31. Gifford, "Trajectories in African Christianity," 283.
32. Haynes, "Moving by the Spirit."
33. Meyer, "Christianity in Africa," 453.

Meyer saw the inclinations of Pentecostal churches as negotiating global flows and notions of identity, Ogbu Kalu talked about how, back in the 1990s, these Pentecostal churches had a big dream. They believed it was God's plan for them to spread their message all over Africa.[34]

Bishop Oyedepo, the leader of Winners' Chapel, is a key player in this movement. His teachings, especially about success and wealth, have a big impact. People listen to him and are influenced by his words. His vision across Nigeria and into Cameroon and more globally is justified in the light of Meyer's and Kalu's theses. But the power of Oyedepo to use his specific teachings on success and wealth to influence members of his church and to empower them to win even more members both in Nigeria and across Africa is significant. After setting up Winners' Chapel in Cameroon, Oyedepo consistently shares his teachings from Nigeria, aiming to reinforce and promote the church's values in these new "mission fields." In the next chapter, we explore the religious ideas and tools Bishop Oyedepo is deploying into Cameroon and discuss their significance for world Christianity in the twenty-first century.

---

34. Kalu, *African Pentecostalism*, 131.

Chapter Five

Power, Persuasion, and Pentecostalism

AMID THE EVER-EVOLVING LANDSCAPE of Africa, two nations, Nigeria and South Africa, loom large, casting vast shadows that define, to a significant extent, the power dynamics within the continent.[1] Yet, for all their evident influence, there remains a dissonance among scholars about the precise terminology to encapsulate the magnitude of their sway.[2] What is it that makes a nation influential? And how do cultural, economic, and spiritual entities within these nations further magnify their impact?

These questions serve as our guideposts as we venture deeper into the tapestry of intra-African power dynamics. Specifically, we examine the case of Nigeria and its ascent as a regional hegemon. Factors such as economic prowess, formidable military presence, and the magnetic pull of its cultural exports have been advanced for its superior power in the sub-region. However, the cinema of Nollywood and the spread of megachurches have also contributed to its dominant position. Further amplifying Nigeria's spiritual gravity are televangelists, whose reported miraculous abilities have not just won them followers but also elevated

1. Ogunnubi and Isike, "Regional Hegemonic Contention," 152.
2. Ogunnubi and Isike, "Regional Hegemonic Contention," 152; Flemes and Wojczewski, "Contested Leadership in International Relations."

Nigeria's reputation as a spiritual powerhouse.[3] It is the relationship between religion and power that forms the basis of this chapter.

One cannot understand the dynamics at play without relating them to the notion of "soft power,"[4] a term coined by Joseph Nye. This concept, which underscores influence without coercion, often through cultural channels, becomes the lens through which we examine the operations of Winners' Chapel, the Pentecostal behemoth birthed in Nigeria. The church's strategic rotation of Nigerian pastors in Cameroon is a testament to the application of soft power. The prevalent belief among many Cameroonians that Nigerian pastors possess a depth of biblical understanding and spiritual insight unparalleled by their own pastors is both intriguing and indicative of the broader dynamic at play. However, the chapter also uncovers other complexities: While Nigerian spiritual teachings and leaders find reverence in Cameroon, a tension simmers beneath the surface. Cameroonian pastors, despite undergoing rigorous training, find themselves eclipsed by their Nigerian counterparts in leadership roles. This is not just a matter of expertise but also indicative of deeper power dynamics, particularly the trust vested by Bishop Oyedepo in his compatriots.

A crucial element in this arrangement of influence is the concept of "spiritual homogenization." Bishop Oyedepo's "Great House Vision" envisions a standardized global identity for Winners' Chapel. To realize this, Nigerian missionaries, seen as vessels of Oyedepo's teachings, are dispatched globally, ensuring the core tenets of the church remain undiluted. But how does a message retain its potency when transmitted across borders? Media, in its myriad forms, becomes the conduit. From Bishop Oyedepo's prolific writings emphasizing the prosperity gospel to the electronic dissemination of sermons and spiritual events, the media bridges geographical chasms, allowing for a unified religious experience. Yet, as this chapter will reveal, all is not harmonious. Voices of dissent rise from the Cameroonian pastors, who, feeling marginalized by the church's Nigerian leadership, call for autonomy and the right to steer their religious course. Their appeal for indigenization echoes across multiple African nations, suggesting a broader pattern of discontent.

In essence, this chapter serves as a voyage into the heart of intra-African Pentecostalism. It attempts to unravel the threads of power, influence, and spiritual governance. How does soft power manifest within

---

3. Ogunnubi and Isike, "Regional Hegemonic Contention," 162.
4. Nye, *Soft Power*.

the realm of religion? And can a balance be struck between maintaining the core tenets of a faith and adapting to the diverse spiritual landscapes of a vast continent?

By using the concept of soft power to analyze the activities of Winners' Chapel in Africa, the argument of this book aligns with broader discourses of diplomacy and international relations. Although the focus of the book revolves around an independent Pentecostal church and its intra-continental dynamics rather than nation-states as a whole, the concept of soft power can be effectively applied to comprehend the mechanisms of power and cultural influence employed by Winners' Chapel in its operations within Cameroon.

Nigerian Missionary Incursions to Cameroon

Since its establishment in Cameroon in 1996, the Winners' Chapel has continued to send missionaries from Nigeria to the country, as mandated by the international headquarters of the church. Apart from the Nigerian national pastor stationed in Ndogbong-Douala, Nigerian missionaries hold the positions of district heads in all four districts of Winners' Chapel in Cameroon.

According to the church's missionary strategy, Nigerian missionaries are expected to spend two years in Cameroon before being deployed to other nations, subsequently being replaced by new Nigerian missionaries. This strategy is implemented to prevent people from becoming too accustomed to one leader and potentially growing weary of them. The regular introduction of new leaders every two years aims to keep the church dynamic, appealing, and innovative. Many adherents of Winners' Chapel, as well as the missionaries themselves, believe that Nigerian leaders possess a superior understanding of the Bible, greater spiritual depth, and superior preaching abilities compared to their Cameroonian counterparts.[5] Therefore, Nigerian missionaries are seen as instrumental in guiding Cameroonians, helping them learn and grow in their understanding of the church, ultimately empowering them to lead Winners' Chapel congregations in Cameroon. As one of my interlocutors remarked, the presence of Nigerian missionaries in Cameroon offers an opportunity for Cameroonian pastors to learn and emulate their practices, enhancing

---

5. Personal interviews with Deaconess Clemantine Ning (pseudonym) in Buea (Nov. 19, 2015).

their performance on the pulpit. "If Nigerian missionaries are coming to Cameroon, it is an opportunity for our own pastors to copy what they are doing, to try to understand from them how they 'caught the fire' and to improve on their performances on the altar."[6]

Evidence suggests that both members of Winners' Chapel and many other Cameroonians are strongly attracted to Nigerian missionaries and preachers, as opposed to Cameroonian pastors. A Cameroonian pastor within the Winners' Chapel expressed frustration over the lack of affirmation received from their compatriots, noting that when a Cameroonian pastor leads a service, the response is often lukewarm, whereas the presence of a Nigerian pastor elicits enthusiastic reactions:

> Our ministries are hardly affirmed by our Cameroonian brothers and sisters. When a Cameroonian pastor goes up to the altar and shouts hallelujah the response is usually cold and lukewarm but if it is a Nigerian the shouts can bring down the ceiling. Cameroonians believe that Nigerians are the ones who can make miracles and that their own anointing is special.[7]

An illustrative example of this pattern can be found in a comparison between the attendance at a crusade organized by a young Cameroonian Pentecostal pastor, which drew only around forty-five people in a venue with a capacity of over one thousand, and a crusade organized by Apostle Johnson Suleman, a prominent and controversial Nigerian Pentecostal apostle, in the same city in 2015. The latter crusade took place at the Reunification Stadium in Bepanda-Douala and saw over sixty thousand attendees, nearly twice the stadium's capacity and ignoring any health and safety regulations. Commentators noted that this was the highest recorded attendance in the stadium's history, surpassing even the massive turnout during a football match between Cameroon and Ghana many years prior.[8]

While it is unfair to directly compare the popularity of a young Cameroonian pastor with an established international figure from Nigeria, similar arguments have been made regarding the preference for Nigerian transnational Pentecostal pastors over their Cameroonian counterparts, or the significant influence and spiritual power of Nigerian Pentecostal pastors and prophets. An example lies within the narrative of liberation,

---

6. Personal interview with Pastor Sako Emmanuel in Douala (Nov. 19, 2015).
7. Personal interview with Pastor Clement Mbambad in Buea (Feb. 4, 2016).
8. Ajei, "Apostle Suleman Johnson's Crusade."

where Cameroonians continue to derive inspiration from the prophetic messages and displays of the late Nigerian prophet T. B. Joshua. The evidence underscores the profound longing within the Cameroonian community to embark on a pilgrimage to T. B. Joshua's Synagogue Church of All Nations in Nigeria, driven by the desire to utilize his blessed religious objects in their quest to confront, dismantle, or transcend the perceived malevolent forces that hinder their socioeconomic progress.[9] This exemplifies the significant impact of T. B. Joshua's teachings and the practices on the collective consciousness of Cameroonians. These observations suggest that Nigerian influence remains strong in Cameroon, particularly within Pentecostal religious circles. The increasing attraction toward Nigerian pastors, their ideologies, and their patterns of ministry can be attributed to their televised displays of miracles and their periodic crusades held in Cameroon.

In public diplomacy, countries may achieve their goals in world politics by inspiring admiration for their values, serving as examples to be emulated, and arousing aspirations for similar levels of prosperity. Powerful actors recognize the necessity of shaping the agenda and attracting others, rather than solely relying on military or economic coercion. This form of influence, known as soft power, co-opts individuals rather than forces them into compliance.[10]

Although the concept of "soft power" primarily applies to diplomatic relations among nation-states, it can be employed in the discourse surrounding transnational Pentecostalism, where a church comprises members from multiple countries, with the originating country wielding significant influence.

This book argues that the popularity of Nigerian Pentecostal transnational actors in Cameroon, the crowded nature of their crusades, and the extensive display of instant miracles and testimonies on television screens all serve as manifestations of the soft power employed by Winners' Chapel to influence the religious landscape in Cameroon. Once Cameroonians are convinced that Nigerians excel in ministry and possess the miracles they yearn for, they willingly yield to Nigerian leadership. This sheds light on the reason why Nigerian missionaries are used to lead Winners' Chapel in Cameroon, presenting an effective strategy that attracts new church members who appreciate the spiritual gifts demonstrated by

---

9. Tanzanu, "Practices and Narratives of Breakthrough," 32–66.
10. Nye, "Public Diplomacy and Soft Power," 94–95.

successive missionaries, as each pastor possesses unique areas of gifting, such as preaching, healing, or prosperity.[11]

If, indeed, Cameroonians believe that Nigerian pastors and missionaries have significant leadership potential and can meet their spiritual and related needs, it can be summarized that, consciously or unconsciously, the concept of soft power has played a role in facilitating the intra-African missionary work of Winners' Chapel in Cameroon, driven by the agenda set by Bishop Oyedepo. Nye's assertion that "the ability to establish preferences tends to be associated with intangible assets such as an attractive personality, culture, political values and institutions, and policies that are seen as legitimate or having moral authority" is pertinent here.[12] If Nigerian pastors can influence Cameroonians to desire what they want, coercion becomes unnecessary. Consequently, Cameroonians willingly embrace the leadership of Nigerian missionaries and see them as representative figures of the founding bishop—who holds spiritual power.

Between Spiritual and Temporal Power Relations

The phenomenon of spiritual and temporal power relations within neo-Pentecostalism relates to how influential spiritual leaders transmit and uphold their spiritual power beyond the context of their ministries' origins.

The presence of Nigerian missionaries in Cameroon can be seen as a manifestation of temporal power structures, serving to realize Bishop Oyedepo's vision and mentor Cameroonian pastors in understanding the vision and operational dynamics of the Nigerian-founded church. Nigerian missionaries, sharing a national and cultural heritage with Oyedepo, are well-positioned to provide the necessary temporal power necessary to transmit effectively and sustain the bishop's spiritual power in Cameroon.[13] A former missionary of the Winners' Chapel in Douala affirms that the church's leadership is committed to realizing Oyedepo's vision of liberating the world from poverty and disease, which necessitates the deployment of missionaries to various locations worldwide, including Cameroon.

---

11. Personal interview with Deaconess Philomena Ekum (pseudonym), in Bamenda (Jan. 10, 2016).

12. Nye, "Public Diplomacy," 95.

13. Personal interview with Pastor Peter Toh (pseudonym) in Douala (Oct. 12, 2015).

The hierarchical nature of the church also contributes to the use of Nigerian missionaries, who seamlessly carry out their duties regardless of their location, ensuring consistency in the church's practices. The missionary further highlights that their presence is due to the current absence of indigenous individuals capable of assuming these hierarchical positions, expressing hope that Cameroonians will soon rise to that level. As he commented:

> One of the things about our church leadership is that they are interested in realising the vision, which God gave to God's servant Bishop Oyedepo to liberate the world from poverty and disease. That is one reason why missionaries are sent from Nigeria to different places all over the world and not only to Cameroon. Our church is also hierarchical and as you flow hierarchically in different functions, you perform your duties. For example, as a Zonal Pastor, the same duties that are expected of me here are the same duties that I would carry out in Nigeria, no difference. My essence of being here is because there are no indigenes that can fit into my hierarchy at this moment, but I hope that very soon they too will come up into that level.[14]

The claim suggests that Nigerian missionaries are stationed in Cameroon not only to advance Oyedepo's vision but also to ensure the effective transmission of his spiritual and charismatic power. The Nigerian missionaries serve as reminders of Oyedepo's leadership, influence, and authority over the church in Cameroon. This spiritual and structural arrangement conforms with Asonzeh Ukah's concept of charismatization, whereby a leader imprints their charisma on group members as a leadership strategy.[15] As Oyedepo cannot physically be present in all the churches established under his leadership, he relies on representatives who embody his views and ideologies and possess the temporal power necessary to transmit his charismatic and spiritual authority.

The missionary's claim also implies that there is currently a perceived lack of qualified Cameroonians who can occupy the positions held by Nigerian missionaries due to their alleged deficiency in expertise. An assistant pastor from Winners' Chapel in Bonaberi supports this notion, emphasizing that Nigerian missionaries are indispensable in instilling the core values of Winners' Chapel in Cameroon. The aim is to ensure

---

14. Personal interview with Pastor Victor Hill, in Douala (Nov. 9, 2014).
15. Ukah, "Redeemed Christian Church of God," 104.

that appointed pastors fully comprehend the church's vision and uphold its core values, avoiding deviations from the established traditions:

> What I think is happening now is that Nigerians are there so that Cameroonians who are aspiring to become pastors and leaders should be catching the fire.[16] Catching whatever makes Winners' Chapel to tick because if you don't get it, you will have a situation where you appoint pastors in churches who do not understand the vision of the church and they start doing funny things. So, you get people who know what Winners' Chapel is, who know the core values of the church and who know how Winners' Chapel functions. People who can easily dictate that this is Winners' Chapel tradition or not. I mean it is just inside you.[17]

These ideas suggest that there is currently a dearth of adequately trained Cameroonians with a comprehensive understanding of Winners' Chapel principles serving in Cameroon. This raises questions about the church's failure to train local leadership over its more than two decades of existence in the country. However, evidence reveals that by 2002 at least three pastors who had trained at the Word of Faith Bible Institute (WOFBI) in Nigeria were serving in Cameroon. Additionally, more Cameroonian pastors have undergone training at WOFBI, with over 120 resident Cameroonian pastors within Winners' Chapel in Cameroon.[18] These pastors wonder why trained Cameroonians have not been given prominent positions in the church despite their education and years of service. As one of the pastors lamented, "you mean when we train in the same schools, we don't qualify to hold the same positions; we don't qualify to enjoy the same social facilities?"[19] The discrepancy between their training and their perceived lack of recognition or access to the same benefits raises concerns.

It appears that the deliberate strategy of deploying Nigerian missionaries to key leadership positions in Cameroon, even in the presence of qualified Cameroonians, indicates another motive. This motive suggests that the founder and leader of the church prefers Nigerian missionaries to oversee the activities of his church due to the belief that his compatriots

---

16. "Catching the fire" here refers to the belief that the Nigerian missionaries possess certain spiritual gifts which Cameroonians lack and therefore the latter need to learn from the former.

17. Personal interview with Pastor Sako, in Douala (Nov. 9, 2015).

18. Personal interviews with Pastor Titus Ngah (pseudonym) in Douala (Feb. 2, 2016).

19. Personal interviews with Pastor Titus Ngah (pseudonym) in Douala (Feb. 2, 2016).

will be more loyal, accountable, and better equipped to maintain and advance the church's original mission. Consequently, Nigerian control becomes essential for upholding the church's unique apostolic commission. Another former pastor emphasized the trust and accountability that Nigerian missionaries offer, comparing this organizational structure to the operations of other enterprises based in Europe, where representatives report back to their original countries to defend their interests:

> Even other enterprises from Europe must report back to their original countries because they must defend their interests and why the organisation was created in the first place. The bishop knows these missionaries because they are mostly Yoruba people like him, and he can easily trust them and hold them accountable. That is the reason why he sends them to Cameroon. But I think they are here on assignment, and they must respect their boss because they are working under a boss who is under God. So, you see like I said this is not a Nigerian church but God's church. For quite some time now, I know that they are looking for a Cameroonian to head the church because for example, you see this matter of authorisation, we learned that it is delaying because it is only Nigerians who are leading the church and then they are asking what might be the benefits that the nation gets from the establishment of the church in Cameroon.[20]

The bishop entrusts Nigerian missionaries to uphold the church's values, recognizing their close connection to him and the need for their oversight in Cameroon. This perspective challenges the notion that Winners' Chapel in Cameroon is solely a Nigerian church, as it is led and governed by Nigerians assigned by the bishop. The narrative also reveals a subtle agenda by the church's leadership, utilizing Nigerian missionaries not only to maintain Bishop Oyedepo's apostolic and spiritual power but also to foster homogeneity across different spheres of the church's influence.

The Homogenization of Winners' Chapel

The homogenization of the Winners' Chapel is the process by which the Nigerian-founded church seeks to replicate its organizational and doctrinal structures, practices, and beliefs in other countries to achieve a certain form of uniformity and standardization across its different branches.

---

20. Personal interviews with Pastor Elias Che (pseudonym) in Douala (Nov. 22, 2015).

This involves a range of strategies, including the replication of church services and programs, the adaptation of a standardized organizational structure, the dissemination of the church's doctrines and teachings, and the use of common symbols, languages, and cultural references.

We have noted that the movement of Nigerian missionaries to Cameroon is not unrelated to the fact that the Nigerian leadership sees Nigerians as embodiments of the vision of Bishop Oyedepo with whom they share a common ethnic identity and affinity. They are also thought to understand the implications of a church mandate that emerged in their home context, and they are best suited for its implementation elsewhere to produce a church that is homogenous in character and practice. This ambition for homogeneity is reinforced by Bishop Oyedepo's claim to a divine mandate, symbolized by the "Great House Vision." Oyedepo writes:

> Our church is not a man's idea but a divine mandate. It is neither seeking nor buying into opportunities but a divine command. This was unveiled in a vision on the 6th of September 1983, at a prayer meeting with staff, where I saw a great house coming down from heaven and breaking into splinter houses as it hit the earth. This is why we do the same thing in all churches, why we have the same prophetic theme, the same teaching focus and the same global identity.[21]

The "Great House Vision" arguably justifies Winners' Chapel intra-African and global identity in light of the divine revelation that Oyedepo claims to have received in 1983. But it also informs our insight into the reasons why the church needs to be homogenous all over the world: "I saw a great house coming down from heaven and breaking into splinter houses . . . this is why we do the same thing in all churches."[22]

The desire to create a single worldwide Winners' Chapel is evident in the leadership's aspiration to clone emerging congregations that mirror the Nigerian church. The exportation of Nigerian practices to Cameroon is a manifestation of this homogenizing objective. The internship program for pastors enlisted for foreign missions in Winners' Chapel is designed to impart "the winning ways and virtues of the commission, including stewardship, accountability, integrity, and loyalty."[23] Bishop

---

21. Oyedepo, *Mandate*, 55.
22. Oyedepo, *Mandate*, 55.
23. Oyedepo, *Mandate*, 55.

Oyedepo emphasizes the importance of these virtues, along with true followership, in the fulfillment of the missionary calling:

> Missionaries must be instilled with the core values of true stewardship, open accountability, responsibility, integrity, and loyalty as the intern is taken through documentation/record keeping and other administrative procedures such as church growth indices records, financial management, budgeting, monthly report preparation. Missionaries are also to learn "true followership" which is required for the fulfilment of any calling particularly to ministry.[24]

The seriousness placed on foreign missions within Winners' Chapel is evident in the rigorous training provided to missionaries to ensure their ability to fulfill assigned tasks abroad, despite potentially challenging circumstances. The missionaries are expected to have a deep understanding of the church, maintain connections with the international headquarters in Nigeria, and demonstrate unwavering loyalty to Bishop Oyedepo. Nigerian leaders, well-versed in their founder's teachings, often occupy leadership positions and actively promote Oyedepo's books and the pilgrimage to the annual conference, "Shiloh," held in "Canaanland" in Lagos.[25]

The homogenization efforts within Winners' Chapel raise questions about the balance between unity and cultural diversity. While standardization and replication may facilitate coherence and organizational efficiency, it may also lead to the suppression of local expressions of faith and hinder the organic growth of indigenous leadership. The emphasis on loyalty to the founder and centralization of power in the Nigerian leadership raises concerns about the potential for hierarchical control and the stifling of individual autonomy within the church. Furthermore, the replication of practices and narratives without sufficient contextual adaptation may undermine the cultural richness and diversity of local expressions of spirituality. That is why it is important to reflect on the implications of homogenization within religious movements and examine how and to what extent the pursuit of unity might be overshadowing the value of cultural and spiritual diversity.

Three areas of practice exemplify the homogenizing ambitions of the Winners' Chapel and their implications for world Christianity: the use of ready-made sermons from Nigeria, the reproduction and use of

---

24. Oyedepo, *Mandate*, 55.
25. Gifford, "Trajectories in African Christianity," 288.

Nigerian testimonies, and the appropriation of media in their intra-African operations.

Nigerian Sermons in Cameroon

An essential aspect of the missionary endeavors undertaken by Winners' Chapel is the use of sermons composed in Nigeria and subsequently transmitted to pastors for proclamation in Cameroon. Bishop Oyedepo asserts that he receives a monthly prophetic message from God, which serves as the foundation for the development of sermons that are subsequently disseminated to all Winners' Chapel congregations worldwide via email or other social media platforms. This practice is designed to ensure uniform teaching among all members of Winners' Chapel, on a weekly, monthly, and yearly basis.

The underlying purpose behind Bishop Oyedepo's endeavor to prepare and distribute sermons from Nigeria for global consumption by his followers is twofold: Firstly, it aims to ensure the faithful delivery of his ideals, thereby reinforcing his authority and spiritual influence, even in locations he has never physically visited. Secondly, this practice serves as a mechanism for safeguarding Oyedepo's divinely inspired vision for Winners' Chapel and his goal to rid the world of poverty and suffering. A former Nigerian missionary and pastor of the Winners' Chapel to Cameroon regards this arrangement with great importance:

> We are people under the authority of Bishop Oyedepo and that is how it must be. Disorderliness is created when there are too many opinions on the same matter. I grew up to learn that too many cooks spoil the pudding but at the same time that claim made me query the issue of teamwork. But then it has also made me know that any institution without a head is a "hydra headed monster" as Bishop Oyedepo often says. I have told you that you don't need to travel the whole of Cameroon in order to do your research, our church is one everywhere and I am here to make sure that it happens that way. As you have noticed each time you come here, I am sitting on this table coordinating issues. I need to put in all the concentration in this world to achieve the goals that the bishop has set for this commission.[26]

---

26. Personal interview with Pastor Dominion in Douala (Nov. 17, 2015).

In this quotation, the missionary reveals various aspects of power, representation, and loyalty within the context of an institutional setting. He highlights the identification of all those working with Bishop Oyedepo as individuals under the authority of the bishop, emphasizing the necessity of maintaining this hierarchical structure. The assertion is made that disorderliness arises when too many opinions on a particular matter exist, implying a preference for a more centralized decision-making process. The notion of "too many cooks spoil the pudding" further supports this viewpoint, suggesting that excessive input or dissenting voices can be detrimental to the functioning of the institution. However, the speaker also expresses a degree of ambivalence regarding the issue of teamwork, indicating that he has contemplated the potential benefits of collaboration. Nonetheless, the prevailing belief, reinforced by Bishop Oyedepo's teachings, is that any institution lacking a clear leader becomes chaotic, akin to a "hydra-headed monster." This metaphor conveys the idea that multiple heads lead to confusion and disarray.

Another aspect of this quotation is the pride that the speaker takes in the extensive reach of the church, highlighting its omnipresence throughout Cameroon. He considered it unnecessary for me to travel extensively, because the church's influence pervades the entire country. His role in coordinating various aspects and their commitment to realizing the goals set by Bishop Oyedepo further exemplifies their loyalty and dedication to the institution.

It is helpful to note that the comments raised from the quotation of the Nigerian missionary to Cameroon offers insights into the power dynamics within the Winners' Chapel and the importance of centralized authority. They reflect the belief that a strong leadership structure is necessary to prevent disorder and ensure the achievement of institutional goals. Additionally, they raise questions regarding the balance between teamwork and the need for a centralized decision-making process. The quotation also illustrates the speaker's loyalty to the institution and their perception of themselves as crucial agents in implementing the bishop's objectives. What we find here is an interplay of power, representation, loyalty, and the management of a religious institution within a hierarchical framework.

Max Weber suggested that the successful establishment of religious movements depends on a process whereby either a prophet himself or his disciples secure the permanence of his preaching and congregation's distribution of grace.²⁷ Oyedepo's charisma revolves around these ideas of grace through his sermons to Cameroonians, which also legitimate his leadership and attract people to his church. However, the problem with this arrangement is that there have been times when pastors have waited for the sermons from Nigeria until 5 a.m. on Sunday morning because the bishop received the prophetic declaration from God late, which consequently delayed the writing up and dissemination of the sermon. Another problem is that in areas where internet access is inconsistent or entirely absent, the churches suffer a great deal because they are unable to receive the sermons on time.

The practice of uniform instruction within a specific denomination or church extends beyond the scope of Winners' Chapel, possible in different ways. Several other religious institutions demonstrate a commitment to providing their members with consistent teachings, which promotes a harmonious equilibrium and facilitates a sense of collective identification among members of the church. For instance, the Presbyterian Church in Cameroon employs a lectionary, prescribing specific texts for sermon preparation. Christians within this church are expected to reflect upon the same text each week. The aim is to ensure comprehensiveness of coverage of the Bible. However, unlike Winners' Chapel, ministers in the Presbyterian Church in Cameroon craft their sermons based on personal inspiration and their aptitude for interpreting biblical texts. Similarly, the Church of Scotland employs a lectionary for sermon preparation by individual ministers. The distinctive aspect of Winners' Chapel lies in the production and circulation of detailed sermon outlines that exhibit significant thematic unity, with the presiding bishop utilizing a variety of texts to substantiate his claims.

The practice was introduced by Bishop Oyedepo following the termination of many pastors who lacked undergraduate degrees, subsequently replacing them with degree holders. Some Cameroonian degree holders were then trained at the church's Bible school in Nigeria.²⁸ Critics of the policy of exclusively recruiting degree holders argue that attending Bible school does not necessarily equate to a divine calling for ministry. Consequently, many degree holders within the Winners' Chapel became a source of embarrassment to both themselves and the churches they served, struggling to deliver effective sermons due to their lack of

---

27. Blau, "Critical Remarks," 307.
28. Personal interview with Clement Mbarbad in Douala (Nov. 17, 2015).

true calling. In response, Bishop Oyedepo decided to prepare sermons in Nigeria and distribute them to pastors for proclamation. One of the drawbacks of this practice is that some pastors simply read the sermons verbatim from Nigeria, impeding creativity within the church.[29]

While the practice of providing uniform teachings within a religious institution may foster a sense of cohesion and shared identity among members, it also raises concerns regarding the potential limitations on individual creativity and interpretative freedom. The reliance on detailed sermon outlines from a centralized source may hinder the development of unique perspectives and fresh insights among pastors. Furthermore, the exclusive recruitment of degree holders based on formal education, without sufficient consideration of their spiritual calling, can result in a disparity between their qualifications and their actual ability to minister effectively to the congregation. This discrepancy may undermine the authenticity and sincerity of sermons delivered within the church. However, if sermons are prepared in Nigeria and sent to Cameroon to maintain the prophetic declarations and unique spiritual power of Bishop Oyedepo and provide similar teaching to Winners' Chapel members outside Nigeria, what might be the reason for the importation and use of Nigerian testimonies in Cameroon?

The Power of Testimony

The phenomenon of testimony holds great significance in Pentecostalism, as in much of the evangelical tradition, representing an individual's personal account of their encounters with God and the transformative effects of their faith on their lives. It serves as a potent method for sharing and disseminating the gospel of Jesus Christ, providing evidence of God's actions as a problem-solver capable of addressing even the most challenging human issues. While testimony is primarily associated with the religious domain, it extends beyond it to encompass other spheres, including the judiciary.[30]

Within the Pentecostal religious imagination, testimony is interconnected with other pneumatic experiences such as prophecy, visions, trances, exorcism, and other signs and wonders attributed to the work

---

29. Personal interview with Pastor Thomas Kont (pseudonym) in Douala (Nov. 21, 2015).

30. J. D. Pluss, "Testimony," in Dyrness and Kärkkäinen, *Global Dictionary of Theology*, 877–79.

and power of the Holy Spirit.[31] This concept is particularly associated with the spiritual authority of influential figures widely known as "powerful men and women of God."

Worship services, whether conducted within church buildings or at large outdoor crusades, serve as the preferred settings for sharing testimonies. Here, individuals are encouraged to recount their stories of salvation, inspiring listeners to follow the same principles in pursuit of their own miracles or supernatural encounters. Testimonies allow Christians to share their experiences of the Holy Spirit's power, its dynamic ability to address personal problems, and its capacity to transcend all facets of life, ultimately bringing about salvation.

Extensive literature exists that articulates the concept of testimonies, unveiling life-altering encounters between individuals and the Holy Spirit, fuelling the revival of Pentecostalism. Scholars have recognized testimonies as a significant church practice worthy of theological investigation. For instance, Vinson Synan's book *Voices of Pentecost: Testimonies of Lives Touched by the Holy Spirit*, presents first-hand accounts from various individuals across different segments of the Pentecostal and Charismatic movements.[32] These testimonies span from the pre-Pentecostal era prior to 1901, including figures such as Saint Augustine of Hippo, Saint Francis of Assisi, John Wesley, Edward Irving, Charles G. Finney, and D. L. Moody.

Synan's work authenticates the experience and beliefs of these individuals based on their own words and understanding. He argues that the belief systems and experiential dimensions revealed in these testimonies contributed to the emergence of "the most buoyant and fast-growing Christian Movement of the last thousand years."[33]

Mark J. Cartledge takes the discussion further in his book *Testimony in the Spirit: Rescripting Ordinary Pentecostal Theology*. He situates the practice of testimonies within the broader context of key themes in Pentecostal worship. Employing a dialogical approach, he analyzes testimonies collected from church members to diversify their worship experiences. Cartledge's main argument is that, in Pentecostal worship, humanity is joined by the heavenly host, and testimony becomes a means

---

31. J. D. Pluss, "Testimony," in Dyrness and Kärkkäinen, *Global Dictionary of Theology*, 877–79.

32. Synan, *Voices of Pentecost*. Also see Anderson, *To the Ends of the Earth*; Anderson et al., *Studying Global Pentecostalism*.

33. Synan, *Voices of Pentecost*, 13.

for worshipers to express the joy and triumph arising from encounters between the human and the divine. Testimonies possess a unique spiritual dynamic that defies conventional standards, whether spiritual or physical, stirring the faith of other members within the same faith community.[34]

However, it is essential to evaluate critically the practice of testimonies in contemporary Christianity. While testimonies hold value as oral narratives within specific faith communities and serve as subjects of scholarly examination, this limited dimension fails to fully capture the broader power and function of testimonies. Furthermore, testimonies have evolved into powerful tools used to legitimize the presence and influence of Pentecostal churches and their founders across international boundaries.

Voices across Borders: The Power of Nigerian Testimonies in Cameroon

Throughout my research on African Pentecostal Transnationalism, since 2012, I have had the opportunity to worship in various Pentecostal congregations. Among these, the Winners' Chapel stands out for its distinctive approach to testimonies. I have personally attended church services and other programs organized by the church in locations such as Douala, Buea, Yaoundé, Bamenda, Tiko in Cameroon, and Edinburgh in the United Kingdom. These programs encompass a range of activities, including Sunday services, Covenant Hour of Prayer,[35] midweek services for Holy Communion, and Satellite Fellowship Meetings held on Saturday evenings.[36] During these gatherings, two forms of testimonies are observable: The first involves individuals and local members orally narrating their personal testimonies to the congregation. The second involves pastors or designated office bearers reading out testimonies from a written document to the congregation. Notably, the second category predominantly comprises testimonies from Nigerian members, reproduced in Cameroon. In comparison to the oral testimonies given

---

34. Cartledge, *Testimony in the Spirit*.

35. This is the name that Oyedepo recently gave to morning prayer sessions of his churches across the world. Church members are encouraged to go to church every morning from 6 a.m. to 7 a.m. in order to ask God for the things they wish to achieve that day.

36. All Winners' Chapel congregations administer the sacrament of Holy Communion every Wednesday evening.

by Cameroonians, Nigerian testimonies tend to be more sensational. To illustrate the difference, I present testimonies from both Cameroonian individuals within Cameroon and a Nigerian individual whose testimony was read in Cameroon.

1. **Testimonies from Cameroonians**

    a. "Difficulty in Conception Destroyed through Divine Intervention"

Two of my sisters were facing difficulties in conception. When I joined this church, I started praying for them. Their names were constantly on my prayer request cards and I kept on believing God to change their stories. The God who answers prayers heard me and visited them. They both conceived and have given birth to wonderful children. I give God the glory and praise.[37]

   b. "Three Years of Barrenness Destroyed Via the Anointing"

My brother and his wife had been searching seriously for the fruit of the womb for the past three years. I took it upon me to pray for them. I continued in prayer for a while, and I also kept on anointing the wife's picture every time I prayed. Today, the story has changed. The God of Winners' Chapel visited them and blessed them with the fruit of the womb. To God be all the glory.[38]

The two testimonies from Cameroonians highlight instances where individuals faced challenges related to conception and barrenness but experienced divine intervention through their involvement in the church. The first testimony recounts how the person prayed for their sisters, believing that God would change their circumstances. As a result, both sisters were able to conceive and have children. Similarly, the second testimony involves a person praying and anointing the picture of their brother's wife, leading to a transformation in their ability to conceive and bear children. Both testimonies celebrate the individual's experiences of divine intervention and attribute their blessings to God. They primarily focus on the personal experiences of the individuals involved, emphasizing the power of prayer and anointing within the context of Winners' Chapel. However, they lack broader contextual information, such as medical

37. Personal interview with Simon Pier (pseudonym) in Douala (Sept. 14, 2016).
38. Personal interview with Perpetua Kudi (pseudonym) in Douala (Sept. 7, 2016).

POWER, PERSUASION, AND PENTECOSTALISM   129

factors or other contributing elements, which could provide a more comprehensive understanding of the situations.

2. **Testimony from Nigeria**

The following testimony is taken from one of the flyers sent out in Cameroon during Shiloh,[39] in 2015, that was held under the theme "from glory to glory." Four supernatural encounter testimonies are mentioned on the flyer: "Triplets after 20 Years of Waiting!" "Four Years Prostate Cancer Humiliated!" "Miracle Marriage!" and "'SS' Turned 'AA'!" We will consider in detail this testimony from a sufferer from sickle cell anaemia.

> For 21 years, I suffered from sickle cell anaemia and was on medications. When I gained admission into Covenant University, I received my healing by faith and was off medication but sometimes I would fall sick and go home. Every Shiloh, my first prayer request was for God to change my genotype to "AA." I almost lost hope, but I continued to key into the prophetic words from this altar. I was at the viewing centre during Shiloh 2013 because I couldn't make it to Canaanland. I keyed into the testimonies of those whose genotypes changed to "AA" and was sure that my testimony was on the way. Lo and behold, after one of the morning sessions at Shiloh 2013, I went for a test and the result was "AA." I went back for a confirmation result and was still "AA." Since then, I have not taken any medication. Now, I am healed and healthy. I give God the glory (Testifier: Omolara, A).[40]

This testifier from Nigeria endured the affliction of sickle cell anaemia for an astonishing span of twenty-one years, relying on medications for sustenance. However, upon gaining admission to Covenant University, he experienced healing through an unwavering faith in God, ceasing the need for medication. Despite occasional bouts of illness necessitating return visits home, the testifier consistently

---

39. "Shiloh," the annual convocation of the Winners' family, is a prophetic annual appointment ordained for both the dominion of the church and the individual members of the Winners' family. This holy convocation was flagged off by the inspiration of the Holy Ghost from the book of Josh 18:1, which states: "And the whole congregation of the children of Israel assembled together at Shiloh and set up the tabernacle of the congregation there. And the land was subdued before them."

40. "Supernatural Encounter Testimonies in Experience Supernatural Change @ Shiloh2015, December 8–12: From Glory to Glory." This is a handbill, several copies of which are in the possession of the author. Collected in Douala during fieldwork 2016.

presented his first prayer request during every Shiloh event, petitioning God for a miraculous transformation of his genotype to "AA." In the face of diminishing hope, the testifier remained resolute, drawing inspiration from the prophetic utterances emanating from the spiritual platform of Bishop Oyedepo. Even though unable to physically attend the Shiloh 2013 event, he virtually aligned himself with those sharing testimonies of transformed genotypes to "AA." Consequently, after a morning session during Shiloh 2013, he underwent a test that astonishingly confirmed his genotype as "AA." Subsequent confirmatory tests further affirmed this miraculous alteration. From that point forward, the testifier has been liberated from medication, enjoying restored health and well-being. All praise and glory are ascribed to God for this remarkable healing.

The testimonies provided by both Cameroonians and Nigerian individuals within the Pentecostal context depict such instances of profound transformation and miraculous interventions. While the Cameroonian testimonies center on prayer and intercessions made on behalf of their relatives struggling with infertility, they lack substantial details that could underscore a sense of extreme desperation. In contrast, the Nigerian testimony, disseminated through a flyer to Cameroonians, showcases a more striking narrative and perhaps less verifiable, since the only evidence is a remotely provided flyer.

If late prophet T. B. Joshua has been shown to manufacture healing miracles, as he certainly has from recent evidence, then we may allow ourselves for a similar possibility in the case of other neo-Pentecostal church leaders. However, it is still important to note how the testifier in our case recounts his personal journey of enduring twenty-one years with sickle cell disease and details the spiritual resolutions he received. The testimony highlights the prolonged suffering endured by the individual, with intermittent experiences of relapse into sickness, further intensifying the complexity of his condition. However, through virtual engagement with testimonies of others who had experienced healing from the same illness and through his connections to the program in Canaanland and to Bishop Oyedepo, the testifier ultimately receives his healing.

The written Nigerian testimony surpasses mere indications of how religious leaders possess the power to bestow healing miracles upon the desperate. It illuminates the multifaceted manifestations of supernatural power and the creation of new relationships that transcend boundaries of time, space, and individuality. The Nigerian testifier forms a personal and intimate connection with the bishop and other sick individuals, even though merely viewing the events through screens. By assuming the same position as those physically present within the church auditorium in Nigeria, and participating in the testimonial atmosphere, the testifier becomes part of a larger collective, empowered to liberate those in bondage. This testimony reflects an enduring characteristic of transnational Pentecostalism, in which reported miracles of healing, deliverance, and prosperity become significant expressions of spiritual power.

The Western mindset may struggle fully to accept or grasp such incredible miracles concerning changes in genotypes, especially considering that medical science recognizes stem cell therapy or bone marrow transplants as the only known cures for sickle cell disease, with such procedures carrying substantial risks and limited availability. But what we learn is that neo-Pentecostal churches in Africa and elsewhere challenge conventional modes of healing, asserting that the supernatural transcends the limitations imposed by time, space, and the vicissitudes of life. Westerners would be more open to the possibility that some of these miracles are genuine, but the expectation of continual miracles places the leaders of such churches under enormous pressure to produce such miracles "on demand," and hence there is the temptation to manufacture the miracle by dubious means.

While the testimonies highlight the agency of spiritual power and the transformative experiences of individuals, it is necessary to engage in rigorous inquiry and analysis to better understand the dynamics at play. Further examination of the cultural, social, and theological factors within the Pentecostal tradition will contribute to a deeper comprehension of how these testimonies shape beliefs, practices, and the construction of meaning within the faith community. Moreover, it is essential to consider the potential implications and consequences of emphasizing miraculous healings as a primary marker of spiritual power and religious legitimacy. The centrality of supernatural interventions in testimonies can inadvertently marginalize individuals who do not experience such extraordinary manifestations of divine favor, and it could also reduce the spiritual credit of any leader who cannot produce such interventions. Additionally, a critical assessment is warranted regarding the reliance on faith-based healing while potentially disregarding or underestimating the significance of medical interventions and healthcare practices.

Are There No Miracles of Power in Cameroon?

The use of Nigerian testimonies within the Cameroonian context, as exemplified in the examples, implies that Cameroonians may perceive themselves as having fewer miraculous experiences or breakthroughs compared to their Nigerian counterparts, leading to a perceived dearth of testimonies. However, it is crucial to acknowledge that Cameroonians also bear witness to the transformative power of God in their lives. For instance, an assistant pastor at the Bonaberi branch of Winners' Chapel joined the church in 2006 following his miraculous healing from a stomach ulcer, an affliction that had eluded resolution through consultations with medical professionals over several years. While still under prescribed medication, he fortuitously encountered an old acquaintance who introduced him to Winners' Chapel in Douala. Through fervent prayers led by the resident pastor from Nigeria at the time, he received his healing and has since been relieved of the need for medication.[41] This illustration demonstrates that Cameroonians too have supernatural encounters worthy of recognition within the Cameroonian context. However, the consistent reliance on Nigerian testimonies in Cameroon serves a specific purpose: to foster commitment and dedication among Cameroonian believers, akin to the perceived commitment of Nigerian members, with the aim of attending similar or equivalent supernatural transformations facilitated by the presiding bishop in Nigeria.

The Practicality of Transnational Testimonies

The ability of testimonies from Nigeria to bridge geographical and cultural boundaries, allowing individuals from different locations to share and receive spiritual experiences and insights is a notable feature in Winners' Chapel transnational operations. These testimonies serve as practical examples of the power of faith and the transformative potential of religious practices. They have fostered a sense of unity and shared belief among diverse communities of Winners' Chapel. Through the transmission of these testimonies, individuals can draw inspiration, strengthen their faith, and find encouragement in their own spiritual journeys.

However, the rather pragmatic approach of using Nigerian-crafted testimonies in Cameroon challenges prevailing paradigms and customary

---

41. Personal interview with Pastor Wanki in Bonaberi, Douala (Sept. 14, 2016).

practices, particularly concerning the interplay between testimonies, their method of communication (whether oral or written), and the specific context in which they are shared. This departure from convention is exemplified in the contrasting approaches to testimonies during the Azusa Street mission and revival of 1906, as discussed by Cecil Robeck. Robeck posits that testimonies played a significant role in congregational worship services during the revival, contributing to its sustained momentum. In this context, individuals shared their spiritual experiences through testimonies, providing comfort and edification to one another.[42]

The reciprocal sharing of testimonies as personal narratives within faith communities proves to be an effective means of disseminating the message of salvation and instilling hope in those who feel disheartened by their circumstances. Matviuk et al. suggest that stories of salvation, healing, hope, and victory are compelling and powerful narratives that open pathways for embracing a life marked by anticipation of the miraculous based on what God has done for others, as shared in their testimonies.[43] Engaging with the personal narratives of those who recount their experiences of salvation allows listeners to verify the circumstances surrounding the testifier's supernatural encounters. However, the lack of open attestation by the Nigerian individuals whose testimonies are used in Cameroon appears to contradict Tony Richie's conception of testimony as a genre of speech, which involves public acknowledgment and profession.[44] It also qualifies Walter Hollenweger's proposition that Pentecostalism is rooted in oral culture, shaped by narrativity rather than a literary culture.[45]

As I have noted earlier, the efficacy of spiritual testimonies hinges significantly on the interplay between the speaker and the audience, a dynamic that is enriched by the immediacy and personal engagement of oral communication. I have wondered whether written testimonies, originating from a context as distinct as Nigeria, hold equivalent sway over audiences in Cameroon. The intuitive response might lean toward skepticism. However, my findings reveal that written testimonies from afar can indeed resonate powerfully with Cameroonian audiences. This unexpected receptivity may stem from the ability of these narratives to mirror the congregants' own experiences, thereby tapping into universal

42. Robeck, *Azusa Street Mission*, 2–4.
43. De Matviuk, "Latin American Pentecostal Growth," 220.
44. Richie, "Translating Pentecostal Testimony," 166.
45. Hollenweger, *Pentecostalism*, 18.

themes and shared human experiences. This phenomenon suggests that the impact of spiritual testimonies is not solely confined to the traditional oral format but can also extend to written narratives, challenging us to reconsider the modalities through which spiritual experiences are communicated and shared across borders.

Although members of Winners' Chapel in Cameroon are aware of the inconsistencies within transnational testimonies, their perspectives sometimes exhibit self-contradictions. Consider the comment of a Winners' Chapel pastor's wife:

> In Winners' Chapel we are taught to always pray saying if God has done something good to a brother or sister, God can equally do it to me. Testimonies make God real, when you know the person testifying, you know what he/she went through, it would be easy for you to believe and then you do the same thing the one did and when you see the results another person will quote you in their prayers to God. For example, if you say that Abraham and Sarah went through the problem of barrenness people will argue that they were Bible people but when you see somebody who says he and his spouse have gone through the same problem for 11 years and God has now given them a child then you don't need to fast and pray to believe the story. It is real, and it builds up your faith and the faith of others.[46]

This comment provides insight into the role of testimonies in Winners' Chapel, emphasizing the belief that God's goodness and miracles can be experienced by individuals through prayer. While the comment highlights the power of testimonies in making God's reality tangible and fostering faith, it also contains contradictions and ambiguities that need consideration.

On the one hand, Comfort Sih's comment underscores the theological principle of believing in the potential for God to bring about positive outcomes in one's life. It encourages individuals to draw inspiration from the testimonies of others who have experienced God's blessings and to have faith in the possibility of similar outcomes. This aligns with the teachings of many religious traditions that emphasize the importance of faith and prayer in seeking divine intervention. However, Sih's comment is ambiguous because it suggests that knowing the personal experiences of the testifier makes it easier to believe and replicate their outcomes. While personal connection and relatability can enhance the impact of

---

46. Personal interview with Comfort Sih (pseudonym) in Yaoundé (Jan. 27, 2016).

testimonies, it raises questions about the role of objective evidence and critical discernment. Testimonies, by their nature, are subjective and rooted in personal perception. Without critical evaluation and discernment, there is a risk of uncritical acceptance and a potential for misinformation or manipulation.

Additionally, Sih's comments present an example comparing the biblical story of Abraham and Sarah's barrenness with a contemporary testimonial experience. It suggests that witnessing a modern-day account of overcoming similar challenges might be more convincing than relying solely on biblical narratives. This raises questions about the hierarchy of authority and the relationship between personal experience and scriptural authority within most Pentecostal churches as represented by this member of the Winners' Chapel. It also brings into focus the potential tension between the interpretive framework of personal experience and the role of scripture in shaping beliefs. However, of greater concern for most Winners' Chapel members in Cameroon is how transnational practices of the church are connecting them to other Winners' Chapel members across the globe and especially to the bishop because, in their view, "a Winner is a Winner."

"A Winner Is a Winner"

One notable advantage of using Nigerian testimonies from Winners' Chapel to instruct and assist Cameroonians in achieving their own miracles is its capacity to stimulate their imagination and establish a consistent identity for the church across different regions. This approach reinforces the notion that regardless of being in Nigeria or Cameroon, "a Winner is a Winner." Thus, the same God who attentively addresses and resolves the problems of Nigerian Winners possesses the capability to do likewise for Cameroonian Winners in Cameroon. Consequently, it explains the reason why Cameroonians tend to perceive Nigerian testimonies as more potent than their Cameroonian counterparts, perceiving no limitations in their applicability within Cameroon. As articulated by another Cameroonian:

> God is one. If miracles are happening in Nigeria, they can also happen in Cameroon and if things were not happening in Cameroon people would not have been joining the church. We have new members coming to our church every day because of the signs and wonders we are experiencing. But I strongly believe that Cameroonians need to hear about these testimonies from

Nigeria because they are more powerful and capable of building up our faith in God. It is also important to maintain the link between Cameroonian Winners' Chapel members in Cameroon and their brothers and sisters in Nigeria but most especially with "Papa" who is the head of the church.[47]

The ideas of this quotation resonate with what André Corten refers to as one of three new religious needs of transnational Pentecostalism: "A strong externalised emotion; a pursuit of the sacred through the representation of frightening powers; and fantasies of dramatic transformation."[48] David Oyedepo has thus suggested that "testimonies are faith boosters and that when one does not appreciate and consider testimonies, one's spiritual understanding is short-circuited, and expectations are crippled."[49] He further states that "every testimony shared is capable of reproducing itself in other lives. It also helps to confirm the efficacy of God's word."[50] In these claims, Oyedepo appeals both to members of his church in Nigeria who believe in his leadership and power, and to everyone who identifies as a Winners' Chapel member, regardless of where they are and come from. It also supports his suggestions that testimonies from elsewhere are capable of replicating themselves in other lives.

According to Michel Foucault's concept of pastoral power, the exercise of power entails possessing knowledge about the consciousness of those subjected to pastoral authority, along with the capacity to direct and influence it.[51] By applying this framework, it seems evident that Nigeria serves as the epicenter of pastoral power, radiating its influence on other countries. Consequently, Nigerian testimonies have gained prominence in the process of evangelizing the gospel within Cameroon, particularly in the context of Winners' Chapel. Further research would be required to substantiate whether Cameroonian testimonies have been reciprocally used in Nigeria.

The use of Nigerian testimonies in Cameroon not only underscores the transcendence of geographical barriers within the shared objectives and practices of Winners' Chapel. It also substantiates one of the widely

---

47. Personal interview with Pastor Joseph Wah (pseudonym) in Bamenda (Jan. 18, 2016).

48. Corten and Marshall-Fratani, *Between Babel and Pentecost*, 110.

49. Oyedepo, *Mandate*, 65.

50. David Oyedepo, "Power of Testimony," obtained from the Facebook page of David Oyedepo's Ministries International, July 19, 2016.

51. Foucault, *Power*, 333.

acclaimed adages of Pentecostalism, emphasizing the notion that distance holds no relevance in the spiritual realm, as prayer and anointing have the power to bridge any gap. This phenomenon is further exemplified by the extensive use of the media in Pentecostalism.

"Present in Their Absence"

Media plays a transformative role in collapsing intra-African space and connecting Pentecostals across international boundaries, allowing them to be present in their absence. Through various media platforms such as books, electronic media, and viewing of church TV programs, Pentecostals are able to bridge geographical distances and participate in religious experiences regardless of their physical location.

Within the context of Winners' Chapel, three media practices emerge as crucial components of their religious experiences across borders: The use of books authored by Bishop Oyedepo, the use of electronic media for connecting the mother church in Nigeria with the Cameroonian daughter church, and the production and distribution of sermon DVDs within Cameroon itself. In this section, I will focus on two specific media practices, namely the use of books and electronic media, with a particular emphasis on what I have called "present in their absence." This concept captures the important sense of connection experienced by Cameroonian believers when participating in special events of the church in Nigeria through electronic media. By examining these media practices, I aim to reveal the dynamic ways in which Winners' Chapel cultivates connectivity, bridges geographical distances, and engenders a feeling of presence among its followers.

Oyedepo's Books

Bishop Oyedepo has authored and published a substantial number of over seventy books,[52] primarily focusing on themes of success and prosperity. Within the church, members are obligated to read at least one of Oyedepo's books each month as a means of personal growth and spiritual edification.[53] Oyedepo's theology is the conventional prosperity gospel,

---

52. See David Oyedepo Ministries International, "Books."

53. Several interviews with elders, deacons, deaconesses and members of the Winners' Chapel in Cameroon, 2014–16.

which insists that the Bible is a contemporary document and the blessings which God bestowed on Abraham and made him wealthy are equally appropriate for Christians today.[54] The influential nature of Oyedepo's books have played a pivotal role in attracting new members to Winners' Chapel.

One compelling testimonial exemplifies the impact of Oyedepo's written works. A university graduate in Yaoundé was introduced to Winners' Chapel in 2010 after reading Oyedepo's book titled *Success Buttons*,[55] gifted to her by a friend. The book proved to be well-crafted, containing biblical illustrations that provided encouragement during her struggles with academic pursuits and living expenses. It instilled in her the belief that success was her inherent right as a Christian, and it effectively paved her path to success as outlined in the Bible. This encounter prompted her to attend Winners' Chapel, where she discovered the church's commitment to delivering the unadulterated word of God. Subsequently, she made the decision to join the church.[56]

Similar testimonies from numerous Winners' Chapel members underscore the deep sense of connection fostered through reading Oyedepo's books, such as *Born to Win*[57] and *Making Maximum Impact*.[58] These texts not only establish a connection to Bishop Oyedepo's teachings but also convey the promised blessings associated with church membership, emphasizing good health, prosperity, wealth, and success.[59]

The teachings propagated by Winners' Chapel are frequently encapsulated in slogans and phrases disseminated through stickers and handbills for evangelistic purposes. Expressions like "I am a Winner," "Winners' Family," "Am Above and Not Beneath," "Over Comers," and "More Than Conquerors"[60] portray the envisioned reality for members of Winners' Chapel—a life devoid of problems, characterized by victorious triumph in all areas. Oyedepo's brand of Christianity emphasizes triumph, blessings, and dominion, asserting that Christians should be distinctively distinguished in every aspect of life.[61] Consequently, adher-

54. Oyedepo, *Winning the War against Poverty*, 30.
55. Oyedepo, *Success Buttons*.
56. Personal interview with Quinta Kom (pseudonym) in Yaoundé (Jan. 27, 2016).
57. Oyedepo, *Born to Win*.
58. Oyedepo, *Making Maximum Impact*.
59. Several conversations and interviews in Douala, Bamenda, Buea, and Douala with significant members and leaders of the Winners Chapel in Cameroon, 2014–16.
60. Kuponu, "Living Faith Church," 174.
61. Oyedepo, *Signs and Wonders Today*, 14.

ents of Winners' Chapel often embrace Oyedepo's belief in the attainment of worldly rewards through access to God's mind via the Bible and other recommended media materials, ultimately overcoming poverty and sickness.[62] But if books inspire confidence and bring liberation, electronic media have proven to be more valuable as an evangelistic strategy.

The Electronic Media

One of the most prominent strategies employed by Bishop Oyedepo to maintain the allegiance of his church members and engender loyalty is the use of electronic media. Within the Cameroonian context, adherents of the bishop's teachings hold the belief that their connection to him and the blessings derived from such connections are not confined solely to those physically present in Nigeria, but extend to those engaging with him through electronic media.

A media manager revealed that all district headquarters of the church have installed satellite dishes, enabling the reception of live transmissions from Faith Tabernacle in Nigeria.[63] It is during the annual "Shiloh" event, observed every December, that the highest level of activity is witnessed. Preceding this event, an extensive publicity campaign is conducted, serving to alert church members and the general public to the forthcoming live broadcast of events in Cameroon. Individuals are encouraged to establish a spiritual connection to the church and the bishop through prayer, thereby ensuring their active participation and acquisition of blessings while observing the proceedings from Cameroon. By forging a spiritual connection with Nigeria through the medium of satellite imagery, members of Winners' Chapel in Cameroon perceive themselves as being spiritually present in Nigeria, despite their physical absence. One of my interviewees aptly remarked, "Though you are not physically present in Nigeria, you are there through prayer and expectation so that what people are experiencing in Nigeria, you can also experience in Cameroon," and the same is true for all the viewing centers across the globe.[64]

---

62. Kuponu, "Living Faith Church," 174.

63. Faith Tabernacle is the name that is given to Bishop Oyedepo's 540,000 seating capacity church auditorium in Nigeria. It is the international headquarters of the Winners' Chapel, where the bishop resides.

64. Personal interview with Ayuk Takang (pseudonym) in Douala (Yaoundé, Jan. 27, 2016).

During significant gatherings presided over by the bishop, the satellite dishes in Cameroon are realigned to face Faith Tabernacle, thereby capturing signals that are then transmitted to sound and video systems, which in turn are broadcast on television screens installed within representative viewing centers in Cameroon. Through this mechanism, members of the church in Cameroon are able to actively participate in the various activities taking place at Canaanland, Nigeria, such as prayer, singing in English and Yoruba, and other applicable practices.

The phenomenon of Cameroonian Winners' Chapel engaging with Yoruba spiritual songs illustrates a complex understanding of faith that transcends linguistic comprehension. This practice embodies a deep trust in the omniscience of the divine, suggesting that the essence of spiritual communion surpasses the boundaries of human intellect. In this context, music in its universal form emerges as a potent conduit for the divine, capable of transmitting emotional and spiritual resonance beyond the confines of language. The harmonies and rhythms inherent in the religious songs facilitate a collective experience of worship that is accessible to all, irrespective of linguistic mastery.

The practice of glossolalia, or speaking in tongues, within various Christian movements offers a parallel to this musical expression. Here, the faithful engage in communication with the sacred through utterances in unfamiliar tongues, which are perceived as the language of the Holy Spirit or a celestial dialect. Singing in Yoruba by non-Yoruba speaking Cameroonians aligns with this tradition, operating under the belief that spiritual efficacy is not contingent upon human understanding, but rather on the intent and the reception of the divine. The incorporation of Winners' Chapel Yoruba worship songs into the Cameroonian Pentecostal practice should be seen as a microcosm of the global Christian exchange, highlighting the fluidity of African spiritual and musical heritage. Such cross-cultural interactions not only enrich the fabric of worship but also signify a broader theological embrace that acknowledges and honors the plurality within the body of Christ. Through this lens, the act of singing in an unintelligible language can become a powerful symbol of unity, celebrating a collective Christian identity that rises above linguistic and cultural divisions.

Boundless Blessings: The Global Impact of "One Night with the King"

On the seventh of November 2014, I had the opportunity to participate in an all-night prayer session in Bonaberi, Cameroon. The event was titled "One Night with the King." It was broadcast live from Nigeria through satellite imagery, with Bishop Oyedepo at the helm. The program was characterized by fervent prayers, uplifting hymns, powerful sermons, and compelling testimonies. However, the pinnacle of the night was the moment the bishop introduced what he referred to as the "blood of sprinkling." In his message, Oyedepo expounded on the concept of "unveiling the wonders of the blood of sprinkling." He declared that we inhabit a kingdom governed by enigmatic forces, and one of the divine mysteries entrusted to Winners' Chapel was the significance of the "blood of sprinkling." The bishop emphasized that this mystery had been bestowed upon him by Jesus himself through direct revelation. He cautioned us that during the service, we would witness the raw manifestation of the blood of sprinkling's extraordinary efficacy. To illustrate the power of the "blood of sprinkling," Oyedepo recounted a remarkable incident involving an elderly woman in the Maiduguri branch church in Nigeria. This woman's left hand had mysteriously lost its blood, causing it to turn pale. However, after the administration of the blood of sprinkling during a "One Night with the King" service, blood instantaneously returned to her hand, and she experienced miraculous healing. To substantiate his claims, Oyedepo cited several scriptural references, including Heb 9:19–21, Heb 12:22–24, and 1 Cor 5:7. We were then reminded that the application of the blood of sprinkling would activate great transformations in our lives. Oyedepo assured us that growth impediments, discomfort, barrenness, business stagnation, and infertility would all be eradicated. Moreover, he made the audacious claim that through the sprinkling, we would be exempted from death itself and even be transfigured into divine beings or divinized, causing demonized individuals to bow in our presence.

In a ceremonial gesture, the bishop blessed the red-colored liquid, which was placed in small buckets on a table at the sanctuary of the church in Nigeria. Similarly, the leaders of the church in Douala, where I was in attendance, had prepared buckets of red-colored water that were virtually blessed by the bishop. To underscore the wide-reaching influence of his ministry and the magnitude of his power and blessings,

Bishop Oyedepo invoked a prayer that encompassed all altars of God in the Winners' Chapel worldwide. He proclaimed:

> All the contents on the altars of God all over the world are declared as the Passover blood of the lamb and whatever the Passover delivered in Egypt, shall be re-enacted in your lives wherever you are. Everyone connected to this prophetic ministry, as the blood touches you tonight, every mark of the wicked drops off you, everything resisting your fruitfulness drops off you.[65]

The congregation, in response, fervently uttered a resounding "Amen" resonating with a great intensity that seemed to reverberate through the foundations of the church building. Subsequently, a group of ushers took hold of the buckets containing the red-colored water and proceeded to sprinkle it upon those present in the Nigerian church. In a parallel manner, our ushers within the Douala church replicated the act. Following the sprinkling of the blood, the bishop allocated six minutes for instant testimonies, allowing individuals from Canaanland-Nigeria and all the viewing centers around the world to share their remarkable experiences.[66]

Within the premises of Faith Tabernacle in Nigeria, the atmosphere was charged with awe-inspiring testimonies. An usher relayed the story of a woman who had experienced the heart-wrenching loss of two previous pregnancies. The medical prognosis for her third pregnancy was grim, as doctors declared it to be abortive, with the unborn child having already perished within her womb. However, following the administration of the blood of sprinkling during the service, a miraculous transformation occurred. The baby, who had been lifeless, suddenly came alive and began kicking, defying all medical expectations. Similarly, within our viewing center in Cameroon, three testimonies of instantaneous healing were shared. One account involved the disappearance of severe neck pain in a young lady, while another recounted the complete alleviation of two months' worth of abdominal pain. The final testimony described the vanishing of a debilitating headache after the sprinkling ritual.

A week after the event, I engaged in a conversation with a church member to get more insights into the experiences encountered during the sprinkling service. My intention was to discern whether extraordinary

---

65. Personal observation in Douala-Cameroon, Dec. 2016.

66. As we watched the events of "Shiloh" in Nigeria from Cameroon, we were also shown other viewing centers intermittently. These included branches of the Winners' Chapel in other African countries but especially in Europe, the United States, Asia, and Latin America.

miracles akin to the ones witnessed in Nigeria, where a deceased child had been miraculously revived within a mother's womb, were also observed in Cameroon. In response, my interlocutor spoke of miracles manifesting in the form of marriages, employment opportunities, and other notable transformations. However, the most striking testimony involved a woman from Kenya who had miraculously healed from a swollen leg during a separate service of "One Night with the King." This woman, having followed the program online from Kenya, adhered to the bishop's instructions by submerging her cancerous, swollen legs into a bucket of water before retiring for the night. Upon awakening the next morning, she discovered that the water in the bucket had turned white, signifying the complete eradication of her ailment. It is worth noting that this last testimony was likely shared during a local church service, a customary practice employed to disseminate remarkable accounts from other locations within Cameroon.

The narrative concerning the transnational transmission of spiritual and charismatic power through electronic and other media platforms extends beyond a mere depiction of Nigeria exerting dominance over its smaller neighbor, Cameroon. It unveils a global network through which Oyedepo disseminates spiritual power to his followers across the world. There is evidence to suggest that the heightened use of electronic media during events such as "Shiloh" stems from the understanding that many adherents of Winners' Chapel are unable to travel to Canaanland in Nigeria for these sacred gatherings. As these events are perceived as unique moments when God employs the bishop as an instrument to shape destinies, the most fitting approach to fostering connectivity is through the transmission of satellite imagery originating from Nigeria where he resides. It is important to recognize that this representation and virtual presence of Bishop Oyedepo across different regions aligns with a divine revelation; Oyedepo claims to have received from God that a time would come when he would stand in one place, speaking, while individuals from all corners of the world would see and even feel his presence.

The interconnectedness between Nigeria and Cameroon, or between Bishop Oyedepo and his Cameroonian followers through electronic media, exemplifies his aspiration to forge a bond within his congregations and among members, regardless of the physical distance that separate them. As Cameroonians watch the events unfolding within the sacred grounds of "Canaanland" on their screens, they tangibly experience a sense of connection to the church in Nigeria and to Bishop Oyedepo himself. The jubilation of singing in unison with brethren from Nigeria and the devotion to Bishop Oyedepo, all without the need to travel physically to Nigeria, epitomizes the innovative ways in which media appropriation manifests within Pentecostal churches, captivating and inspiring members of the church and their adherents.

Viewing and Touching as Extensions of Faith or Lack of It

The appropriation of media in the manner I have depicted is not exclusive to Winners' Chapel; other African Pentecostal churches also engage in similar practices. Examples include the Redeemed Christian Church of God (RCCG), led by Pastor Enoch Adeboye, and the Synagogue Church of All Nations, established and overseen, until lately, by the late Prophet T. B. Joshua. In Cameroon, T. B. Joshua's Emmanuel TV enjoys considerable popularity, as numerous Cameroonian Christian households tune in to witness the spectacular displays of healing miracles and supernatural encounters. However, what sets Winners' Chapel apart from Emmanuel TV is the distinctive practice employed by the latter, wherein viewers were often encouraged by Prophet T. B. Joshua to place their hands on the screen during prayers. By doing so, viewers sought to establish a stronger connection with the prophet, anticipating the reception of prayers and healing from Nigeria. In contrast, followers of Winners' Chapel perceive this practice as an expression of weak faith. As one missionary from the church revealed:

> Doctrinal matters differ per church. For example, one of the pillars of Winners' Chapel is faith and with faith you connect to God. You must not touch something to benefit from the blessing because we believe according to scripture that touching is even an extension of lack of faith. You can sit where you are and benefit from what is happening in Nigeria just by viewing what is happening in Faith Tabernacle. That is faith and expecting results in Cameroon just like those who are physically present in Nigeria is already faith. So that is faith.[67]

It is reckoned here that touching is indicative of inadequate faith, while observation is regarded as an extension of faith. Nonetheless, whether television screens are touched by viewers or merely observed, what holds significance is the evolving perception among Cameroonians regarding

---

67. Personal interview with Titus Ngah (pseudonym) in Douala (Nov. 13, 2015).

Nigerian "men and women of God" as possessing heightened spiritual potency, enabling them to transmit blessings to their Cameroonian viewers through electronic media. This practice exemplifies how media can profoundly influence individuals' religious perceptions and their understanding of God. Furthermore, it demonstrates how Pentecostal leaders employ electronic media to shape the religious worldview of their adherents across international borders and sustain their loyalty.

When Marleen De Witte reflected on the process of making, broadcasting, and watching the *Living Word* program of the International Central Gospel Church Ghana, she showed that the format of televisualization of religious practice creates charisma, informs ways of perception, and produces new kinds of religious subjectivity and spiritual experience.[68] What De Witte shows is the relationship between religion, charisma, the media, and loyalty. Oyedepo stands out as the charismatic personality of the Winners' Chapel *par excellence*. He is capable of transmitting his spiritual power, blessing, and influence on other lands by the use of the media. By engaging his followers through electronic media and keeping their loyalty to him in this way, Bishop Oyedepo fits into what Boas Shamir et al. refer to as "the Motivational Effects of Charismatic Leadership."[69]

They argue that charismatic leadership has its effects by strongly engaging followers' self-concepts in the interest of the mission articulated by the leader.[70] Max Weber spoke of the charismatic leader's ability to "arouse task-relevant motivation by tapping followers' needs for esteem, power, and/or affiliation."[71] The evidence is in Winners' Chapel where members believe that through the media they can be in the same space as their leader and receive his blessing for their enrichment. In media parlance, Birgit Meyer variously describes this evolution as "mediation and immediacy: Sensational forms, semiotic ideologies and the question of the medium."[72] Meyer argues that the media evoke or authorize sensations of spiritual powers as immediate and real; "media are prone to 'disappear' or become 'hyper-apparent' in the act of mediation."[73] These conceptions reveal how electronic media collapses transnational space

---

68. De Witte, "Altar Media's Living Word," 174.
69. Shamir et al., "Motivational Effects of Charismatic Leadership," 577–94.
70. Shamir et al., "Motivational Effects of Charismatic Leadership," 577–94.
71. Weber, *Toward a Theory of Spiritual Leadership*, 693.
72. Meyer, "Mediation and Immediacy," 23–39.
73. Meyer, "Mediation and Immediacy," 23–39.

in such a way that Winners' Chapel becomes a single sacral community under the bishop irrespective of where people are located.

The Fluidity of Spiritual Things and the Power of Faith

The use of media in Winners' Chapel for missionary purposes, as previously elucidated, can be understood through various conceptual lenses. These include the fluid nature of spiritual domains, the construction of the church's identity transcending international boundaries, and the indispensable role played by Bishop Oyedepo. Furthermore, these observations raise questions regarding the agency and autonomy of Cameroonian church members, pastors, and leaders, both within Cameroon and beyond. Another interlocutor aptly contextualizes these notions.

> There are two elements here: The first revolves around the notion that in the spiritual realm, distance does not matter. The second pertains to faith. Faith is projected as a belief that transcends physical presence. As the adage goes, "all things are possible to him that believes." These issues are intricately intertwined, and while I hesitate to talk about sensitive spiritual matters here, it appears to be working for them. Personally, these were practices and exercises we engaged in, practices that continue to be embraced and celebrated within Winners' Chapel. I believe it forms part of their identity; it is what nurtures the congregation's loyalty and ensures the church's progression. It creates an atmosphere, a driving force that sustains momentum. However, I do perceive inherent challenges within this construct. For example, if the bishop were absent, would there be someone capable of assuming his position, embodying the same charisma? Perhaps the wife? The two sons? Yet, if these individuals were not present, complications would inevitably arise. It appears to me as an Empire, despite the fact that it ought to be a church where elders partake in ministry, where their roles are functional. It should include the essence of a church, rather than an Empire. I often refer to it as a divine triangle, with one person at the apex, while the rest support and maintain this individual's position. One cannot simply step into his place. In my opinion, the most effective approach to ministry or church would resemble a boulevard, where everyone grows, collectively engaging in ministry within a local church, all united in their service to the Lord. In

1 Peter 5:1–3, we encounter the concept of a church where Peter implores the elders to actively participate in leadership.[74]

Rosalind Hackett's scholarship explores how Pentecostal churches accord privileged status to electronic media as suitable platforms for transmitting their teachings and expanding their empires.[75] She argues that electronic media has revolutionized the religious landscape by facilitating transnational and homogenizing cultural flows, thereby elevating the "connections between these movements and the networks they create to new, global levels."[76] The notion of cultural flows being homogenized can be linked to certain Yoruba cultural elements, with observers suggesting their permeation into Cameroon through the agency of Winners' Chapel, owing to the Yoruba background of its founder/leader. Two aspects of "cultural infiltration" are discernible:

The first relates to the way Nigerians revere pastors as God's servants in a very literal sense. According to this perception, the Yoruba community regard pastors as demi-gods, or semi-divine entities, mirroring the Yoruba traditional worldview where kings are elevated and their pronouncements unchallenged. This tradition has found its way into Nigerian Christianity and is now transported to Cameroon through the endeavors of Winners' Chapel missionaries, who actively propagate this paradigm. Consequently, it has become commonplace to hear Cameroonians referring to Nigerian missionaries as "Daddy" while offering unwavering loyalty. The missionary or pastor assumes the role of the quintessential person of God, whose authority remains unquestioned. J. D. Y. Peel, who more than any other scholar has studied the Yoruba religions, convincingly illustrates how Nigerian Pentecostalism experienced a transformative shift in the 1980s, transitioning from a holiness agenda to one concerned with combating evil in the world, an evolution that Peel interprets as a reversion to Yoruba traditional religious culture.[77]

The second aspect of cultural infiltration discussed here, and as earlier referred to, pertains to the songs and music used in Winners' Chapel in Cameroon. These songs predominantly originate from the Yoruba culture, and Cameroonians are expected to sing them. This has led some

74. Personal interview with Pastor Victor Bong (pseudonym) in Douala (Feb. 2, 2016).
75. Hackett, "Charismatic/Pentecostal Appropriation," 258.
76. Hackett, "Charismatic/Pentecostal Appropriation," 258.
77. Peel, *Christianity, Islam, and Oriṣa Religion*, 199.

Cameroonians to perceive it as a means of suppressing their own cultural heritage in favor of Nigerian culture. As one respondent expressed:

> It seems like the Cameroonian style of worship is being phased out, as indigenous worship styles incorporating instruments such as xylophones in French Cameroon or drums in English Cameroon, as well as songs in Meta, Muganka, and Douala, are not given prominence. Instead, Yoruba songs and Brass Band music are prevalent. While there may be no issue with the band itself, the manner in which Cameroonians imitate what they see on Nigerian television, including dance, singing, and even preaching, is seen as detrimental to Cameroonian cultures. The Nigerian missionaries are also promoting this, and it is as if it is not done the Nigerian way it is not authentic, in this way there is no real creativity over the years. This results in the repetition of the same songs in Cameroon, eroding local traditions, cultures, and values. It appears as a mere copy-and-paste exercise, where Nigerian-style preaching is copied and pasted into the Cameroonian context.[78]

The main argument regarding the use of media in Winners' Chapel Cameroon is that Bishop Oyedepo's books and electronic media are employed as evangelistic strategies to attract members to the church and, more crucially, to solidify the transmission of his spiritual power, thus legitimizing his presence in Cameroon while operating from Nigeria. This highlights how the accessibility of new media fosters new mediation practices, which in turn impact and are impacted by changing power dynamics between followers and leaders.[79] The concept within Winners' Chapel revolves around the effectiveness of transmitting transformative spiritual power or successfully conveying the spiritual power of Bishop Oyedepo to his followers who believe they benefit from it. The presence of Nigerian missionaries plays a strategic role in achieving these objectives and provides the temporal power required to sustain the church's external branches.

Asonzeh Ukah's interpretation of Max Weber's theory of charisma resonates with the analysis I make in this section. Ukah posits that charismatization involves the recognition and acceptance of the charismatic leader's legitimacy by their followers. However, charismatic authority is

---

78. Personal interview with Pastor Job Molewe (pseudonym) in Buea (Nov. 18, 2015).

79. Meyer, "Impossible Representations."

often unstable and necessitates a process of routinization to establish a secure foundation for the exercise of authority and legitimacy. For this to be achieved, "the personal authority of the leader is vested on his representatives and officials in such a manner that they now share in the aura of his or her office."[80]

In our case, the personal authority of Bishop Oyedepo is vested in his representatives and officials, allowing them to share in the aura of his office. Nigerian missionaries assume these roles, sharing, transmitting, and legitimizing Oyedepo's power in Cameroon, while Cameroonian pastors play marginal roles. The shifting power dynamics between Nigerian missionaries and indigenous Cameroonian pastors reflects aspects of Nigerian Pentecostal consumerism and the hegemony of Winners' Chapel missionaries in Cameroon. Consequently, indigenous pastors in Cameroon feel alienated and discriminated against.

"We Are Foreigners in Our Own Nation"

The presence and leadership of Nigerian missionaries within the Winners' Chapel in Cameroon have sparked conflicts and contestations with Cameroonian indigenous pastors, revealing feelings of discrimination and alienation among the Cameroonians. One particular area where power dynamics come to light is the timing of Nigerian missionaries' arrival in Cameroon and their continued occupancy of key leadership positions within the church. The subsequent paragraphs will suggest a form of hegemony from the Nigerian leadership in Cameroon and comment on the resulting sentiment among Cameroonian church pastors who now perceive themselves as foreigners in their own country.

The administrative structure of Winners' Chapel in Cameroon is primarily dominated by Nigerian missionaries. While Cameroonian indigenous pastors have been responsible for planting new congregations, Nigerian missionaries consistently occupy leadership positions and oversee the most prosperous churches. One possible explanation for this phenomenon, as mentioned earlier, is that Nigerian missionaries provide a direct connection to the church founder for the effective transmission of spiritual power and the implementation of his vision.

However, Cameroonian pastors raise concerns that Nigerian missionaries should be involved in planting new churches rather than

---

80. Ukah, "Redeemed Christian Church of God," 170.

inheriting thriving ones established by them. This resistance is evident in a 2015 memorandum signed by all full-time Cameroonian indigenous pastors of the church, which questioned why Nigerian missionaries, instead of the pastors who planted the churches, are leading larger congregations, residing in superior housing, and driving cars, while their wives receive salaries.[81] Examples of churches originally planted and established by Cameroonians, but now led by missionaries, include Bamenda, Tiko, Buea, Limbe, Biyamassi-Yaoundé, Ndogbong and Bonaberi in Douala.

An Inversion of Missionary Patterns

The conception of mission in Winners' Chapel, where expatriates replace indigenous pastors who have planted churches, deviates from the typical pattern of mission work, where expatriates initiate church planting and gradually transfer responsibility to indigenous pastors over time. The reason behind Winners' Chapel reliance on indigenous pastors for church planting, followed by their replacement with expatriate missionaries, seems to be aimed at integrating the newly established congregations into the power structures and ethos of the organization as defined in Nigeria. This is why the Nigerian leadership sometimes overlooks the Provincial Council of Winners' Chapel in Cameroon, which consists of both Nigerian missionaries and Cameroonians, tasked with overseeing the church's administration.[82] Furthermore, the Nigerian leadership has failed to convene a general assembly for several years,[83] avoiding any forum where concerns about the legitimate position of Cameroonians within the church could be addressed.

This means that the exercise of power by Nigerian missionaries in Cameroon involves marginalizing other constituted authorities within the church and suppressing dissenting groups. As a result, Cameroonian pastors have raised concerns, questioning whether the Nigerian administration of the church in Cameroon can be characterized as "dictatorial" or as resembling a "Communist government"![84] The evidence suggests

81. CPU WMA-Cameroon, "Our Observation and a Call for an Extraordinary General Assembly Meeting with all Full-Time Pastors and the National Church Committee," A memorandum addressed to the National Pastor of Winners Chapel Cameroon, dated May 4, 2015, obtained by the author.

82. CPU WMA-Cameroon, "Our Observation."

83. CPU WMA-Cameroon, "Our Observation."

84. CPU WMA-Cameroon, "Our Observation."

that Cameroonian pastors face difficulties in influencing any meaningful change or expressing their grievances to the hierarchy of Winners' Chapel, both in Cameroon and Nigeria. This is evident from the response received by Cameroonian indigenous pastors when they submitted the memorandum in 2015 to the Nigerian leadership, outlining thirty-five points that highlighted their sense of alienation within the church in their own country. This is the rather poignant reply that they received:

> It has come to our notice that full time pastors under the aegis of Cameroonian pastors Union (CPU) wrote the national pastor some unscrupulous things and copied the various hierarchies. This is quite embarrassing, ungodly and not the spirit of this commission (Mandate section 18 . . .). At this juncture, we would like all our pastors who are not part of this anti-mandate practice to dissociate themselves in writing within 24 hours.[85]

The reply reflects an exertion of power and authority by the leadership of Winners' Chapel in Cameroon within the context of the Cameroonian Pastors Union (CPU). The national pastor, as the central figure of authority, reprimanded full-time pastors who had expressed dissenting views or criticisms by labeling their actions as "unscrupulous," "embarrassing," and "ungodly." The directives to dissociate themselves from the "anti-mandate practice" within twenty-four hours further demonstrates the exercise of authority to control and discipline the behavior of pastors.

Some of the lessons that can be drawn from the contentious relationship between Nigerian missionaries and Cameroonian pastors include the areas of authority and control, silence and obedience, limits on freedom of expression, organizational culture, and implications for pastors. However, some of the alleged "unscrupulous things" are specified in the following questions posed by Cameroonian indigenous pastors in their memorandum:

- Tell us why you (Nigerians) don't show compassion to a suffering pastor, his family members when they are abandoned in hospital without any help. And even when one dies you abandon his corpse like what happened to late pastor Ngwa who was from Bamenda. But when it concerns you Nigerians, your wives or children, big amounts of money are released. What do you take us for?

---

85. National Disciplinary Committee Cameroon, "Re: Cameroonian Pastors Union (CPU): Warning to Stop Every Attempt to Corrupt Pastors to Lie to Leadership to Protect your Evil Doings against God." Letter dated May 11, 2015, obtained by the author.

- Tell us why Cameroonians don't have the right to benefit all the advantages of staff in this country as provided by the Mandate. For example, Annual Leave, Leave Allowance, or other bonuses like out of station allowances? All these are only for Nigerians. Why? Seeing you force us to produce results in a very poor work environment.

- What gives you the right to abuse, slight, shout at and beat Cameroonian pastors as you did beat pastor Manga in Douala and sent him out like a goat? Even Bishop Oyedepo for whom we are all working does not treat pastors this way. Can you make a pastor? Do you know we are God's servants and not your children?

- Also tell us why in two different meetings we were separated from Nigerian pastors (never called to attend). What were you hiding from us?

- Tell us why you Nigerian pastors in Cameroon don't respect the church Mandate, the constitution of World Mission Agency (WMA) Inc in Cameroon and even our legislation as a Nation?

- Tell us why is it that anytime a church grows in the hand of a Cameroonian pastor he is ejected from the church for a Nigerian to take over? Is it because of our incompetence as the regional said here on the altar or because that is what the Mandate says?[86]

The conclusion of the memorandum is even more forthright:

> With all these and many more, we can conclude that you Nigerians do take us for fools and see our government as incapable as you come into the nation without any work contract as it should be, do what you want, and go with what you want without any fear. You call us foreigners in our own nation; you take us as slaves for the Nigerians in our own country. We think enough is enough.... And let us warn you, we will not tolerate any form of intimidation this time around.[87]

This acrimonious exchange between Nigerian missionaries and Cameroonian pastors in Winners' Chapel reveals a lack of constructive dialogue and a determination by the Nigerian church leadership to suppress perceived rebellion from their Cameroonian colleagues. The Cameroonian

---

86. CPU WMA-Cameroon, "Our Observation."
87. CPU WMA-Cameroon, "Our Observation."

pastors, feeling alienated within the church, lodged complaints about what they perceived as a Nigerian arrangement aimed at exploiting Cameroon's resources for their personal benefit. However, the response from Winners' Chapel leadership was unfavorable, and communication between the Cameroonian pastors and the church's leadership in Nigeria was seemingly blocked. The Nigerian church leadership appeared determined to quash any perceived rebellion from their Cameroonian colleagues. They were expected to dissociate themselves from the union of Cameroonian pastors which in the view of the missionaries was "ungodly and not the spirit of this commission." However, the Cameroonian pastors did not relent in their efforts.

In an attempt to seek resolution, the Cameroonian pastors turned to the Nigerian high commissioner to Cameroon for assistance. In a letter dated May 18, 2015, titled "Pleading for your intervention to contact the presidency of Living Faith Church Worldwide aka Winners' Chapel International,"[88] the pastors expressed their concerns about barriers at the international level preventing communication and physical contact with Bishop Oyedepo. They also raised issues related to delayed salary payments, noncompliance with Oyedepo's vision, and irregular transfers that negatively affected their children's education. The letter further highlighted at least four additional significant points that bolster the evidence supporting the claims made by the Cameroonian pastors:

- Cameroonian pastors are now mature enough—mentally and spiritually—to manage churches under the World Mission Agency Inc. (WMA) in Cameroon.
- In this regard, the WMA should with immediate effect stop sending missionaries pastors from Nigeria to manage Cameroon churches.
- By implication, Nigerian pastors working under the WMA, on mission in Cameroon, should be withdrawn and sent elsewhere within the next one month so that pastors from Cameroon would also have the privilege to see the WMA Inc. president and even communicate with him, from a distance or at close range, if need be.

---

88. CPU WMA, "Re: Pleading for Your Intervention to Contact the President of Living Faith Church Worldwide aka Winners' Chapel International." Letter addressed to the Nigerian high commissioner to Cameroon, dated May 18, 2015, obtained by the author.

- In place of the constitution of Living Faith Churches Worldwide, the internal Rules and Regulations under WMA Inc. Cameroon should be scrupulously implemented in Cameroon. By so doing, Pastors of the same level will enjoy the same advantages and make the Liberation Mandate a reality and not a dream to those in the Commission.[89]

"Give Us the Chance to Lead Our Own Churches!"

The preceding lines express a strong sentiment that Cameroonian pastors are now capable, both mentally and spiritually, of effectively managing churches under the World Mission Agency Inc. in Cameroon. As a result, the suggestion is made for the WMA to cease sending missionary pastors from Nigeria to oversee churches in Cameroon. It is also implied that Nigerian pastors currently serving under the WMA in Cameroon should be relocated elsewhere. This will create an opportunity for Cameroonian pastors to have direct access to the president of WMA Inc. and enable communication between them, either from a distance or in person, if necessary.

To ensure equitable treatment and to uphold the vision of the Liberation Mandate, the letter proposes that the internal rules and regulations under WMA Inc. Cameroon be meticulously implemented in place of the constitution of Living Faith Churches Worldwide. This would ensure that pastors at the same level receive the same benefits and contribute to making the Liberation Mandate a reality for those within the commission. It is a call for greater autonomy and empowerment of Cameroonian pastors within the organization, advocating for a shift in power dynamics and the implementation of internal structures and guidelines that would promote fairness, equality, and the fulfillment of the organization's mission.

I was unable to find any response letter from the Nigerian high commissioner to Cameroon in relation to the concerns raised. However, the available evidence suggests that the Cameroonian pastors are still facing challenges in resisting what they perceive as domination by Nigerian missionaries. It also indicates their desire for the indigenization of the church in Cameroon, as they feel confident in their ability to lead and contribute to realizing the Liberation Mandate of Bishop Oyedepo.

A notable aspect of these contestations is the apparent efforts, whether intentional or unintentional, by Nigerian missionaries to hinder

---

89. CPU WMA, "Re: Pleading for Your Intervention."

any prospect of indigenization within Winners' Chapel in Cameroon. If this is indeed the case, it contradicts Bishop Oyedepo's earlier commitment to indigenization, as demonstrated when the African Gospel Invasion (AGIP) shortlisted indigenous missionaries from African countries in 2000, subsequently assigning them to newly established churches.[90] This initiative bears comparison with the euthanasia of mission propounded by Henry Venn in the nineteenth century, advocating for the development of indigenous leadership within missions. Venn had suggested that "as early as possible local leadership should replace the missionary."[91] However, despite the passage of over twenty-seven years since Winners' Chapel was established in Cameroon, the concept of indigenization appears to be neglected.

It is worth noting that Cameroon is not the only African country where Nigerian Winners' Chapel missionaries are involved in church leadership and administration; similar situations are found in South Africa, the Democratic Republic of Congo, Ivory Coast, and Ghana. In Ghana, for instance, the control and perceived exploitation from the Nigerian leadership prompted the secession of one of the affluent Winners' Chapel churches, resulting in the establishment of Winners' Chapel Ghana, independent from Winners' Chapel International.[92] A Ghanaian bishop owns the former while Oyedepo owns the latter.

This separation of ownership suggests that Bishop Oyedepo's preference for Nigerian missionaries over indigenous pastors in different African countries may be an attempt to avoid losing church branches to strangers, as occurred in Ghana. In light of this, one may conclude that, in solving one problem, Bishop Oyedepo has inadvertently created another by fostering a categorization within his movement. This categorization portrays the Nigerian missionaries as owners or landlords, while the Cameroonian pastors are depicted as caretakers or tenants, potentially rendering them foreigners in their own land. The paradigm adopted by Winners' Chapel, where Nigerian missionaries are sent to lead churches planted by Cameroonians, represents a reversal of earlier mission patterns in which missionaries established and subsequently handed over churches to indigenous leaders.

The evidence suggests that Nigerian missionaries maintain absolute control and authority over Cameroonian pastors, exercising power over

90. Kuponu, "Living Faith Church," 37.
91. Warren, *To Apply the Gospel*, 28–29, 63, 85.
92. Gifford, *Ghana's New Christianity*.

them rather than sharing power with them. While Cameroonian pastors attempt to resist the power of Nigerian missionaries by questioning and seeking answers, the latter are determined to suppress the former and prevent any form of indigenization within the church in Cameroon. Nevertheless, within the leadership and power structure of the Nigerian missionaries, there is potential for the provision of social capital and empowerment to Cameroonian pastors.

Chapter Six

The Socioeconomic Impact of Winners' Chapel

IN A WORLD MARKED by dynamic shifts and evolving paradigms, the role of religious institutions has taken on an intriguing transformation. This chapter examines the socioeconomic impact of Winners' Chapel in Cameroon, unveiling a compelling narrative of the church's evolution from a purely spiritual entity to a formidable influencer in the realms of both faith and finance within the region.

Scholars of religion and world Christianity have noted how Pentecostalism, a religious movement deeply entrenched in spirituality and fervent worship, is undergoing a remarkable evolution.[1] What was once primarily a conduit for spiritual nourishment has blossomed into an influential force shaping social behavior, ameliorating economic well-being, and embarking on an ambitious mission to alleviate poverty, offer employment opportunities, and channel vital capital into communities.[2] The endeavors of Pentecostal churches are multifaceted and commendably

1. Danny McCain, "The Metamorphosis of Nigerian Pentecostalism: From Signs and Wonders in the Church to Service and Influence in Society," in Miller et al., *Spirit and Power*, 160–77.

2. Danny McCain, "The Metamorphosis of Nigerian Pentecostalism: From Signs and Wonders in the Church to Service and Influence in Society," in Miller et al., *Spirit and Power*, 160–77.

diverse. On the one hand, they engage in humanitarian activities, establishing robust welfare systems for the needy, launching relief initiatives to aid victims of civil unrest, and significantly contributing to educational empowerment. Beyond the purely spiritual realm, their commitment to addressing fundamental societal needs have become evident through health initiatives and pioneering water projects. In the case of Winners' Chapel, the church's borehole project, in Ndogbong-Douala, ingeniously bridges the gap between the practical need for clean water and the spiritual beliefs surrounding its healing properties.

Economically, Winners' Chapel stands out as a paragon of commitment to stimulating entrepreneurship, fostering job opportunities, and promoting social capital. The church is not merely an employer to hundreds; it serves as an incubator of entrepreneurial spirit among its followers, persuading them to establish businesses within the heart of Cameroon, rather than seeking opportunities abroad.

Yet, beyond commendable humanitarian and economic contributions, the most profound influence of these Pentecostal institutions arguably resides in their ability to inspire spiritual and behavioral transformation among their members. As we shall see, the heart-warming testimonials, like that of a woman who metamorphosed from alcohol addiction to being "drunk with the Holy Spirit," underscores the potent power of Pentecostal Christianity to induce a seismic shift in values and foster personal development.

Nonetheless, it would be remiss to overlook the challenges and criticisms that accompany the influence of Pentecostal churches. Some narratives allude to the complex interplay between believers and the institution, pointing, for example, to the dual nature of power that religious institutions can wield. While people may experience economic empowerment, the church's demands sometimes lead to feelings of disempowerment, shedding light on the important balance that individuals must navigate between faith and personal well-being. The chapter ends with an unveiling of Winners' Chapel's pivotal role in catalyzing the birth of independent churches in Cameroon. These emergent congregations are spearheaded by individuals who have been impacted by their experiences within Winners' Chapel. Their divergence into separate religious ventures underscores the enduring influence of Bishop Oyedepo and Winners' Chapel, even as they forge unique spiritual pathways.

The Community Impact of Winners' Chapel

Bishop Oyedepo's "Mandate" outlines the humanitarian services of Winners' Chapel as a mission to rescue and assist mankind, particularly in areas affected by war, natural disasters, waterborne diseases, and other endemic challenges.[3] In Cameroon, the church has established a welfare system to support the less fortunate members of society. Each congregation has a Welfare Committee responsible for assessing applications and determining eligibility for assistance.[4] The welfare scheme operates in two main ways: Firstly, there are designated Sundays, known as "Operation Andrew,"[5] when church members are encouraged to invite their less fortunate neighbors and friends to benefit from donated food items, clothing, and other valuable items.[6] Secondly, the church provides financial aid to unemployed members for starting small businesses or covering medical expenses. To qualify for assistance, individuals must be active members of a Satellite Fellowship,[7] which serves as a growth organ of the Winners' Chapel. New church members are initially identified at Satellite Fellowships before being incorporated into the church as full members, who in turn recruit other members. According to Oyedepo, "each one has a part to play in growing the body so as to actualize a high rate of multiplication of the church."[8]

Applicants seeking financial support for business or medical bills discuss their needs with the leader of the Satellite Fellowship and complete an application form provided by the church. The form is then

---

3. Oyedepo, *Mandate*, 406.

4. Personal interview with Pastor Dominion in Douala (Nov. 17, 2015)

5. The concept of Operation Andrew that requires church members to bring a friend to church has probably been borrowed from the Billy Graham Evangelistic Association. It is based on the fact that when Andrew heard what John had said about Jesus, the first thing he did was to find his brother Simon and tell him, "we have found the Messiah," and he brought Simon to Jesus (John 1:41). This is surely one way the Winners Chapel uses to recruit new members into the church, even though the pastors do not totally agree with that but rather claim that their gifts are a matter of charity and nothing else!

6. Personal interview with Elder Emmanuel Yele (pseudonym), in Douala (Nov. 7, 2015).

7. Oyedepo sees Satellite Fellowships as growth organs of the church within the parishes made up small numbers of church members who meet every Saturday in the home of a chosen leader, who may be an elder, deacon, or deaconess. Satellite Fellowships act as the care center of the church and provide a platform where young people in the faith can ask questions and receive answers. It provides spiritual care and practical attention for the needs of individuals. See also Oyedepo, *Mandate*, 71.

8. Oyedepo, *Mandate*, 72.

submitted to the leader, who forwards it to the Welfare Committee. The committee decides the amount to be given, regardless of the requested sum. While some members may express dissatisfaction with the partial amounts received, it is important to acknowledge that the provision of any form of assistance by Winners' Chapel contributes significantly to alleviating the burdens faced by its members. Examples include members receiving sums ranging from 200,000CFA to 60,000CFA to start small businesses such as Call Box.[9]

The church also contributes toward empowering Cameroonians in their educational pursuits through donations and prayers. At the beginning of each school year and during periods of public exams, congregations organize church services where students are prayed for and school materials are anointed with olive oil and donated to beneficiaries.[10] This initiative aims to support the less fortunate by providing books, pens, pencils, and sometimes school fees.

Many believe that the prayers offered by church pastors and elders, along with the anointing of these materials, ensure success and protection against any threats to one's future. A member of the church in Douala told me that her success in the 2008 General Certificate of Education was due largely to the blessings and anointing that she received during such a prayer session. She had failed the exam twice while attending another church, the Presbyterian Church in Cameroon, despite the many prayers that went along with her preparations. In her former church, the pens and other writing materials were never anointed with olive oil.[11] The anointing she experienced in Winners' Chapel contributed to her success.

Anointing with olive oil in Winners' Chapel is seen as a means to empower individuals for success in a world that is often viewed as precarious. Asamoah-Gyadu's concept of "unction to function" in Pentecostal/Charismatic Christianity highlights how the anointing with olive oil enables progress and success.[12] By incorporating the use of olive oil

---

9. Personal interview with Pastor Cyprian Kum (pseudonym) in Douala (Nov. 9, 2015). A Call Box is a makeshift box produced out of plywood and fortified with planks. It usually has space which can contain an individual who provides quick telephone communication services to passers-by for money. Customers are usually charged per minute of communication.

10. Personal interview with Pastor Collins Bua (pseudonym) in Douala (Nov. 12, 2015).

11. Personal interview with Deaconess Denicia Kolo (pseudonym) in Bamenda (Nov. 21, 2015).

12. Asamoah-Gyadu, *Contemporary Pentecostal Christianity*, 121.

in their practices, Winners' Chapel aims to empower individuals not only through physical gifts but also through spiritual blessings. Some branches of the church allocate approximately 200,000CFA each year to purchase books and school supplies for children in their communities, further contributing to educational empowerment.[13]

One dimension of spiritual and physical empowerment experienced by members of Winners' Chapel in Cameroon is demonstrated during specific church services. Attendees are instructed to bring or acquire olive oil, which they pour into their palms. The pastor leads prayers and declarations, proclaiming that all problems will vanish after the anointing. Participants are then invited to apply the oil on their foreheads or any afflicted body part. They are also given the option to consume the oil while making personal declarations for financial breakthroughs, healing, and career advancements. This practice serves as a symbolic act of empowerment within the context of Winners' Chapel.

Charitable Endeavors in Times of Displacement

In addition to the empowering rituals stated above, Winners' Chapel engages in charitable endeavors aimed at assisting individuals affected by displacement caused by war and civil unrest. In 2015, the church dispatched relief materials worth 5 million cfa to the northern regions of Cameroon, supporting victims of Boko Haram insurgency. These relief items, including rice, other food supplies, and clothing, were contributed by church members and supplemented by church funds.[14] Such charitable actions align with the teachings of Jesus, who promises eternal life to those who serve the needs of others: "For I was hungry and you gave me something to eat, I was thirsty and you gave me something to drink, I was a stranger and you invited me in, I needed help and you clothed me, I was sick and you looked after me, I was in prison and you came to visit me."[15] The beneficiaries of Winners' Chapel's assistance are never coerced to join the church, emphasizing the church's commitment to altruistic motives.[16] These humanitarian services are particularly significant given the staggering statistics of individuals affected by various tragedies, as

13. Personal interview with Pastor Job Molewe (pseudonym) in Buea (Jan. 18, 2016).

14. Personal interview with Pastor Pierre Mua (pseudonym) in Douala (Nov. 17, 2015).

15. Matt 25:35–40, New International Version.

16. Personal interview with Pastor Victor Hill in Douala (Nov. 20, 2015).

evidenced by the United Nations' estimate of over two million people displaced from their homes in Nigeria and Cameroon, with many residing in refugee camps such as Minawao in the northern regions of Cameroon.[17] Therefore, the relief program initiated by Winners' Chapel emerges as a valuable initiative to address pressing humanitarian needs.

Bridging the gap between their tangible humanitarian services and their dedication to fulfilling the essential needs of communities, Winners' Chapel has not only offered relief to those affected by war and civil unrest but has also turned their focus inward, to daily struggles faced by the local populace. Recognizing the pivotal role of water—both as a physical sustenance and a spiritual metaphor—the church's efforts extend beyond mere relief provision. In a similar vein of service and with a parallel commitment to holistic well-being, Winners' Chapel's involvement in quenching physical thirst has become a precursor to healing souls.

Quenching Thirst and Healing Souls

Winners' Chapel has significantly contributed to fulfilling basic needs within communities in Douala, such as the provision of clean drinking water. In 2010, the national headquarters of Winners' Chapel in Ndogbong undertook the creation of a borehole to alleviate an impending water crisis in the region. Despite the water supply provided by SNEC[18] Cameroon, the growing population and demand necessitated alternative measures. Prior to the construction of the borehole, community members often resorted to purchasing water from commercial vendors or endured long journeys to obtain water during interruptions in the SNEC supply.[19] To address this challenge, Winners' Chapel installed a borehole on the exterior wall of the church in the Ndogbong neighborhood, offering free access to clean water for the public. The maintenance of the borehole is entrusted to the church, serving as a demonstration of their commitment to community welfare and their efforts to meet the essential needs of individuals in the region.[20]

17. Kindzeka, "AU: Return of Nigerian Refugees."

18. The National Water Supply Company of Cameroun (SNEC) is a mixed economy structure company with the legal personality and financial autonomy. See Oumar and Mbonigaba, "Assessment of the Performance."

19. Personal interview with Pastor Peter Toh (pseudonym) in Douala (Oct. 12, 2015).

20. Personal interview with Pastor Collins Bua (pseudonym) in Douala (Jan. 14, 2016).

THE SOCIOECONOMIC IMPACT OF WINNERS' CHAPEL 163

Figure 3: Picture of borehole in Ndogbong-Douala fixed on the wall of the church fence and conspicuously carrying the picture of Bishop Oyedepo and his wife, Faith Oyedepo. Photo by the author.

The water project in Ndogbong neighborhood serves as a valuable asset, not only addressing the issue of water scarcity but also reportedly providing healing properties. The perceived healing effects of the water are attributed to the prayers conducted by the anointed authorities of the church during the inauguration of the borehole.[21]

Testimonies from two individuals offer evidence to the water's healing potency. One account involves a member of another Pentecostal church who, guided by the Holy Spirit, felt compelled to drink from the tap and later discovered the alleviation of his stomach pain. Subsequently, he shared his testimony during a morning prayer session at Winners' Chapel.[22] The second example pertains to a member of Winners' Chapel who, upon hearing the testimony of the previously healed individual,

---

21. Personal interview with Pastor Wanki in Douala (Nov. 9, 2015).
22. Personal interview with Pastor Wanki in Douala (Nov. 9, 2015).

decided to consume the water in hopes of curing a throat ailment. Miraculously, her condition improved as well.[23]

Scholars concur that traditional Pentecostal churches historically regarded the reliance on scientific medicine as indicative of deficiency in faith. According to Allan Anderson, Pentecostals were initially skeptical toward modern medicine because it was seen as conflicting with a reliance on divine healing. This skepticism was rooted in the Pentecostal emphasis on faith, prayer, and the expectation of miraculous interventions, with the belief that turning to scientific medicine might signify a lack of faith in God's power to heal.[24]

Anderson's work is critical for understanding the complex relationship between Pentecostalism and scientific medicine, highlighting how traditional Pentecostal churches have navigated their faith's healing practices in the context of modern healthcare advancements. Many Pentecostal churches are now actively engaging in tangible efforts to promote health programs within their communities. This transformation reflects an evolving perspective and an increasing willingness among Pentecostal congregations to combine spiritual beliefs with practical initiatives to enhance overall well-being.

From the miraculous healing testimonies arising from the water project in Ndogbong to more structured health campaigns, Winners' Chapel embodies the merging of faith and pragmatism in promoting health and well-being. While the waters of Ndogbong attest to the spiritual potency believed by the congregation, they also hint at a broader commitment: the tangible promotion of physical health. This convergence of faith-driven healing and proactive health initiatives underscores the evolving role of Pentecostal churches in today's world. Rather than solely focusing on spiritual wellness, there is a burgeoning emphasis on holistic health—encompassing both spiritual and physical dimensions. With this understanding, we now turn to the multifaceted ways Winners' Chapel is championing the cause of health and well-being in their communities.

Promotion of Physical Health

Winners' Chapel actively engages in organizing health campaigns and programs aimed at raising awareness of prevalent diseases and educating

23. Personal interview with Pastor Enoch in Douala (Jan. 14, 2016).
24. Anderson, *Introduction to Pentecostalism*.

people on preventive measures. For instance, Winners' Chapel Douala conducted a public, free health campaign in 2011, offering consultations and laboratory tests for diseases such as HIV/AIDS, malaria, typhoid, and general blood tests.[25] The campaign was facilitated by medical officers who attend the church and other hired medical practitioners, with the church sponsoring free treatment for those in need.[26]

Winners' Chapel also supports existing medical institutions in Cameroon, fostering connections between the church and beneficiaries. Notably, in 2010, Winners' Chapel made a significant contribution by donating hospital equipment worth 10,000,000cfa (approximately 20,000 USD) to the Chantal Biya Foundation[27] in Yaoundé.[28] This donation included essential medications, anti-malarial drugs, antibiotics, oxygen cylinders, as well as provisions such as rice and milk for children. The senior pastor of Winners' Chapel Nfouda, Yaoundé, at the time, led the delegation in delivering these gifts and expressed admiration for Chantal Biya's efforts in addressing healthcare needs. This act aimed to support humanitarian work in the country and establish a long-lasting relationship between the Chantal Biya Foundation and Winners' Chapel in Cameroon.[29]

Within the local community of Ndogbong-Douala, Winners Chapel has provided financial support for medical bills when its members were admitted to the Lanquintinie Hospital in Douala.[30]

Winners' Chapel's commitment to the well-being of its community, as seen through its health promotion endeavors, goes beyond the realm of physical health. While their proactive measures in raising health awareness and supporting medical infrastructure are commendable, their holistic approach does not end there. From the corridors of health clinics to

25. Personal interview with Pastor Titus Ngah (pseudonym) in Douala (Nov. 18, 2015). Personal interview with Pastor Enoch in Douala (Nov. 12, 2015).

26. Personal interview with Pastor Titus Ngah (pseudonym) in Douala (Nov. 18, 2015). Personal interview with Pastor Enoch in Douala (Nov. 12, 2015).

27. The Chantal BIYA Foundation is an apolitical, non-denominational, and non-profit humanitarian association, created by Mrs. Chantal Biya, wife of Cameroon's head of state, in 1994 "in order to raise national and international awareness on the fight against poverty, disease, misery and all types of exclusion in urban and rural areas. The main aim of the Chantal BIYA Foundation is to assist vulnerable segments of the population and combat hardship"; see Republic of Cameroon, "Chantal BIYA Foundation."

28. Yufeh, "Cameroon: Winners Chapel Donates"; personal interview with Pastor Peter Toh (pseudonym) in Douala (Oct. 12, 2015).

29. Yufeh, "Cameroon: Winners Chapel Donates"; personal interview with Pastor Peter Toh (pseudonym) in Douala (Oct. 12, 2015).

30. Personal interview with Elder Philemon in Douala (Jan. 12, 2016).

the bustling arenas of job markets, the church has seamlessly transitioned its mission into nurturing socioeconomic resilience among its members. As we take the discussion further into the church's initiatives, we uncover its dynamic role in fostering social capital and promoting economic empowerment, underscoring its vision of creating a spiritually enriched, healthy, and economically stable community. The next sections shows how the church, through its networks and ethos, has become a nexus for job opportunities, entrepreneurial spirit, and the sharing of social wealth.

Nurturing Social Capital and Economic Empowerment

Beyond direct social services, the church offers opportunities for members to connect and gain employment. Affluent members or business proprietors are encouraged to consider fellow church members for job vacancies within their companies before seeking external candidates. The pastor acts as a mediator by announcing job descriptions and qualifications during church services, and interested individuals are invited to meet privately with the pastor in his office.[31] This practice, termed as "positive discrimination," focuses on benefiting active church members by advertising job opportunities internally before they are made public.[32]

The church's approach aims to empower its members first before reaching out to others. By emphasizing shared values and virtues between employers and employees within the same church community, Winners' Chapel fosters confidence in the reliability of its members as potential candidates for various roles. Scholars refer to this practice as the provision of social capital, which creates advantages and additional resources for individuals through their network of relationships.[33]

The importance of social capital is that it provides the space for meeting of individuals, one of whom may have the possibility to offer a job and the other seeking a job. In this case, the church to which both employer and employee belong provides a continuum for meeting each other's needs. Crucial to this process is the role of the pastor as the one who encourages church members to seek opportunities for the less privileged members of the church. The provision of social capital is important because it makes possible the achievement of certain ends

---

31. Participant observation in Douala (Nov. 7, 2015).
32. Personal interview with Pastor Victor Hill in Douala (Nov. 9, 2015).
33. Adogame, *African Christian Diaspora*, 103.

that would not be attainable otherwise.[34] In addition to providing social capital, Winners' Chapel enables members to create their own employment opportunities, further promoting economic empowerment within the community.

Entrepreneurial Spirit and Economic Impact

Winners' Chapel fosters an entrepreneurial spirit among Cameroonians through teachings that inspire them to take responsibility for creating job opportunities. Notable Sunday services and themes, such as "Day of Alliance with Progress," "Day of Alliance with Favour," "Day of Alliance with Supernatural Success," "Covenant Day of Fruitfulness," and "Covenant Day of Business and Career Breakthrough,"[35] reflect the church's focus on motivating members to pursue these themes faithfully through prayer and commitment. The teachings encourage individuals to seek their breakthroughs within Cameroon, instilling confidence that God will bless them in their homeland rather than seeking prosperity in distant Western countries. Consider this remark from one of the pastors:

> We teach our members that Cameroon is Africa in miniature indeed and that what they are seeking in faraway western countries can be achieved in Cameroon if they rely on God and make some efforts. Ask the Holy Ghost, "what can I do to change my environment?" And he will help you. You don't need to travel to America or Europe to be rich and to live a good life. Everything is in this country. We pray for them, and we anoint them for unlimited breakthroughs in life.[36]

The pastor's counsel reinforces the psychological empowerment of Cameroonians, dissuading them from embarking on treacherous journeys across the Mediterranean Sea in search of better economic opportunities. At the time of this counsel, it was particularly relevant due to the alarming number of African lives lost during attempts to cross the Mediterranean.[37] In 2022, it was estimated that 2,062 migrants died while

---

34. Coleman, "Social Capital," S95–S120.

35. I was present in all these days and observed how the church services were concentrated around the major themes while the pastor encouraged people to engage into impossible adventures in life because God can always give people what they ask for. Anointing of the church members always accompanied the final prayers.

36. Personal interview with Pastor Sam in Tiko (18/01/16).

37. The BBC reported that at least 200 Senegalese were among the more than 750

crossing the Mediterranean Sea. However, the accurate number of deaths recorded in the Mediterranean Sea cannot be ascertained. Between 2014 and 2018, for instance, about twelve thousand people who drowned were never found. In July 2023, UNICEF estimated that the number of children who lost their lives while attempting to cross the Mediterranean Sea to reach Europe doubled in the first half of the year compared to the same period last year.[38]

By encouraging individuals to create jobs within Cameroon, Winners' Chapel aims to deter its members from risking their lives in pursuit of the "golden fleece" abroad. This empowering message has inspired young Cameroonians to develop their talents and make a positive impact on their homeland.

Two pastors of Winners' Chapel, who were once students at the University of Buea, have successfully established the Institute of Management and Financial Accounting (IMFA) in Buea and the International College of Accounting and Sciences in Molyko-Buea.[39] These entrepreneurs credit their prosperity to the teachings of Bishop Oyedepo, which they learned while attending Winners' Chapel. Rather than succumbing to pressure to travel abroad, they chose to invest in their own businesses in Cameroon.[40]

Other members of the church have been encouraged to embark on great adventures because of Oyedepo's teaching and are grateful for how useful their connections with the Winners' Chapel have been in comparison to their experiences in former churches:

> When I compare my time in the Apostolic Church and now in Winners' Chapel, I can say that this church (Winners' Chapel) has been very helpful to me. The teachings of Bishop Oyedepo to his followers are unique. He teaches us to make wealth, he teaches the principles of financial prosperity. Then there is this captivating teaching that he always mentions about our place in the supernatural which makes me to understand that we can

---

migrants who died when a boat capsized off the coast of Libya on April 2015. These migrants were not fleeing war, as would be expected of citizens of Syria, who need to flee from their country, which is being ravaged by war and civil unrest. The Senegalese were economic migrants. BBC News, "Rescue Hopes Fade."

38. Knaus, "Children Drowning in the World's Inaction."
39. Personal interview with Pastor Sam in Tiko (Jan. 18, 2016).
40. Pastor Sam claims that the two proprietors later delivered their testimonies to the church on how the Winners' Chapel had provided them with the confidence to begin their own businesses.

do all things through Christ. So, it gave me the courage to take a big adventure. I started this Orphanage, which by the grace of God is doing very well even though it is not the kind of business I would have liked to do. I see it as a calling from God rather than a business.[41]

The positive impact of Winners' Chapel is highlighted in this quotation, particularly in comparison to the individual's previous experience in the Apostolic Church. The speaker acknowledges the significant support he received from Winners' Chapel, attributing it to the unique teachings of Bishop Oyedepo. These teachings encompass principles of financial prosperity and the belief in the supernatural abilities granted through Christ, fostering the individual's understanding that he is capable of achieving anything. This newfound understanding instilled the speaker with the courage to embark on a substantial venture, namely the establishment of an orphanage. Although not aligned with his initial business preferences, the individual perceives this endeavor as a divine calling rather than a purely commercial undertaking.

It is evident from the analysis that Winners' Chapel, under the guidance of Bishop Oyedepo, plays a significant role in shaping the speaker's belief and actions. The teachings on wealth creation and financial prosperity resonates with the individual, inspiring him to pursue new opportunities and take risks. Moreover, the emphasis on the supernatural and the notion that all things are possible through Christ instills a sense of empowerment and self-confidence. This spiritual perspective becomes the impetus for his philanthropic endeavor, the orphanage, which he perceives as a divine mission. In this quotation, we find the transformative power of religious teachings and their influence on personal aspirations and actions. It underscores the ability of religious institutions, such as Winners' Chapel, to inspire individuals to go beyond conventional career choices and engage in activities driven by a sense of divine calling.

The notion that Cameroonians can achieve their life goals without venturing to the Western world recalls a claim previously made by Bishop Oyedepo at the inception of his ministry. Initially, Oyedepo believed that a successful Pentecostal leader needed to study under renowned figures in the faith gospel, such as Kenneth E. Hagin, Oral Roberts, and T. L. Osborn. However, just as Oyedepo was preparing to embark on a journey to the United States, he claims to have received a divine revelation that

41. Personal interview with Isaiah Kum in Douala (Nov. 12, 2015).

the blessings he sought were not contingent upon studying abroad. "The things that you seek do not come from abroad but from above. You are not going to America."[42] Guided by this instruction, Oyedepo abandoned all plans to travel to the United States for training, relying instead on God's direct tutelage in the school of the Holy Ghost, which he found immensely valuable.[43] It is worth noting, however, that Oyedepo's subsequent excitement upon being informed by the management of a hotel in the United States that he would be spending the night in a room once occupied by Kenneth Copeland seems contradictory. Oyedepo offered a prayer on that occasion, expressing his admiration for Copeland's ministry and requesting that the works manifested through Copeland also became active in his life:

> God, you know how much I love Copeland's ministry, how much I appreciate your hand upon his life, how much he has affected our world for you, how much he has proved the devil wrong in demonstrating that you bless those you have called. Lord, as I go to sleep on this bed tonight, let those works in Copeland begin to work in me.[44]

Furthermore, the bishop has recounted a visit he made to Tulsa in 1986 to learn from Kenneth Hagin, whom he referred to as the "superhero" of the faith message. During one of Hagin's speaking sessions, Oyedepo claims to have had a transformative encounter where he witnessed a transfiguration of Hagin's face. Overwhelmed by this experience, Oyedepo's heart burst with emotion, and he openly wept. He asserted that the spirit entered him, altering the entire trajectory of his ministry, and he immediately acquired the serene manner of ministration exemplified by Kenneth Hagin.[45]

These accounts suggest that Oyedepo drew inspiration for his preaching and teaching styles from North American proponents of the faith gospel. Whether his primary influences came from American faith gospel preachers like Kenneth Copeland, whom he frequently invites to his Faith Tabernacle in Canaanland,[46] or from Pastor Adeboye, who

---

42. Oyedepo, *Mandate*, 18–19.
43. Oyedepo, *Mandate*.
44. Oyedepo, *Mandate*, 140.
45. Oyedepo, *Mandate*, 133.
46. Kenneth Copeland was one of the officiating ministers at the thirty-fifth anniversary of the Living Faith Church Worldwide in Nigeria along with Pastor Enoch Adeboye in May 2016.

ordained him, or even from the late Benson Idahosa, the pioneer of the prosperity gospel in African Pentecostalism, what remains significant is that Oyedepo's ideas are empowering local Cameroonians who, in turn, create employment opportunities and impact their communities. While these ideas have undoubtedly provided impetus for Cameroonians to strive toward entrepreneurship, it is important to acknowledge that the church itself has directly employed individuals in Cameroon.

Direct Employment

Winners' Chapel, through the World Mission Agency (WMA), provides employment opportunities for both youth and adults in Cameroon.[47] The church employs individuals across its approximately 135 congregations in various positions, including resident pastors, assistant resident pastors, associate pastors, office assistants, church accountants, office secretaries, bookshop attendants, studio attendants, IT technicians, security officers, and cleaners. Recruitment is conducted through interviews, and upon hiring, employees sign a contract that includes adherence to specific rules and regulations, including compulsory membership in Winners' Chapel and tithing obligations.[48]

Monthly salaries for employees varied depending on the position held, ranging from 30,000CFA (approximately £42 or $50US) for cleaners and security officers at the lower echelon to 428,707CFA (approximately £535 or $714US) for the highest-paid Cameroonian, who is also the longest-serving full-time pastor of the church.[49] The church's monthly expenditure on salaries for approximately 182 workers in Cameroon, in 2020, amounted to about 15,237,500CFA (approximately £21,000 or $25,375US), totalling approximately 182,850,000CFA (approximately £250,500 or $304,490US) annually.

---

47. The World Mission Agency is the name with which the Winners Chapel identifies its foreign branches. This is the umbrella name, which consists of churches and other investments such as schools that the church might possess wherever it is established.

48. "Living Faith Church Worldwide (aka) Winners Chapel International, Stewardship Covenant for all Ordained Workers and Service Unit Leaders." Obtained in Douala by the author in January 2016.

49. "World Mission Agency INC, Winners Chapel International Manpower Schedule, 2015." Document containing the names of workers of the Winners' Chapel posts of responsibility, current monthly salaries, and year of entry. Obtained in Douala by author in January 2016. Personal interview with Pastor Enoch in Douala (Jan. 2016).

While there is a discrepancy between the highest and lowest earners, the minimum salary of 30,000CFA paid by Winners' Chapel aligns favorably with the average minimum wage approved by the Cameroonian government, of 28,246CFA per month.[50] Consequently, Winners' Chapel's contributions modestly alleviate the country's unemployment rate and poverty. According to the 2013 report from the International Labour Organisation, Cameroon has a population of approximately 20 million people, with a staggering 30 percent unemployment rate and about 75 percent underemployment.[51]

One important aspect of employment within Winners' Chapel is the training provided to individuals before their employment. The church offers low-cost training programs to individuals with lower qualifications or who have dropped out of school. The Bible school, WOFBI, trains pastors and other leaders. This training has provided opportunities for individuals to acquire jobs that sustain their families, often surpassing the prospects offered by government positions. Consider the following comments by a pastor and accountant of the Winners' Chapel in Cameroon:

> I started working with Winners' Chapel in Cameroon since 1996 as a receptionist in the home of the first missionaries from Nigeria. Since then, I have grown in this church in my faith and commitment and today I am one of the pastors and church accountants! I thank God. It is the Winners' Chapel that has made me who I am because if not for this church I am not sure what I will be doing and whether I would have the kind of satisfaction that I have working under the anointing of a great man of God like bishop Oyedepo. I had dropped out of school because of lack of sponsorship before I came in contact with this church during its early beginnings. From the time I was employed my life has changed. I am married with two kids and can take care of my family without any problems. I am so grateful that bishop Oyedepo had this vision for a church like this in Cameroon.[52]

This pastor initially dropped out of school due to financial constraints after obtaining a primary school graduation certificate. After completing the WOFBI program, which is equivalent to a post-secondary school certificate, he obtained a salary comparable to that of a secondary school teacher in Cameroon, along with additional benefits. He also claims that

50. Cameroon 2013 Human Rights Report, "Executive Summary."
51. Ukuh, "Youth Unemployment Challenge."
52. Personal interview with Pastor Nanje in Douala (Nov. 19, 2015).

working with the Winners' Chapel provides him with both financial stability and a unique spiritual anointing associated with Bishop Oyedepo, which he credits for bringing unstoppable breakthroughs in his life.

The personal testimonies of individuals employed by Winners' Chapel reflect their gratitude for the opportunities provided by the church. They appreciate the chance to serve and make a living through their services, as well as the distinctive spiritual benefits derived from Bishop Oyedepo's anointing. These benefits inspire hope and confidence in overcoming life's challenges. The employment opportunities and spiritual impact provided by the church have created a sense of reliance on its founder, whom followers perceive as a powerful man of God with special revelations and understanding of God's workings. The anointing is regarded as a catalyst for healing, empowerment against supernatural evil, and the realization of success and prosperity.

The concept of anointing as both a spiritual-symbolic and physical sacramental act holds significant prominence within African Pentecostalist discourses. The case of Winners' Chapel reveals its multifaceted approach in providing anointing to its members and workers. As demonstrated by Asamoah-Gyadu, anointing in contemporary African Pentecostal thought serves three primary purposes: healing the sick through prayer, empowering individuals and fortifying them against supernatural evil, and reversing the effects of evil to facilitate success and prosperity in various aspects of life.[53] Bishop Oyedepo is viewed by his followers as a powerful figure who engages conversations with God, possessing unique revelations and an understanding of divine workings that have the potential to transform lives. As suggested by Asamoah-Gyadu, the intensity of a charismatic leader's anointing is contingent upon the effectiveness of their ministry and the frequency with which their prayers yield positive outcomes in people's lives.[54]

As we trace the journey of many who have been under the influence and guidance of Winners' Chapel, we see a consistent theme of transformation and empowerment. The church, through its employment opportunities, provides individuals with the tools they need to not only better their financial situation but also to foster spiritual growth. For many, this holistic approach is an antidote to the various issues plaguing their lives.

---

53. Asamoah-Gyadu, *Contemporary Pentecostal Christianity*, 123.
54. Asamoah-Gyadu, *Contemporary Pentecostal Christianity*, 120.

As seen in the pastor's testimony, the impact of the church's teachings and the anointing of its leaders is profound.

The direct employment and support provided by the church seem to function as a stepping stone toward achieving a more stable and prosperous life, both materially and spiritually. This trajectory of positive change is mirrored in the personal journeys of many congregants, as they transition from a state of physical "drunkenness" with alcohol to a state of spiritual "drunkenness" with the Holy Spirit. The juxtaposition of these two states, physical intoxication with substances and spiritual exhilaration with faith, offers a poignant commentary on the church's transformative influence. Just as employment under the church's guidance can lead to financial and personal growth, so too can its spiritual teachings guide individuals away from detrimental habits and toward a fulfilling relationship with God.

From "Drunkenness with Wine" to "Drunkenness with the Holy Spirit"

The phenomenon of converts to Pentecostal churches celebrating their spiritual experiences and the perceived improvements in their lives has been widely observed. These individuals attribute their positive transformations to the teachings and engagements within Pentecostal communities, which have fostered a heightened sense of responsibility. Thus, a member of Winners' Chapel in Bamenda could testify that "these days I am rather drunk with the Holy Spirit than drunk with wine."[55] This quote highlights the metaphorical conceptualization of "drunkenness" in both secular and religious contexts, where being "drunk with the Holy Spirit" is seen as a superior state compared to being intoxicated with wine. The testimony also illustrates how "born-again" Christianity, and the influence of Winners' Chapel, can reconstruct individual's lives and promote a family-oriented lifestyle.

In her past association with a historic mission church, the convert regularly consumed alcoholic beverages alongside her pastors, resulting in frequent intoxication. At that time, she believed that drinking alcohol was acceptable due to the shared practice among congregation members and spiritual leaders. However, her membership in Winners' Chapel has prompted a departure from these detrimental habits. In addition

---

55. Nofuru, "Rise in Pentecostalism Conversions," para. 7.

to financial savings, she attributes her family's healing and transformation to the power of the Holy Spirit. Previously afflicted by poor health, she and her son found no relief through modern medical treatments or traditional healers. Furthermore, her husband's promiscuity had caused concerns of infidelity and financial wastage. Since joining the Winners' Chapel, however, they have experienced miraculous healing and the abiding presence of the Holy Spirit, leading to improved health and a reformed husband. These profound changes are attributed to the transformative power of being born-again.[56]

This account reflects a common narrative among converts, illustrating the perceived benefits of Pentecostal conversion, particularly within the context of Winners' Chapel. Such testimonies often emphasize the role of divine intervention and the spiritual experience in fostering personal growth and the resolution of various life challenges. The contrast drawn between being "drunk with the Holy Spirit" and being intoxicated with wine symbolizes a transformative shift in the individual's values and priorities. It highlights the conviction that spiritual fulfillment and reliance on divine power surpasses worldly indulgencies and their associated consequences. These testimonies serve to reinforce the belief among converts that their lives have been positively impacted by their affiliation with Pentecostalism and the teachings and practices of Winners' Chapel.

Scholarly discourse on born-again Christianity, particularly within the field of religion, has long recognized its significance in the lives of its adherents. Birgit Meyer, for instance, has argued that converts to Pentecostal Christianity undergo a complete break from their previous sinful lives.[57] In the context of my earlier narrative, it is striking how the woman metaphorically conceptualizes the contrasting implications of drunkenness in secular and religious contexts. This example aligns with Michael Castor's proposition that conversion entails a paradigmatic shift, involving not only a complete departure from past sinful lifestyles but also the restructuring of familial relationships.[58] Thus, conversion serves as a process of re-socialization, drawing away from the world of sin and introducing them to a family-oriented life.

However, while it is evident that Winners' Chapel in Cameroon provides employment opportunities and empowers Cameroonian citizens in various ways, it is crucial to examine critically the broader implications

---

56. Nofuru, "Rise in Pentecostalism Conversions."
57. Meyer, "Make a Complete Break," 316–49.
58. Goliama, "Gospel of Prosperity."

of these contributions to the country's economic landscape, particularly in terms of resource exchange between the mother church in Nigeria and the daughter church in Cameroon.

Economic Footprints and Comparative Influence

In terms of employment opportunities provided to Cameroonians, the significance of Winners' Chapel within the national context may be relatively limited. However, when compared to other transnational churches like the RCCG, Winners' Chapel demonstrates a comparatively stronger commitment to employing local individuals. The RCCG had fewer than one hundred church branches in Cameroon in 2017 and employed approximately eighty-nine pastors,[59] with an average monthly salary of 35,000CFA.[60] As a result, some leaders and members of Winners' Chapel asserted that Winners' Chapel was the most influential Pentecostal church in Cameroon, particularly with regard to its contributions to the economic and social spheres:

> The contributions that Winners' Chapel is currently making to the economic and social life of Cameroon are amazing. Just after twenty years we have been able to establish more than two hundred churches, employing over two hundred Cameroonians who can earn bread for their families. We have got at least one permanent church structure in each regional headquarters of this country and that is development. Look at other churches like Redeemed, they are still struggling to reach where we are, and I tell you that in the next ten years you will see the structures that we will have in this land.[61]

Winners' Chapel was lauded by its members for remarkable contributions to Cameroon's economic and social fabric. In over two decades, the church established over two hundred churches, providing employment opportunities to more than two hundred Cameroonians. Moreover, it

---

59. Numbers are from Redeemed Christian Church of God, Central African Region: A document listing all the Redeemed Christian Church parishes in Cameroon with the dates of establishment and pastors in charge. The author obtained the document from the resident pastor of the Redeemed Christian Church of God-Shepherd House, Bonaberi, in Douala during fieldwork in Cameroon in November 2015.

60. Personal interview with Pastor George Njonyu, pastor of Shepherd House-Redeemed Christian Church of God, Bonaberi, Douala (Nov. 20, 2015).

61. Personal interview with Pastor Peter Amah (pseudonym) in Tiko (Jan. 18, 2016).

had erected at least one permanent church structure in each regional headquarters, which is viewed as a sign of development. In comparison, other churches, such as RCCG, were perceived as struggling to attain a similar level of success. Proponents of Winners' Chapel confidently predict significant growth and expansion in the coming years.

However, despite the achievements of Winners' Chapel among Pentecostal Charismatic churches in Cameroon, its contributions pale in comparison to classical Pentecostal churches like the Full Gospel Mission Church. In 2000, the Full Gospel Mission reported 518 assemblies and a membership of over 59,062. Additionally, the church operates several educational institutions, including nursery and primary schools, a bilingual teacher training college, a technical college, and a secondary school. It also has health centers in Garoua and Yaoundé, which it hopes to transform into hospitals, along with additional health centers and a printing press, opened in Bamenda in 1986.[62] Unfortunately, obtaining statistics on the number of Cameroonians employed by the Full Gospel Mission Church is challenging. Nonetheless, data collected by Robert Akoko in 2007 suggests that the contributions of the Full Gospel Mission Church far surpass those of Winners' Chapel in Cameroon. This disparity is likely due to the Full Gospel Mission Church's ownership of various institutions where more Cameroonians are employed. And also, the fact that the Full Gospel has existed in the country for a longer period. Akoko argues that the motivation for Pentecostals, fuelled by the prosperity gospel, to engage in business sectors played a pivotal role in overcoming the economic crisis that effected Cameroon in the 1990s.[63]

The relevance of Winners' Chapel evokes mixed perceptions among the population at large, encompassing feelings of uncertainty, suspicion, as well as conviction in the church's potential to instigate change and transformation in Cameroon. Given the multifaceted and conflicting ideas held by communities and individuals regarding large-scale transnational religious organizations, it is crucial to examine areas of ambivalence in their operations.

---

62. Akoko, *"Ask and You Shall Be Given,"* 62.
63. Akoko, *"Ask and You Shall Be Given,"* 62.

The Challenges of Social Capital

The limited presence of social institutions beyond the few churches owned by Winners' Chapel in Cameroon has sparked controversy, prompting questions about the church's societal role. This is particularly noteworthy considering that in Nigeria, Winners' Chapel possesses a network of educational institutions ranging from nursery schools to universities. These schools not only provide employment opportunities but also supplement the educational efforts of the Nigerian government at the federal and state levels.[64] The two universities owned by Winners' Chapel are quite prominent throughout Nigeria.[65] One would expect that as the church expands beyond national borders, it will make similar investments to contribute to social development. Such endeavors would enhance church-related activities and fulfill the comprehensive proclamation of the evangelical church's message. This message often emphasizes the inseparability of biblical evangelism, social responsibility, Christian discipleship, and church renewal.

Leaders of Winners' Chapel recognize the importance of this engagement and express their willingness to pursue such goals in Cameroon. They argue that the church has made efforts to establish schools but has faced obstacles from the Cameroonian education authorities. Each time they have submitted applications to open schools, they have been rejected on grounds that the church must be legally registered before establishing additional institutions.[66] For example, in January 2016, the national pastor of Winners' Chapel Cameroon visited the prime minister's office in Yaoundé, where the church's application documents were received. The authorities assured that they would review the documents and make recommendations to the president of the republic for signing a decree recognizing the church.[67] According to a local council financial chairperson of Winners' Chapel, once the president signs the decree, the church has plans to construct a hospital and university that would serve the entire Central African region. Cameroon has been chosen as the host

---

64. Omotoye and Opoola, "Church and National Development."

65. The first university of the Winners' Chapel was created in 2002 and named Covenant University, and the second, Landmark University, was created in Omu-Aran, the native town of Bishop Oyedepo, in 2010.

66. Personal interview with Pastor Enoch in Douala (Oct. 12, 2015).

67. Personal interview with Pastor Enoch in Douala (Oct. 12, 2015).

for these projects due to its high number of Winners' Chapel congregations in Africa, second only to Nigeria.[68]

Nigerian missionaries have expressed their frustration over the lack of cooperation from Cameroonian state authorities regarding the perceived investment plans of the church. Some speculate that the Cameroon government is aware of contributions made by Winners' Chapel but is hesitant to legalize the church due to concerns that such recognition would extend to other Pentecostal churches, which harbor questionable motives.[69] However, available evidence suggests that the Cameroonian state authorities may be cautious about granting legal status to Winners' Chapel, because they are skeptical of the true intentions of the church and the potential benefits they bring to the Cameroonian people. Two significant issues contribute to this skepticism.

Firstly, none of the Cameroonians working with Winners' Chapel in Cameroon was registered with the Caisse Nationale de Prévoyance Social (CNPS),[70] meaning there would be no pension for them upon retirement. In 2015, an indigenous Cameroonian pastor from Winners' Chapel reported to the state authorities, prompting the church administration to submit a list of workers along with their respective years of entry into the ministry.[71] Instead of providing a comprehensive list of over 182 full-time workers, the authorities submitted a list of only 78 workers, falsely indicating that the first worker was employed in 2012, instead of 1996.[72] Further investigations revealed that the submitted list had been manipulated and reduced the true years of entry and salaries of the workers.[73]

68. Personal interview with Elder Emmanuel in Douala (Nov. 7, 2015).

69. Personal interview with Pastor Clement in Douala (Jan. 18, 2016).

70. The National Social Insurance Fund (CNPS) ensures, within the framework of the general policy of the government, the various benefits provided in the legislation of social protection and the family. As such, it covers three branches of social security including: family benefits, old age, invalidity, and death pensions/occupational risks. http://www.cnps.cm/.

71. Personal interview with Pastor Paul Menyole (pseudonym) in Douala (Feb. 4, 2016).

72. Personal interview with Pastor Paul Menyole (pseudonym) in Douala (Feb. 4, 2016). Also from "World Mission Agency INC, Winners Chapel International Cameroon." A document containing names/number of workers of the Winners' Chapel in Cameroon, years of entry, and their salaries. This is the list with the wrong information, a copy of which is with this author, obtained in Douala in February 2019.

73. Personal interview with Pastor Victor Bong (pseudonym) in Douala (Feb. 2, 2016). Also from "World Mission Agency INC, Winners' Chapel International, Manpower Schedule." A document containing number of workers of the Winners' Chapel in Cameroon with their actual years of entry and salaries. Obtained in Douala by the author.

Consequently, the Cameroonian Pastors Union demanded an explanation from the national pastor, questioning why the true years of entry of Cameroonian pastors were not forwarded to CNPS and inquiring about the status of those who had been working since 1996.[74] The union also sought clarification on why workers who had served the commission since 1996 were falsely listed as starting work in 2012.[75]

Secondly, the issue of social investment made by Winners' Chapel in Cameroon has sparked controversy, with claims suggesting that the church has made significant contributions when there is little evidence to support such assertions. According to a reliable source and indirect information, it is alleged that the Nigerian church authorities wrote a letter to the presidency of the Republic of Cameroon, stating that the church had constructed schools and other social facilities within the country. This action may have been an attempt to appease the Cameroonian state authorities and obtain authorization for the church's operations, as it currently operates in an illegal capacity.[76] However, upon discovering the existence of this letter, the Cameroonian Pastors Union raised further inquiries to the national pastor, seeking clarification regarding the locations of the purportedly constructed Centre for the Blind, orphanage, and schools as indicated in the letter addressed to the presidency of the Republic of Cameroon.[77]

The concerns raised by the Cameroonian Pastors Union highlight the need for transparency and accountability. The questionable practices regarding workers' years of entry and salaries, along with the failure to register employees with the CNPS, seems to contribute to suspicions of the Cameroonian state authorities. There is no doubt that the unresolved issues surrounding employment and social security undermine the credibility and perceived benefits that Winners' Chapel claims to bring to the Cameroonian society.

The claim that the Nigerian church authorities wrote a letter to the presidency of the Republic of Cameroon, asserting the construction of schools and other social facilities, adds another layer of complexity to the discussion. Granted, this action can be seen as an attempt to appease the Cameroonian state and gain authorization for their operations, considering their current illegal status. However, it raises concerns about the

---

74. CPU WMA-Cameroon, "Our Observation."
75. CPU WMA-Cameroon, "Our Observation."
76. Personal interview with Pastor Clement in Douala (Feb. 4, 2016).
77. CPU WMA-Cameroon, "Our Observation."

motivations behind such claims and whether they are primarily driven by a desire for legitimacy rather than a genuine commitment to social justice and empowerment.

It is plausible to suggest that the church hierarchy made these assertions in an attempt to gain authorization from the Cameroonian government,[78] with the intention of subsequently carrying out the proposed investments. However, if Winners' Chapel resorted to such tactics to secure legal recognition from the Cameroon state, the government might be perceiving their actions and claims as potentially detrimental to the well-being of its citizens, despite the employment opportunities they provide. This interpretation could help explain why the church has not been granted legal recognition in Cameroon.

Power Dynamics and Economic Disparities

It appears that Winners' Chapel is content with confining its activities in Cameroon to opening churches, which generate funds for investment projects in Nigeria and allows for greater control by the Nigerian leadership. Consequently, some individuals perceive the underlying issue to be a struggle for power and control over potential investments in Cameroon. The fundamental question has been: Who will ultimately have authority over these investments, the Cameroonians or the Nigerians, given that the church is owned by the latter? Consider a lament from another Cameroonian pastor:

> We have been fighting the idea of opening at least one Primary school in this country. We have been asking the Nigerian national pastors who come to this country to apply for authorisation from the government to open schools, but they don't listen or simply don't want to do it. At one time we had decided that we were going to ask for authorisation to open a Primary school but in the last meeting we had, the Nigerian pastors who were heading the church said if schools were opened it would be their wives administering them because they cannot have their wives who are

---

78. One of my respondents suggested that the government of Cameroon might be delaying the recognition of the Winners' Chapel in Cameroon because the church has not established any schools or hospitals. He had advised the national leaders of the church to try to establish at least one primary school because most of the older mission churches started with such services before opening congregations. My respondent did not in any way justify that they had lied to the government about opening any schools or orphanage because he never knew that I had this information.

graduates working under Cameroonians who have been trained as Primary School teachers with basic professional qualifications from Teachers Training Colleges. They vowed that if their wives are not going to be directors of the schools, they were not going to open them. But we collect large sums of money each year including all the Shiloh offerings and transfer to Nigeria where they keep building Universities... Universities where we cannot send our children, even though we are pastors of this commission, because the fee is too high, and we cannot afford.[79]

This quotation highlights the complex relationships between Winners' Chapel, the Cameroon government, and the local communities, with significant implications for governance, economic empowerment, and the equitable distribution of resources. The statement portrays a struggle within the church regarding the establishment of primary schools in Cameroon. The Cameroonian pastors express their desire to open schools and have repeatedly urged the Nigerian national pastors to seek authorization from the government. However, the Nigerian pastors either do not listen or are unwilling to pursue this course of action. The crux of the matter lies in the insistence of the Nigerian pastors that their wives should be appointed as directors of any potential schools. Their stance reflects a reluctance to have their well-educated wives work under Cameroonian educators who possess basic professional qualifications from teacher training colleges. This assertion raises concerns about power dynamics, control, and a potential disregard for local expertise and professionalism. It suggests that the Nigerian pastors prioritize maintaining control over the educational institutions rather than empowering the local community and adhering to principles of equitable distribution of resources.

Moreover, Pastor Wah's words shed light on the financial aspects of Winners' Chapel's operations by revealing that substantial sums of money, including offerings collected during events such as Shiloh, are transferred to Nigeria. These funds are used for building universities that, according to the Cameroonian pastors, are unaffordable for them and their communities. This situation highlights a disparity between the financial capabilities of the church and the practicality of providing affordable education for its own members and the local community.

---

79. Personal interview with Pastor Lazarus Wah (pseudonym) in Bamenda (Feb. 2, 2016).

The Ambivalent Nature of Social Capital

One way to look at the challenges surrounding social capital within the context of intra-African Pentecostalism is the dynamics of resource flow between the mother church in Nigeria and the daughter church in Cameroon. It requires a comprehensive analysis that emphasizes a balanced and inclusive approach, giving priority to the needs and aspirations of local communities, while fostering collaboration and dialogue among stakeholders.

Afe Adogame has drawn on Peggy Levitt's concept of social capital in the African Christian diaspora, where immigrants bring with them a range of norms, practices, and social resources to their host societies, which Levitt refers to as "resources."[80] Over time, immigrants adapt and transform these resources, which subsequently become the content of social remittances sent back to their home communities.[81] Although Adogame's focus on African immigrants in Europe and the United States differs significantly from our examination of the Winners' Chapel from an intra-African perspective, the notion of remittances and resources remains pertinent to both contexts. Levitt's concept of social remittances suggests that ideas, behaviors, and social capital flow from receiving to sending communities.[82] If resources flow from the USA back to Nigeria, Levitt's model would also lead us to expect a flow from Cameroon back to Nigeria, which is what we find. However, a crucial distinction between the two remittance models lies in the economic disparity between the USA and Cameroon. The USA, as the wealthier partner, benefits from the transfer of resources, while Cameroon, as a significantly poorer country, would benefit from resources flowing in the opposite direction. From a moral and empowerment standpoint, the direction of resource flow should be different. However, according to Levitt's argument, the flow aligns with the existing pattern.

In the case of intra-African movements, considerations of economic justice and empowerment would suggest that ideas, resources, and behaviors should ideally flow from sending to receiving countries, enabling organizations to fully establish themselves in their new contexts. This would promote the ideas and principles that form the foundation of the organization's operational framework as defined in its country of origin.

80. Adogame, *African Christian Diaspora*, 118.
81. Adogame, *African Christian Diaspora*, 118.
82. Adogame, *African Christian Diaspora*, 118.

Within the context of global migration, it is understandable that immigrants feel a responsibility to send money to their friends and relatives in Africa once they settle into their new host countries. However, it is important to acknowledge that immigrants also contribute to the economies of their receiving countries through the payment of taxes on their income and by participating in various benefits such as pension schemes. This creates a triangular trajectory of benefits, where immigrants provide services in the receiving countries and receive rewards, subsequently benefiting their family members through remittances.

While the concept of remittances as a source of social capital is applicable to immigrants in Europe and the United States, its application to organizations like Winners' Chapel and other African Pentecostal churches in their intra-continental operations raises questions. These churches are often perceived as empowering the receiving countries. However, there appears to be an ambivalence regarding the contributions of Pentecostal churches to social capital in Cameroon, particularly in terms of the flow of resources and remittances between the Nigerian mother church and the Cameroonian daughter church. This flow, though complex, seems to be predominantly unidirectional in favor of the mother church.

The funds used to pay the workers employed by Winners' Chapel in Cameroon come from the Cameroonian congregation's tithes and offering.[83] Additionally, the church in Cameroon pays the missionaries sent from Nigeria to control the church as national leaders and overseers of the wealthier and more established congregations in Cameroon. Cameroonian workers are not registered for social insurance, leaving them without job security. A finance committee chairman of one of the most financially buoyant congregations reported that, until 2013, the church used to send the balance of all its monetary collections to Nigeria after running its services. From 2013 onward, only 40 percent (still a significant percentage) of the total income including all tithes has been sent back to Nigeria.[84]

Historical precedents of transnational remittance practice within Winners' Chapel are evident and not limited to Cameroon. For instance, Ukah Asonzeh's study of the Christian Missionary Fellowship and Winners' Chapel in Cameroon, titled "Piety and Profit: Accounting

---

83. Personal interview with Pastor Samuel Anang (pseudonym) in Douala (Nov. 9, 2015).

84. Personal interview with Elder Emmanuel Yele (pseudonym) in Douala (Nov. 7, 2015).

for Money in West African Pentecostalism,"[85] reveals the existence of a "remittance ratio" system. This system assigns a financial quota to each congregation for monthly reparation to the international headquarters in Nigeria, with the amount varying depending on the financial viability of the parish.[86] Paul Gifford previously reported that the Accra branch of Winners' Chapel in Ghana was required to remit $60,000 USD to Nigeria each month during a crisis in 2004.[87] Ukah's findings further indicate that Winners' Chapel has a policy of closing congregations, particularly in semi-urban areas, that fail to meet their remittance ratios or that demonstrate unproductivity.

In Cameroon, the Douala church has financial oversight over other Winners' Chapel churches in the country, and they remit their ratios to Douala for onward transmission to Nigeria, often done through cash transfers via public transport to potentially conceal the magnitude of outflow from Cameroon.[88] In one occasion, armed robbers on the way stole the money that was being transported to Nigeria and no concerns were raised to avoid police intervention.[89] It is noteworthy that Winners' Chapel demands remittances to be sent to Nigeria even if the sending countries incur debt as a result. This is exemplified in the case of Cameroon, where the Douala national headquarters acquired a bank loan for property purchase and was repaying the loan while remitting only 10 percent of total income to the Lagos church at the time of Ukah's research.[90] The current remittance ratio for Cameroon is reported to be 40 percent, possibly indicating the completion of the loan repayment.[91]

One could make a reasonable argument that financial contributions from all branches of Winners' Chapel worldwide to the international headquarters in Nigeria are necessary to support the church's mission work. However, the current remittance practices within the church, particularly within the intra-continental context, involve substantial amounts of money. This raises concerns, especially when these funds originate from countries lacking permanent Winners' Chapel buildings, job security, social facilities, and adequate working conditions.

85. Ukah, "Piety and Profit," 633.
86. Ukah, "Piety and Profit."
87. Gifford, *Ghana's New Christianity*.
88. Ukah, "Piety and Profit," 633–48.
89. Ukah, "Piety and Profit," 633–48.
90. Ukah, "Piety and Profit," 633–48.
91. Personal interview with Kennedy Kum (pseudonym) in Douala (Nov. 7, 2015).

Consequently, the notion that Winners' Chapel in Cameroon creates social capital within the nation appears to be more of a rhetorical concept than a tangible reality.

It is worth noting that other transnational Pentecostal churches engage in the practice of transnational and intra-continental remittances on a similar scale to that of Winners' Chapel. A case in point is the Redeemed Christian Church of God (RCCG), as demonstrated in the following passage:

> Each individual parish of the Redeemed Christian Church is linked to the Lagos International headquarters, through an evolving hierarchical administrative structure. At the central organizational level, local parishes are required to make monthly financial contributions through administrative, zonal headquarters to RCCG International headquarters. This includes 10 per cent of total tithes and offerings of all RCCG fellowships, 30 per cent of tithes and 10 per cent of offerings of all parishes dedicated by the General Overseer or not.[92]

Afe Adogame highlights the hierarchical administrative structure within the Redeemed Christian Church of God and its financial contributions system. Each local parish is connected to the Lagos international headquarters, and this connection is facilitated through an evolving hierarchical administrative framework. At the central organization level, the RCCG mandates that local parishes make monthly financial contributions. These contributions are made through administrative and zonal headquarters, ultimately reaching the RCCG International headquarters. The financial contributions comprise 10 percent of the total tithes and offerings collected by all RCCG fellowships. Additionally, 30 percent of tithes and 10 percent of offerings from all parishes, regardless of whether they were dedicated by the general overseer or not, are also included in these contributions. This financial system demonstrates the RCCG's emphasis on centralized control and financial commitment from its local parishes. The requirement for monthly contributions serves as a means of resource mobilization and financial support for the RCCG's overall operations, projects, and mission work. The specific percentages allocated to different types of financial contributions indicate a structured and organized approach to resource allocation within the church. From an organizational perspective, this system ensures a regular flow of financial

---

92. Adogame, *African Christian Diaspora*, 119.

resources to the RCCG International headquarters, enabling the central administration to manage and coordinate the activities of the entire church. However, it also raises questions about the degree of financial autonomy and decision-making power held by individual parishes, as their contributions are predetermined and governed by the central administrative structure.

There is a discernible pattern suggesting that the phenomenon of remittances, particularly in a specific direction, is a prevalent trend among African Pentecostal churches. This raises the crucial inquiry regarding the extent to which these practices contribute to the empowerment of the communities in which they have expanded their influence. In the case of Winners' Chapel in Cameroon, the evidence suggests a paradoxical outcome: the very individuals whom the church claims to empower are confronted with the potential for disempowerment.

A Journey of Faith: Power, Powerlessness, and Empowerment

In 2022, I interviewed a man in Buea, Cameroon, whose story embodies the interplay of power, powerlessness, and empowerment. This individual, like many others in the continent, sought solace and hope in a religious setting and had lessons to learn.

In the year 2000, the man in question was at a crossroads, grappling with the aftermath of a job loss that had cast a shadow over his life. It was during this tumultuous period that a friend invited him to a "Shiloh" event at the Winners' Chapel, Buea. The service was led remotely from Nigeria by Bishop Oyedepo and held a promise of transformation. In a moment of prophetic declarations, Bishop Oyedepo proclaimed that anyone who had suffered losses could reclaim their blessings by simply believing in the divine word. With unwavering trust, my interlocutor embraced this proclamation, anchoring his hopes in the bishop's words. Miraculously, just two days after the culmination of the "Shiloh" program, he received a phone call from the Mobile Telecommunications Network head office in Douala, offering him a job opportunity he had previously sought.

This extraordinary turn of events, following Bishop Oyedepo's declaration, strengthened his belief that the Nigerian bishop's divine conduit had reshaped his destiny. Thus, he fully immersed himself in the Winners' Chapel, drawn by its electrifying worship, potent prayers, and the prevailing atmosphere of ambition, prosperity, and wealth accumulation. But, as time unfolded, the enthusiasm of his newfound faith began to wane. The mounting financial demands from the church, including tithes amounting to a tenth of his salary, weekly offerings, and an incessant multitude of church programs, began to weigh heavily on him. His once-thriving family life now teetered on the brink of dissolution due to his dwindling presence at home. It became apparent that what he had initially perceived as empowerment was, in fact, a subtle form of disempowerment. The relentless demands had drained not only his financial resources but also his time and family relationships. In response to these challenges, he made a conscious decision to return to the Presbyterian Church, seeking a quieter and more balanced Christian life. Nonetheless, he acknowledged that his time in the Winners' Chapel had enriched his spiritual journey in certain facets, particularly in the realms of prayer and commitment to achieving tangible results.

This narrative underscores the multifaceted dynamics of power within religious institutions. Initially, the man's encounter with the prophetic proclamation of Bishop Oyedepo illustrates the significant power wielded by religious leaders, capable of instilling hope and catalyzing life-altering changes in the lives of their followers. The subsequent job offer crystallizes the transformative potential of faith in the face of adversity. However, this story also reveals the power imbalance inherent in religious settings, where individuals may feel compelled to surrender significant resources, both financial and temporal, in pursuit of spiritual empowerment. In this context, empowerment becomes a double-edged sword, potentially leading to a sense of disempowerment when it infringes on one's financial stability and family bonds. Ultimately, the decision of the man to return to the Presbyterian Church underscores the quest for self-empowerment and a harmonious life balance, suggesting that empowerment can take diverse forms depending on individual needs and circumstances within the complex realm of religious experiences.

Pathways of Faith

Winners' Chapel has instilled spiritual vibrancy within the Cameroonian religious mosaic, and the country has witnessed the rise of new sources of spiritual life. Born out of a shared experience within the Winners' Chapel, at least three noteworthy independent Pentecostal churches have emerged, each carving a niche in the spiritual landscape of the country. These are the Gospel of Power Chapel, Harvest Bible Chapel, and Ambassadors of Christ, all founded in the city of Douala. These churches stand as a testament to the resilience and faith of their founders: Pastors Greenfield Nchia, Ebua Kum, and Tebah John, respectively.

Each of these pastors underwent rigorous training at the Word of Faith Bible Institute (WOFBI), immersing themselves in theological teachings and dedicating their lives to the service of the Lord. The journeys of Pastors Greenfield and Ebua within the Winners' Chapel took them through various roles, both in Cameroon and abroad. Despite their dedicated service, a feeling of marginalization within their home country prompted them to re-evaluate their paths. Driven by a conviction and vision to create an inclusive space for their fellow Cameroonians, they decided to embark on independent spiritual journeys. Their ministries, while rooted in the teachings they acquired, have evolved to cater to the unique spiritual needs of their congregations. A brief exploration of the lives and profiles of these three pastors reveals a shared narrative of breaking free from constraints and establishing churches that resonate with their perceived individual callings.

The Gospel of Power Chapel

Pastor Greenfield's spiritual journey began with the Presbyterian Church in Cameroon. However, it was in 2001,[93] while studying for a pharmacy degree at the University of Buea, that his path took a transformative turn following an encounter with Pastor Song, who led a passionate campus ministry in Buea. Greenfield felt a stirring in his soul, leading him to commit himself wholeheartedly to Christ. In 2002, a new door opened for Greenfield when he joined Winners' Chapel. As the years passed, his dedication to the church and its mission deepened. By 2008, he had taken the mantle of full-time pastor with the church. Seeking to further deepen his understanding, Greenfield embarked on a journey to Lagos to study at WOFBI. Upon his return in 2009, he was ordained as a full-time pastor for the Winners' Chapel in Cameroon. Greenfield planted churches

---

93. My research findings suggest that most people who join Pentecostal/Charismatic churches from historic mission churches often have a conversion narrative professing that they were never born again in the former churches or had not given their lives to Christ. That is to say, even though they attended church in those former years, they were never fully committed or had not received the "baptism of the Holy Spirit."

in Limbe and Tiko and served as an overseer for the Winners' Chapel in the northern regions of Cameroon and as a missionary in Chad. His tenure in Bonaberi, Douala, saw a remarkable transformation. Under his leadership, a budding church, with an initial membership of two hundred, blossomed into a vibrant community of eight hundred members. However, an abrupt transfer to Bafoussam, replacing him with a Nigerian missionary, left Greenfield questioning the motives and the path set before him. He could not help but wonder if his successful expansion of the church, leading to increased financial contributions, made the Nigerian leadership prefer one of their own to oversee the rewards of his labor. Was there a place for Cameroonians in the future of the church? His contemplations took on a deeper hue when, after conducting his first service in Bafoussam on June 16, 2013, a sweeping government order led to the immediate closure of nearly all Pentecostal churches, including Winners' Chapel. This closure persisted for a challenging six months. Undeterred, Greenfield devised a way to keep the congregation connected, organizing them into two groups for regular worship sessions. He kept the flame of faith burning, even in these trying times, but began to seek answers from God about the direction his life was taking. Why had he been uprooted from Bonaberi? Why were the churches closed upon his arrival in Bafoussam? Intense periods of prayer and fasting led him to a revelation: his journey with Winners' Chapel had ended. Upon conveying his decision to the national pastor, and after consultations with the executive secretary in Nigeria, Greenfield was granted permission to leave. A few weeks later, with renewed purpose and faith, he laid the foundation for his own independent church in Douala, the Gospel of Power Chapel International. It was not just a departure from his former church but a response to what he perceived as injustice in Cameroon and, above all, an answer to a divine call to start his own ministry.[94]

The Harvest Bible Chapel

Pastor Kum's spiritual journey began on foreign soil. While studying biomedical sciences at the University of Kaduna, Nigeria, he was introduced to the Abundant Life Faith Ministries in Akwaibom. This encounter in 1994 marked his transition to born-again Christianity. On his return to

---

94. Personal interviews with Pastor Greenfield Nchia in Douala (Dec. 10, 2015); Tanku, "Cameroon's President Orders."

Cameroon in 1996, he felt a strong connection with Winners' Chapel. However, his true calling came after a fervent three-day prayer session at the Unification Stadium in Douala. Recognizing his faith and dedication, Winners' Chapel granted Kum a scholarship to WOFBI in Nigeria. After a year of intensive study, he was ordained as a full-time pastor in 2002. His pastoral journey was marked by notable assignments, from serving in Northern Nigeria to venturing as a missionary in the Democratic Republic of Congo. Back in Cameroon, he served in various regions, including Yaoundé and Buea. While the decision of Winners' Chapel to "indigenize" its establishments across Africa initially seemed promising to Pastor Kum, he quickly realized the challenges. Despite his commitment to the church, he found himself being shuttled between Cameroon and the DRC. This frequent relocation posed challenges for his family, especially his children's education. It was during this difficult period that Pastor Kum's path took an unexpected turn. Feeling disillusioned with the inconsistencies in his assignments and other challenges within the church, he began contemplating a new direction. His decision to pursue further studies led him to Liberty Baptist Theological Seminary in Lynchburg, Virginia, USA, where he aimed to earn a master's degree in church planting and leadership. It was here that fate intervened. Leaders of the Harvest Bible Fellowship came to Liberty to lecture on church planting. Intrigued, Pastor Kum approached them, inquiring about the possibility of establishing a partner branch in Cameroon. Their affirmative response set the wheels in motion. Upon return to Cameroon, the Harvest Bible Chapel came into existence on October 1, 2012. This was not just another church; it was a branch of a renowned fellowship that boasted over 156 branches globally, with its roots in Virginia. For Pastor Kum, this was a departure from his past with Winners' Chapel and Bishop Oyedepo. He views his Harvest Bible Chapel as a representation of the true, selfless gospel of Jesus Christ. His journey, which was marked by challenges and revelations, culminated in the establishment of a church that he believed offered boundless opportunities for the people of Cameroon, something he felt was missing in his previous affiliation.[95]

---

95. Personal interview with Pastor Ebua Kum in Douala (Feb. 2, 2016).

The Ambassadors of Christ

Pastor Tebah's spiritual journey unfolds against the backdrop of his Presbyterian roots. On March 14, 1993, while studying in Nigeria, he experienced a meaningful transformation. His encounter with a breakaway Charismatic Renewal Ministry from the Roman Catholic Church introduced him to the concept of the "Full Gospel,"[96] a message that would become the catalyst for his conversion. In 1999, Tebah joined the Winners' Chapel. He did not merely attend; he wholeheartedly engaged in various roles, from being an usher to leading the youth, chairing the marriage committee, and serving as a dedicated deacon. His commitment to the church was unwavering. A pivotal moment arrived when Winners' Chapel expanded its reach from Ndogbong to Bonaberi, and Tebah generously opened his home to host the church for several months until a suitable rented space was found. His dedication did not go unnoticed.

In 2010, Tebah's journey took another significant turn as he was ordained. Under the mentorship of Pastors Wisdom from Nigeria and Greenfield Nchia from Cameroon, he honed his pastoral skills and deepened his connection with the church. However, he testifies that it was on the twenty-fifth of April 2012, at precisely 5:05 p.m., that his life's purpose was unveiled. While driving to a prayer meeting, Tebah experienced a divine revelation. God instructed him to become his ambassador, proclaiming liberty to the captives. The message was clear: "my son I want to talk to you, get a pen and a paper and write this down... my word is living, and I am sending you as my ambassador to take and proclaim liberty to the captives." God further commanded him not to take any action at that moment but to remain in Winners' Chapel for adequate preparation for the task. Preparation was needed, God's timing was perfect, and Tebah spent two years diligently preparing for the mission. In 2014, the call to ministry became undeniable. Tebah reached out to his district and national pastors, seeking their blessings and support for his newfound purpose. The leaders of Winners' Chapel endorsed his journey, reaffirming his divine calling. The establishment of his church came at a challenging time when state authorities were closing churches and resisting the opening of new Pentecostal congregations. Despite these obstacles, Tebah's faith prevailed, and he saw this as an affirmation of his ministry. A parting gift from Winners' Chapel reinforced his divine mission. A

---

96. This is in reference to the classic Pentecostal formulation of the four-fold Gospel of Jesus Christ as Savior, Sanctifier, Healer, and Coming King.

book titled *Making Full Proof of Ministry: Understanding Your Calling in Life and Ministry*,[97] authored by one of his favorite pastors, Dr. Enenche, symbolized their continued connection and support.

Tebah's transformation from a Presbyterian with no pastoral aspirations to the founder of the Ambassadors of Christ was guided by the teachings of Winners' Chapel. He had imbibed the ethos of "Kingdom service,"[98] a concept championed by Bishop Oyedepo himself. According to Oyedepo, giving time, talents, and resources to the church yields heavenly rewards. He quotes scripture to suggest that "our labour in the Kingdom is what determines our wages here on earth and Kingdom service is a vital key to supernatural blessings."[99] Tebah was a testament to this teaching. Although the Ambassadors of Christ operates independently with full autonomy, Tebah maintains a strong spiritual connection with Bishop Oyedepo. He continues to draw inspiration from Oyedepo's books and online programs, considering Oyedepo not just as a mentor but a guiding light on his journey of faith.

Across the narratives of Pastors Greenfield of the Gospel of Power Chapel, Pastor Kum of the Harvest Bible Chapel, and Pastor Tebah of the Ambassadors of Christ runs a shared motif: Winners' Chapel's significant influence in catalyzing their spiritual journeys and the subsequent establishment of their independent churches. Their stories spotlight Winners' Chapel's unintended legacy in Cameroon, as an incubator for new-age Pentecostal leaders. All three pastors, through different paths and unique experiences, embraced the teachings and ethos of Winners' Chapel. Yet, amid their unwavering dedication, they each encountered moments of introspection and revelation that propelled them toward individual spiritual directions. Whether it was Greenfield's feeling of being replaced after his monumental efforts or Kum's pursuit of broader horizons and just gospel practices from other evangelical churches, these personal moments were pivotal. Tebah's divine revelation while driving, signalling his grand purpose, resonates with a sense of destiny, just as the others felt their unique callings.

One consistent theme is the ethos of empowerment embedded within the teachings of Winners' Chapel. Even as these pastors chose to part ways from the main church, the spiritual foundation laid by the church remained intact. Pastor Tebah's story, for instance, embodies

---

97. Enenche, *Making Full Proof of Ministry.*
98. Personal interview with Pastor Tebah John in Douala (Nov. 12, 2015).
99. Oyedepo, *Mandate*, 156.

Bishop Oyedepo's teachings of "Kingdom service." His evolution from a passive Presbyterian to the founder of a thriving church, inspired and guided by the tenets of Winners' Chapel, is indicative of the transformative potential the church bestows upon its devotees. However, a discerning observation across the narratives reveals an element of tension. There is an evident push-pull between the individual aspirations of these Cameroonian pastors and the overarching influence of the Nigerian-based church. This tension, while causing personal tribulations for each person, ironically, proved instrumental in their spiritual growth, prompting them to create their independent Pentecostal entities.

As we have analyzed the complex interplay of spiritual journeys, political power, and the ever-changing dynamics of Christianity, the role of Winners' Chapel in Cameroon cannot be understated. The stories of Pastors Greenfield, Kum, and Tebah illuminate the church's profound, albeit often unintentional, role as a catalyst for the birth of independent Pentecostal ministries. These narratives highlight the push and pull between the localized spiritual aspirations and the overarching, sometimes overpowering, influence of international institutions.

The nuanced interplay of power dynamics, missionary zeal, and individual agency becomes even more complex and intriguing when we shift our focus to the global stage. The shifting sands of world Christianity have brought the "global South," once the receiving end of missions, to the forefront as the new missionary hub. The concept of "reverse mission" captures this transformation. However, what stands out is not just the shift in the source of missionary endeavors but also its multidirectional nature. The missionary flow is no longer a one-way street from the global North to the South; it is complex, multidirectional, and multifaceted. This, however, raises an even more profound question: As churches from the global South assume the role of spiritual vanguards in the North, why are African Pentecostal churches, like Winners' Chapel, also turning their gaze to neighboring African nations? Does this signify a new form of intra-African mission work, or is it a reflection of "reverse mission in reverse"? These questions will be pursued in our final chapter.

Chapter Seven

Dynamics of Mission and the Politics of Pentecostal Power

THE CONCEPT OF "REVERSE mission" or "mission in reverse" has gained significant traction in the field of religious transnationalism, highlighting the shifting dynamics of world Christianity. The phenomenon embodies a broader theme of religious and cultural exchange that defies traditional colonial and post-colonial narratives. This reversal challenges the historical unidirectionality of religious influence from the global North to the global South, indicating a more complex, interdependent relationship between these regions. Traditionally, mission efforts were predominantly carried out by Europe and North America, with missionaries venturing out from these regions to Africa, Asia, and Latin America. However, in recent decades, there has been a notable reversal in the direction of mission, as Christianity in the global South has experienced rapid growth while organized Christianity in the Western world has witnessed a decline.[1]

Proponents of the reverse mission project justify this shift by invoking the divine mandate to spread the gospel worldwide; the perceived secularization of the West emphasizing scientific reasoning over spirituality; the decline in church attendance and membership, and the belief that African, Asian, and Latin American churches are uniquely positioned to

1. Jenkins, *Next Christendom*.

address moral decadence in the Western world.[2] One of the arguments is that African, Asian, and Latin American Christians and churches are driven by a determination to re-evangelize the "former heartlands" of Christianity in the West. This is exemplified by statements like "Europe: A Prodigal Continent! Europe: A Mission Field in Need of Church Attention" displayed on the notice board of the Redeemed Christian Church of God (RCCG) International headquarters in Nigeria.[3] Further evidence in support of the idea is provided by the increasing number of ministers from the Northern Hemisphere, serving in Western churches, a topic to which I return in the conclusion.

The evolving missionary agenda, with mission bases now established in the global South and the exportation of missionaries, does not stand in direct opposition to the earlier operations of Western missionaries in the global South. It is essential to note, however, that despite apparent contradictions and rhetorical complexities within the concept of reverse mission, the dissemination of the gospel in regions where Christianity is in decline and moral standards are diminishing is a crucial endeavor. It is upheld by individuals who bring the gospel and their faith from different parts of the world, and their commitment should not be disregarded.[4] The significance lies in the fact that the "non-Western world," which historically received missions until the late twentieth century, has now emerged as a sending force. This emergence of the "global South" as the new gravitational center of Christianity marks a watershed moment for the reversal and multidirectionality of missionary endeavors.

The "Reverse Mission in Reverse"

Within the broader context of global religious trends, a telling question comes to mind: As the forces of secularization lead to religious decline in the Northern Hemisphere, resulting in the global South assuming the mantle of Christianity's new gravitational center and even exporting missionaries to former heartlands of the faith, why do certain African Pentecostal churches engage in missionary activities within other African countries? Is this a manifestation of another form of "reverse mission" or

---

2. Robert, *Christian Mission*; Ma and Ross, *Mission Spirituality and Authentic Discipleship*.
3. Adogame, *New Currents and Emerging Trends*.
4. Kalu, *African Pentecostalism*.

an instance of the "reverse mission in reverse"? These initial reflections sparked my curiosity and prompted the exploration of the movement of African-founded Pentecostal churches across the African continent, ultimately shaping the trajectory and title of this book, *Intra-African Pentecostalism and the Dynamics of Power*.

The Power of African Pentecostalism

As suggested by its title, this book claims to make an original contribution to the field of religion and transnationalism. Departing from conventional approaches prevalent in contemporary studies, which primarily focus on the intercontinental movement of African Pentecostal churches to Europe within the framework of a "reverse mission," the book takes an intra-African perspective. While African Pentecostal churches establish themselves within the European diaspora to rekindle religious fervor and combat apostasy, they simultaneously traverse the African continent to revive existing churches and infuse them with a problem-solving form of Christianity. However, this book proposes that power dynamics and the quest for influence underlie the operations of transnational Pentecostal churches, compelling them to transcend local boundaries. Examining the complex relationships between transnational Pentecostal actors such as missionaries, and their counterparts in African receiving countries, the book has set out to supply fresh insights into the encounters, contestations, and resistance that emerge between "founder-leaders" and recruited workers within intra-African Pentecostal churches. Moreover, it enriches our understanding of the socio-cultural contexts in which the interplay of migration, mission, and power unfolds on the African continent.

The vibrancy and diversity of Christianities in Africa hold immense promise for world Christianity, partly due to the active sending of missionaries within the continent and beyond. Pentecostal churches in Africa are more successful because of the ingenuity of their leaders to claim and focus on spiritually explaining, predicting, and controlling the events of suffering people. However, the adoption of free-market practices by Pentecostal churches, including business strategies, excessive fundraising, ostentatious displays of wealth by leaders, and well-publicized instances of clerical misconduct, raise concerns about an uncertain future for many individuals and Christian groups in Africa.[5] While acknowledging the

---

5. Ukah, *African Christianities*, 18.

spiritual empowerment and developmental benefits offered by Pentecostal churches to their adherents and communities, this critique sheds light on how some churches have become potent agents capable of influencing the socioeconomic fabric of societies, for better or for worse. It calls attention to the negative developments that tarnish the transformative potential of an otherwise socially and economically impactful religion.[6]

This book has investigated a Nigerian Pentecostal church and its complex power dynamics within the context of Cameroon. However, it would be helpful to adopt a reverse perspective, where scholars delve into the dynamics of power within a Cameroonian-founded church in Nigeria or another African country. An example for consideration could be the Cameroonian-founded Christian Missionary Fellowship International, which has established branches in Nigeria. Another fruitful area for future research lies in examining the extent to which nation-states engage with the practices of transnational Pentecostal churches and the manner in which they operate within their new "mission fields." Additionally, deeper research can be conducted on other transnational Christian churches, including historic mission denominations, to chart the patterns of religious transnationalism and power in their missionary engagements. Such investigations will complement the works of scholars like Emma Wild-Wood, whose notable study *Migration and Christian Identity in Congo (DRC)*, sheds light on crucial aspects of identity within the realms of mission and migration.[7] Wild-Wood's research primarily focuses on the interaction between social and religious changes that arise from the expansion of the Anglican Church in Congo, and the transformative impact of migration on religious identities. The study encompasses two distinct groups of migrants: Urban migrants who relocate from rural areas to cities within Congo, and international migrants who depart from Congo to other countries. Through a nuanced analysis, the author argues that migration engenders a multifaceted process of adaptation and negotiation of religious identities, ultimately leading to the fluidity of religious identity among Congolese Christians.[8] Moreover, the book reveals how migration gives rise to new forms of religious expression, particularly Pentecostalism, which challenges the long-standing dominance of established Christian denominations in Congo. Wild-Wood's work provides

---

6. Ukah, *African Christianities*, 18.
7. Wild-Wood, *Migration and Christian Identity*.
8. Wild-Wood, *Migration and Christian Identity*, 1.

an insightful analysis of the relationship between migration and religious identity and the question of power.

Temporal Authority and Control

As previously noted, Pentecostal church leaders and founders wield significant power and authority over their congregations, ensuring unwavering loyalty. Through preaching, teaching, and spiritual guidance, they meticulously shape the beliefs, practices, and values of their constituents. Within the specific context of our studies, missionaries of the Nigerian Winners' Chapel play a pivotal role in the church's endeavors in Cameroon, projecting an image of indispensability. However, it is crucial to note that my arguments extend beyond the mere pursuit of control by the Nigerian Winners' Chapel for its own sake. Their engagements reflect a distinct understanding of spiritual power and the means by which it is to be transmitted and preserved. The hegemony established by Nigerian missionaries manifests in subtle ways: The Nigerian leadership insinuates that Cameroonians are incapable of crafting their own sermons and positions Nigerian testimonies as appropriate models for Cameroonian believers to emulate in their quest for miracles. Even more subtle is the underlying indication that Nigerian testimonies serve to encourage Cameroonians to contribute financial resources toward the expansion of Oyedepo's religious empire in Nigeria, in exchange for divine miracles.

This strategic focus on Nigeria as the center of power, radiating blessings to the rest of the world, is reinforced through the influence of the electronic media, which ensures that Oyedepo's blessings permeate the Cameroonian landscape and sustain unwavering loyalty to the founding bishop and spiritual repository. While Oyedepo effectively wields his authority through the media channels, his missionaries in Cameroon serve as instrumental agents in consolidating and perpetuating this power dynamic. Their presence and influence within the local context solidify the authority of the Nigerian leadership, reinforcing their message and maintaining a firm grip on the allegiance of Cameroonian believers. According to their perspective, the successful transmission of spiritual power from Oyedepo to his followers hinges upon their indispensable role.

This reminds us of the crucial relationship in many religious movements, namely the relationship between temporal power, the exercise of control, and the transmission of spiritual authority. While Western societies often tend to separate these dimensions, many indigenous societies perceive them as inseparable facets of power. In these contexts, the establishment and preservation of authority structures are deemed necessary for the effective transmission of spiritual power, thereby fostering success. An example of such "spiritual power for success" can be found in Garry Trompf's exploration of the extraordinary charismatic power known as *Mana* in Oceanian primal religions.[9] In Melanesian primal religions, *Mana* represents a form of power. Triumph and ongoing security are attributed to the confirmation of a mandate of rule by the spirit-world.[10] Within this framework, certain individuals are regarded as possessing *Mana* or unique spiritual gifts intended for the betterment of their societies or the groups they lead. Applied to our context, this concept would imply that for Bishop Oyedepo to fulfill his mission in Cameroon and other countries, he must ensure the unobstructed flow of his *Mana*. This necessitates the establishment of appropriate temporal power structures, embodied in the form of missionaries, to sustain and extend the reach of his spiritual authority and charismatic efficacy beyond the boundaries of Nigeria.

Drawing a quite different parallel, we can discern a resemblance to the understanding of spiritual power within the Roman Catholic Church. In this context, the unbroken succession of apostolic authority is considered indispensable for the successful transmission of the power of the spirit. It is important for bishops to maintain communion with the Vatican and demonstrate filial obedience to the pope, as any disruption in this chain of authority would impede the flow of apostolic spiritual power. Consequently, the religious community in question would cease to be recognized as part of the One Holy and Apostolic Church, infused with the spirit of God.[11] The understanding within Roman Catholicism is that the papacy's spiritual dependence and ecclesial authority is said to depend on his "temporal power," that is the Vatican City as a sovereign state over which the pope rules.[12] Both the Roman Catholic Church and Winners' Chapel thus underscore the criticality of unbroken apostolic succession for the effective transmission of spiritual power.

---

9. Garry Trompf, "Pacific Islands," in Swain and Trompf, *Religions of Oceania*, 140.
10. Garry Trompf, "Pacific Islands," in Swain and Trompf, *Religions of Oceania*, 141.
11. Rubinstein, "'New' New Catholic Encyclopedia," 22.
12. Dulles, *Models of the Church*.

The presence of Winners' Chapel missionaries in Cameroon is underpinned by a spiritual rationale that emphasizes the inseparable connection between actual power over individuals and the institutions, and the preservation of spiritual power within the Cameroonian context. This particular ecclesiology, which underscores the interplay between temporal power and spiritual authority, has effectively persuaded Cameroonians to believe that access to the power of the spirit for success necessitates submission to the authority of uniquely Spirit-empowered Nigerian "men and women of God," exemplified by Oyedepo.

Social scientists would classify this religious theory as an instance of hegemony, where individuals acquiesce to their own subjugation due to the allure of the ideology espoused by those in power. This ideology is deeply ingrained in social structures, laws, and cultural practices, shaping individuals' perceptions of reality and influencing their behaviors and choices. The hegemony of transnational religious movements within world Christianity has significant implications for global trends in the twenty-first century. It challenges traditional notions of sovereignty and national identity, as religious ideologies that transcend borders come to influence domestic policies and social attitudes. Furthermore, the rise of digital media has accelerated the spread of these ideologies, creating new frontiers for religious engagements and conflict. The interconnectedness between religion, power, and global trends underscores the importance of understanding the mechanisms of hegemony in transnational religious movements. As these movements continue to shape global discourse on morality, governance, and social cohesion, their influence on world Christianity and beyond will be a critical area of study for social scientists, policymakers, and religious leaders.

Thomas Tweed draws upon the insights of William James and Emile Durkheim to propose that religions possess both individualistic and collective dimensions. According to his analysis of the Jamesian perspective on religious life, there are individuals who experience an original and potent religious encounter, which subsequently becomes transmitted through institutional channels. This transmission enables others to engage with the religious experience in a secondary manner.[13] According to William James, personal, potent religious encounters can profoundly affect individuals. These are original experiences often described as mystical or revelatory, and they serve as the foundation for an individual's

---

13. Tweed, *Crossing and Dwelling*, 64.

faith. Such experiences are deeply personal, yet their power and authenticity can be compelling to others. Spiritual leaders often emerge from those who have had such profound encounters. Their role then becomes one of transmitting this experience to others, though the nature of this transmission is inevitably different from the original encounter. The spiritual leader's articulation of their encounter can inspire and influence their followers, offering a framework within which others can interpret their own religious feelings and experiences.

The transmission of a leaders' personal experience is facilitated through institutional channels, as suggested by Tweed's analysis. This institutionalization includes the creation of rituals, doctrines, and religious narratives that allow followers to engage with the leader's experience in a secondary manner. While the followers may not have the original visionary experience themselves, the structure provided by the institution allows them to access the essence of that experience. Institutions also offer collective practices that reinforce the leader's teachings and experiences, creating a shared religious environment. This collective dimension, informed by Emile Durkheim's perspective and our understanding of the transmission of Winner's Chapel practices to Cameroon such as sermons and testimonies, emphasizes the social and community aspects of religion. It suggests that the power of religious institutions lies in their ability to create a collective consciousness, a shared belief system and moral community that supports and is supported by the spiritual experiences of its leaders and adherents. By understanding the dual nature of religious experience, we can see how spiritual leaders such as Oyedepo are pivotal not just in guiding followers but also in shaping the collective identity and practices of their religious communities. The evidence in our study suggests that the "original, powerful religious experience" is situated in Nigeria, firmly embedded within the practices and values defined by the Winners' Chapel, such as sermons and testimonies. These elements are transmitted to the Cameroonian church, where they are accepted, occasionally questioned, but frequently appropriated for the benefit of the congregations. Despite the evidence pointing toward the hegemonic influence exerted by Nigerian missionaries, Cameroonians continue to actively promote and engage with the church.

"Follow Those Who Know the Road"

The statement "follow those who know the road" is commonly cited by members of the Winner's Chapel in Cameroon to explain their preference for Nigerian missionaries over local Cameroonian pastors. This preference stems from the persuasive influence and "soft power" of the church, which promotes Nigerian missionaries as more sanctified, skillful, and capable of performing miracles. Consequently, Cameroonians have placed their trust in the leadership of these missionaries, at times to the extent of prioritizing them over their own compatriots.

This trend aligns with observations by Kincheloe et al., who noted that oppression can endure in societies when individuals view their lower social status as natural or unavoidable, especially when benefits are unevenly allocated across different groups.[14] In the case of Cameroon, Nigerian missionaries exert influence through their practices, and Cameroonians often adopt a subordinate role, conforming to the Pentecostal methods and influences from Nigeria. Power, in this sense, comes from the ability to wield both tangible and intangible resources to sway others into actions they might not otherwise take, ensuring results that favor those in command.[15]

Ingie Hovland's research demonstrates how modern charismatic churches use various media, including tapes, videos, sermons, and books to extend their influence across borders.[16] These tactics are also used by dominant churches to keep their international congregations loyal to the parent church. Nevertheless, as people become more conscious that yielding to such dominant structures is unnecessary to access the benefits they offer, the spiritual and worldly power of authoritative figures begins to wane.

Contestations and Empowerment

Amid the interactions between Nigerian missionaries and indigenous Cameroonian pastors, certain full-time Cameroonian pastors are actively resisting the power and influence exerted by the missionaries. They firmly believe in their own competence to lead the church in Cameroon and aspire to establish it as an indigenous Cameroonian church. Cameroonians

---

14. Kincheloe and McLaren, "Rethinking Critical Theory," 87–138.
15. Dahl, "Concept of Power," 201–15.
16. Hovland, "Christianity, Place/Space," 331–58.

also seek fair treatment and recognition for their contributions to the vision and mission of Bishop Oyedepo. However, the determination of the Nigerian-dominated leadership to dismiss claims to authority and self-determination and label Cameroonians as "foreigners in their own nation" underscores the pervasive and formidable nature of Nigerian domination within Cameroon. These contestations remind us of the concept of "rational power" as expounded by political scientists, which posits that power is a causal relationship between states in international relations.[17] Their conception of relational power hinges on Max Weber's notion of power as "the probability that one actor within a social relationship will be in a position to carry out his own will despite resistance."[18]

The concept of "rational power" in political science, which denotes a structured influence among nation-states, may not precisely translate to the ecclesiastical authority within a religious organization. Yet, the friction between Cameroonian pastors and Nigerian missionaries reflects a complex interplay of relational power, informed by Max Weber's definition, where resistance to centralized control is evident. This tension raises questions about the potential for an indigenous evolution of the church's leadership and governance, diverging from control of its Nigerian counterpart. The conflict underscores a need for a more equitable power distribution that respects the autonomy and contributions of the Cameroonian clergy, fostering a church that is both locally resonant and globally connected. The question is about how religious organizations can balance the vision of their founding leadership with the aspirations and cultural contexts of their diverse congregations. However, while some Cameroonian pastors are showing resistance to Nigerian authoritative power from within the church, others choose to resign and establish independent ministries as a means of self-empowerment. The intertwining dynamics of disempowerment and empowerment observed in transnational missionary operations broaden our understanding of spiritual power and its manifestation and serve as a linchpin for studying other perspectives of empowerment in transnational Pentecostalism.

---

17. Pustovitovskij and Kremer, *Structural Power and International Relations*, 3.
18. Weber, *Theory of Social and Economic Organization*, 152.

The Paradigmatic Nature of Transnational Power

The paradigmatic nature of transnational power in the missionary activities of Winners' Chapel refers to the distinctive characteristics and patterns that shape the exercise of power in Cameroon. It encompasses the conceptualization, structuring, and manifestation of power, and its impact on believers and collective communities.

The power dynamic we find in the operations of Winners' Chapel is not unique but a common feature of transnational Pentecostalism. In some cases, church leaders continually renegotiate their roles to give them more power. This is exemplified by David Maxwell in his analysis of the ZAOGA Pentecostal church. Maxwell's research illustrates that the proliferation of roles in the expansion of transnational Pentecostal churches gives rise to authoritarianism within the church hierarchy, while also provoking resistance from some of its remote branches. According to the study, the leader of ZAOGA, Archbishop Guti, has assumed multiple functions such as apostle, prophet, culture-broker, and community leader. These roles intertwine to create what scholars refer to as the Pentecostal "big man" within Africa's contemporary social landscape.[19] Similar examples can be found in figures like Mensa Otabil and Duncan-Williams from Ghana, Nevers Mumba from Zambia, and Simeon Kayiwa from Uganda. While these Pentecostal leaders often advocate for a pan-African ideology that resists historical Western missionary dominance and calls for African independence and egalitarian church structures, they paradoxically develop structures of authoritarianism and power within their own churches on the African continent. As Maxwell notes, while ZAOGA resists external missionary dominance, it produces its own internal authoritarianism as a means to maintain cohesion among its large and diverse constituency.[20]

The exercise of control from the headquarters of ZAOGA in Zimbabwe reveals tensions between the mother-headquarters church and its branches in other cities and countries. The leadership imposes local Zimbabwean tenets on these external branches, which has resulted in opposition and conflicts from branches in Mozambique, South Africa, and England. These opposing branches perceive the influence of ZAOGA

---

19. McCauley, "Africa's New Big Man Rule?," 1–21.
20. Maxwell, *Gifts of the Spirit*, 218.

leaders as a form of Zimbabwean cultural dominance, despite continued adherence to the evangelical message by ZAOGA followers.[21]

The Power of a Pentecostal Prophet

The transnational operations of Winners' Chapel, ZAOGA, and other neo-Pentecostal churches reveals power dynamics that are linked to spiritually powerful church leaders. In the case of Winners' Chapel, the evidence suggests that the expansion of the church coincided with the expansion of roles attributed to Bishop Oyedepo within his religious empire, including that of prophet and end-time apostle. Bishop Oyedepo declared in the year 2000 that his calling as a prophet had been confirmed by the Lord on October 4, 1981, during a five-day period of seeking divine guidance. This retrospective claim to prophethood is notable, as it applies to the initial stages of his preaching career in 1981.[22]

The status of a prophet is important for leaders of neo-Pentecostal churches because it grants them unquestionable authority. This explains why many Pentecostal church founders, who initially served as pastors, eventually adopted the title of prophet. The prophetic title helps religious leaders to exert their influence more fully, maintain order in their movements, and restrict their members from expressing opinions that are contrary to the ones that prophets promulgate.[23] Bishop Oyedepo consistently reminds his followers that doubting prophetic utterances is tantamount to opposing God himself.[24] The consequences of opposing the prophet can be severe, sometimes resulting in death. For instance, when a group opposed Oyedepo's plan to relocate the church from its original site in Lagos to its present location at Canaanland, two adults in the instigator's family tragically passed away within a short period, and the instigator himself died in a car accident, allegedly at God's intervention.[25]

Prophets are believed to possess other remarkable qualities that benefit their followers. For instance, when God reveals something to Bishop Oyedepo as the prophet, he has the ability to pronounce and deliver the divine message to the people. Similarly, he claims to possess the

---

21. Maxwell, *Gifts of the Spirit*, 218.
22. MacTavish, "Pentecostal Profits," 152; Oyedepo, *Mandate*, 32.
23. MacTavish, "Pentecostal Profits," 152.
24. MacTavish, "Pentecostal Profits," 152.
25. Oyedepo, *All You Need*, 105–7.

power to heal people through his pronouncements or through the touch of his garments. Bishop Oyedepo recounts an incident where a man with a seventeen-year spinal injury was instantly healed upon touching his clothes while he walked through the congregation toward the pulpit.[26]

One of the findings in this book is that representatives of Bishop Oyedepo in Cameroon are dedicated to promoting the supernatural power and unique abilities of the bishop. A Nigerian missionary attested to Oyedepo's prayerful ability to orchestrate the transfers and appointments of pastors across the world every two years through supernatural means. The bishop would present a comprehensive list of transfers and appointments, and in some cases, names that were initially included on the list would disappear after the bishop's prayers, as God did not approve of their assigned positions.[27]

The complex interplay of authority and faith within African Pentecostal prophetism as evidenced by the roles of prominent figures like Bishop Oyedepo of Winner's Chapel and other independent Pentecostal church founders and leaders, such as Apostle Johnson Suleman of the Omega Fires Ministries, Dr. Paul Enenche of Dunamis, and the late prophet T. B. Joshua, underscores the potent combination of religious charisma and transnational influence. Bishop Oyedepo's retrospective claim to a prophetic calling and his subsequent elevation to a status that equates questioning him with opposing God illustrates the impact of prophetic authority. His narrative of healing and divine intervention bolsters his spiritual credentials, further solidifying his authority within and beyond his church. The emphasis on the influence and unquestionable authority of figures like Oyedepo within African Pentecostal movements warrants us to examine the darker side of such unrestrained power and spiritual leadership.

The story of late Prophet T. B. Joshua, a prominent Nigerian Pentecostal leader, offers a stark look into the dangerous blend of power and potential abuse within religious leadership or African Pentecostal prophetism. T. B. Joshua, who passed away on June 5, 2021, was at the center of a BBC investigation following his death. This inquiry involved interviews with over thirty people once connected to Joshua's Synagogue Church of All Nations (SCOAN). The investigations led to a three-part documentary that peeled back the curtains on the secretive world Joshua had created. It brought to light allegations of abuse ranging from

26. Oyedepo, *All You Need*, 105–7.
27. Personal interview with Pierre Kom (pseudonym) in Douala (Sept. 20, 2016).

harassment and rape to manipulation and the orchestration of fake miracles. According to those who spoke to the BBC, these issues were well-known within the church, yet no actions were taken to investigate them. Shockingly, the accusations of sexual abuse spanned over two decades. Moreover, the documentary uncovered how the church went to great lengths to hide the truth behind a tragic incident in 2014, when one of SCOAN's guesthouses collapsed. The church presented a narrative to its followers through Emmanuel TV, repeatedly showing a clip of the building just before the collapse with what appeared to be an aircraft overhead. This led many, including a woman who tragically lost her daughter in the collapse, to believe the building had been bombed, a story purportedly crafted to deflect blame from the structural issues at play.[28]

When T. B. Joshua began his ministry in 1987, he initially addressed both the spiritual and economic deficits prevalent among Nigerians and the broader African populace. He deftly merged elements from Christianity, Islam, and indigenous African belief systems, before eventually committing to Christianity. The stark disparity between the widespread poverty, the uncertainty of life, and the oppressive conditions faced by many Africans contrasted vividly with his televised philanthropy, his dedication to fostering spiritual growth, and his own unassuming way of life. Such stark juxtaposition garnered him immense affection from millions within Nigeria and globally.

A key aspect of Joshua's, and arguably many Pentecostal leaders', appeal was his focus on religion's capacity to explain, predict, and exert control. He aimed to provide spiritual explanations for the tribulations facing ordinary Africans, to predict or forecast their futures, and claimed to perform miracles that could alleviate their dire circumstances. Joshua was also a pioneer in embracing televangelism. In 2004, when Nigeria prohibited the broadcast of unverified miracles, a measure presumably influenced by Joshua's practices, he circumvented this restriction by launching Emmanuel TV via satellite and subsequently online.[29]

Pentecostalism operates on the premise of a dichotomous reality: the physical and the spiritual, with the latter having dominion over the former. Adherents believe that those endowed with charismatic gifts can access the spiritual realm and garner insights to elucidate, foresee, and

---

28. Sahara Reporters, "BBC Investigation Unveils"; see Northcott and Spooner, "TB Joshua"; Northcott et al., "TB Joshua Exposé."

29. Sahara Reporters, "BBC Investigation Unveils"; see Northcott and Spooner, "TB Joshua"; Northcott et al., "TB Joshua Exposé"; Wariboko, "TB Joshua Scandal."

sway physical outcomes. This pursuit of divine intelligence is foundational. Additionally, Pentecostal epistemology or its philosophy of knowledge is poetically summarized by Nigerian, and by extension, African practitioners as "it does not make sense, but it makes spirit,"[30] suggesting that decisions, while perhaps illogical by secular standards, are considered rational, justifiable, and ethical within their spiritual framework. Furthermore, there is a significant conviction in the Pentecostal narrative that societal renewal can spontaneously arise from existing social dynamics, signifying a belief in miraculous interventions capable of transforming the current plight of Pentecostal adherents.

However, it would be a mistake to overlook the heightened susceptibility of those enduring economic hardship and poverty to the allure of religious demagogues and authoritarian figures in the African religious landscape. So, what factors would have contributed to T. B. Joshua's seeming invulnerability to critique? At least three considerations have been suggested as pertinent. They reflect a broader pattern among some Pentecostal prophets who lead independent ministries: First, Joshua founded an independent Christian denomination that achieved extraordinary success, thereby operating without external accountability. He was beholden solely to his own conscience and to the divine authority that he believed had chosen and consecrated him. I wonder how a religious figure of such unbridled autonomy might be perceived by the eminent nineteenth-century British historian, politician, and writer Lord Acton. Known for his penetrating observation that power has a corrupting influence, and that its absolute form invariably leads to total corruption, Lord Acton also noted that those who are considered "great" are often morally compromised. Second, Joshua's reputation for performing miracles seemed to overshadow and excuse his vulnerabilities, with the enabling complicity of his followers, who were entranced by the allure of his fantastical displays. His excesses were not anomalies but a reflection of deeper, underlying tendencies that were characteristic of his Synagogue church. Lastly, the allegations bring to light a disconcerting absence of regulatory vigilance on the part of Nigeria and various other African nations, where the rights of citizens are compromised under the pretext of spiritual authority. Religious figures, in some instances, appear to function with impunity, unhindered by the constraints of legal frameworks. In the realm of African politics, T. B. Joshua was no stranger to the halls

---

30. Wariboko, "TB Joshua Scandal," para. 11.

of power, having drawn various heads of state to his place of worship for spiritual support, whether to secure a political victory or to give thanks for one already achieved. A case in point was the late Atta Mills of Ghana, who, on the first Sunday following his electoral win on January 11, 2009, attended the Synagogue to partake in a ceremonial thanksgiving for his triumph.[31] Such high-profile endorsements bestowed upon Joshua a layer of untouchability, despite his controversial practices. This phenomenon is not isolated to Joshua alone; it shields numerous self-styled prophets in Africa, enabling them to act with little regard for legal accountability or ethical responsibility.

Paul Gifford's characterization of Africa's contemporary Christianity as an "enchanted religious imagination" captures the extraordinary allure and influence of African neo-Pentecostal churches, as they possess the capacity to assuage the practical challenges that people face daily, and instill hope.[32] While Gifford's observation accurately portrays how neo-Pentecostal churches present themselves, his central argument suggests that this form of Christianity lacks the potential to drive development. Gifford's experience at the Eighth General Assembly of the World Council of Churches in Harare in 1998 exemplifies the contrasting approaches taken by the World Council of Churches (WCC) and the Universal Church of the Kingdom of God, a Pentecostal church of Brazilian origin in Harare. The World Council of Churches focused on addressing global issues such as the debt crisis in developing countries, women's rights, minority group rights (including sexual minorities), intellectual property rights, child soldiers, the status of Jerusalem, the detrimental effects of unrestricted capital flows, and the urgency of tackling climate change. In doing so, the WCC viewed these challenges through a structural lens, employing socio-political and economic realities as guiding factors for theological reflections. Conversely, Gifford's encounter with the Universal Church of the Kingdom of God in Harare revealed a markedly different emphasis. The Pentecostal church primarily addressed personal concerns, including unemployment, homelessness, illness, infertility, business failures, and the quest for a life partner. Moreover, the religious imagination and theological orientation of the Universal Kingdom of God's members were

---

31. Sahara Reporters, "BBC Investigation Unveils"; see Northcott and Spooner, "TB Joshua"; Northcott et al., "TB Joshua Exposé"; Wariboko, "TB Joshua Scandal."

32. Gifford, *Christianity, Development and Modernity*, 13.

shaped by a worldview permeated by spirits, demons, and spiritual powers, believed to be responsible for the adversities encountered in life.[33]

Afe Adogame further substantiates the prevalence of a spiritual worldview in Pentecostal religiosity by exploring the concept of "Spiritual terrorism within and beyond borders: Pentecostalism and ritual emplacement." Adogame contends that the elaborate rituals within Winners' Chapel are designed to combat spiritual attacks related to sickness, unemployment, social insecurity, death, emotional distress, hunger, poverty, and various other life challenges.[34] A compelling testimony from one of Adogame's respondents at the Lagos branch of Winners' Chapel in 2002 exemplifies this perspective:

> On the night of December 30, 2001, I woke up with a holy anger in me because I was in a bank with nothing to show for it. I told God in a prayer that I want a change and I was led to multiply my present monthly tithe by three. Also, in the month of November, when there was a call for sacrificial offering, I gave the whole of my November salary, and then during Shiloh in December, when the call for prayer request was made, I told God that I needed a job in an international oil company, and if not in an oil company, I want it in a reputable bank. To the Glory of God, between Shiloh and now, I've secured a job in an international oil company and two offers from two reputable banks. I give God all the glory.[35]

This personal testimony describes a transformative moment of "holy anger" that prompted the individual to seek change in his financial situation. The quotation reflects a fusion of spiritual devotion with material aspiration characteristic of neo-Pentecostalism. The individual's prayer is not just a general plea for employment but specifically targets high-status, lucrative positions, revealing an intertwining of faith with a particular vision of economic success or a blend of the spiritual and the ambitious, even greedy, that is part of the prosperity gospel. Such prayers reflect and propagate a materialistic ethos, potentially overshadowing the spiritual and altruistic aspects of religious life.

The attribution of success solely to religious acts raises questions about the complex interplay of personal agency, external circumstances, and the role of divine intervention. It is crucial to recognize that

---

33. Gifford, *Christianity, Development and Modernity*, 3.
34. Adogame, *African Christian Diaspora*, 93.
35. Adogame, *African Christian Diaspora*, 93.

individual experiences can be subjective and not necessarily replicable for everyone. This type of testimonial narrative may create unrealistic expectations and place undue pressure on individuals who may not achieve similar outcomes despite their devotedness or acts of faith. Additionally, it is important to critically examine the social and economic factors that contribute to job opportunities and financial success, which extend beyond individual religious practices.

To comprehend the remarkable success of Bishop Oyedepo's ministry and his Winners' Chapel, one must recognize the claim to divine authorization and supernatural power that his followers affirm and actively seek to benefit from and promote. This perspective resonates with Peter Blau's interpretation of Max Weber, particularly when Blau discusses the legitimizing values of charismatic authority. Blau argues that charismatic leaders and their missions are inspired by supernatural forces. Such leaders provide guidance to a new social movement, and their followers and disciples become converts dedicated to spreading the new gospel. Their devotion to the leader and the belief that his pronouncements embody the spirit and ideals of the movement generate the group's willing obedience to his commands.[36] The success of Winners' Chapel, in terms of its intra-African power dynamics, primarily hinges on the perception among its adherents that Oyedepo is a spiritual giant capable of orchestrating their destinies, both within Nigeria and through the use of temporal power structures that facilitate the effective transmission of spiritual powers to individuals beyond Nigeria.

Conclusion

The transformative narrative presented in this book illuminates the complex interplay between power and mission in World Christianity. It illustrates how religious transnationalism and the shifting epicenters of Christianity are reshaping spiritual landscapes.

One striking theme that I have expanded in this chapter is the concept of "reverse mission." Traditionally, the West, with its affluence and dominant cultural narratives, took the lead in spreading Christianity to the global South. However, with the robust growth of Christianity in regions like Africa, Asia, and Latin America and the decline in the West, these "new" epicenters of faith have felt the call to "re-evangelize"

---

36. Blau, "Critical Remarks," 131.

the West. For example, I currently serve as parish minister for Newport-On-Tay Church of Scotland, while individuals of African descent also hold positions as parish priests in the Roman Catholic Church and the Episcopal Church, in the same small town. These denominations are predominantly composed of individuals of white or Scottish heritage. Across the Tay Bridge in Dundee, there exists a cluster of Nigerian churches, including the Redeemed Christian Church of God, with a sizable membership of over two hundred worshipers, and Winners' Chapel International with over one hundred worshipers. The establishment of Nigerian churches in Europe, which mostly cater to the spiritual needs of Nigerians and Africans more broadly, suggests a significant departure from the older missionary endeavors of the Western world in the global South, where churches were established by missionaries to cater to the spiritual needs of Africans. In contrast, the three of us from Africa ministering in Newport-On-Tay did not establish the churches; rather, we encountered them. The demographic composition of the churches my colleagues and I pastor positions us a minority, as we primarily serve the Scottish population and a small number of other European migrants residing in Scotland. Nonetheless, we are participating in what can be considered a "reverse mission" project, despite not being formerly commissioned by any mission organization from Africa, and despite not being the initiators of the churches we currently pastor. However, in this context, the concept of "reverse mission," as currently interpreted, elicits intrigue. The situation in Newport-On-Tay, where I, a Nigerian and a South African, serve predominantly Scottish congregations, exemplifies this reverse flow of mission. But more than mere numbers of the directionality of mission, the depth of the change is found in the underlying dynamics. Western missionary endeavors in Africa aimed primarily at Africans, and that is what is happening with myself and colleagues serving predominantly Scottish or European churches. This points to a much more integrated and holistic approach. However, other African neo-Pentecostal churches in Dundee predominantly serving Africans in Europe does not equate to a reversal of earlier missionary endeavors to Africa. Moreover, how is it that missionaries are now criss-crossing the continent of Africa with a gospel that is already saturated in the continent? In a more nuanced turn, I have spoken of the "reverse mission in reverse" within the African continent suggesting that the dynamics of religious expansion are not just about the North-South dichotomy but also involve sophisticated power plays within regions. The exploration of power dynamics, whether in the context of Winners' Chapel or the ZAOGA neo-Pentecostal Church, reveals the complex relationships and, often, the struggle for dominance and control within religious structures in the intra-African perspective.

The concept of power is a compelling angle to reflect on transnational Pentecostalism. The rise of powerful religious leaders within the new epicenters of faith in Africa is paradoxical. While they resist the historical dominance of Western Christianity, they also establish authoritarian structures within their own denominations. They become central figures of authority, whose words and actions shape and direct the belief systems and practices of millions. The experience and influence of Bishop Oyedepo exemplify how one leader's spiritual charisma can be wielded as both a source of empowerment and control. Furthermore, the concept of the "Pentecostal Prophet" and their vast influence testifies to the charismatic nature of this strand of Christianity. Prophets are seen not just as spiritual leaders but as intermediaries between the divine and the congregation, wielding immense spiritual power. This centralization of power in the figure of the prophet can lead to a scenario where challenging or questioning the prophet is equated with opposing God, with the consequences of potential abuses as seen in the case of late Prophet T. B. Joshua.

The canvas of world Christianity is painted with complicated strokes of multi-directional influences, and our discussions bring to the fore the deeper nuances of power and authority within this expansion. Indeed, leadership in neo-Pentecostal churches in Africa stands at the nexus of these narratives. The expansion of faith is not a mere geographical spread but involves a complex interweaving of power, leadership, and authority. As world Christianity finds its footing in new terrains, the leaders that champion its cause wield significant influence, sometimes overshadowing the very grassroots spirit they seek to nurture.

In essence, as the Christian faith continues its march across the globe, it is tasked with balancing its core theological principles with the convoluted power dynamics inherent in its diffusion. The resilience and adaptability of Christianity, showcased by its global diffusion, is a sign of hope. Yet, the challenges brought forth by power and authority remind us of the continuous need for reflection, adaptability, and a genuine commitment to a faith that is truly inclusive. Recognizing these dynamics is essential, for in the interplay between spiritual authority and human agency lies the true essence of a faith that seeks to be truly global.

Bibliography

Aderigbe, Ibigolade S. "Religious Traditions in Africa: An Overview of Origins, Basic Beliefs, and Practices." In *Contemporary Perspectives on Religions in Africa and the African Diaspora*, edited by Ibigolade S. Aderigbe and Carolyn M. Jones Medine, 7–29. New York: Palgrave Macmillan, 2015.

Adogame, Afe. *The African Christian Diaspora: New Currents and Emerging Trends in World Christianity*. Bloomsbury: London, 2013.

———. "Conference Report: The Berlin-Congo Conference 1884: The Partition of Africa and Implications for Christian Mission Today." *Journal of Religion in Africa* 34:1 (2004) 186–90.

———. "Contesting the Ambivalences of Modernity in a Global Context: The Redeemed Christian Church of God, North America." *Studies in World Christianity* 10:1 (2004) 25–48.

———. "A Home away from Home: The Proliferation of the Celestial Church of Christ (CCC) in Diaspora-Europe." *Exchange: Journal of Missiological and Ecumenical Research* 27:2 (1998) 141–60.

———. "Reverse Mission: Europe—A Prodigal Continent?" Undated paper. Accessed Apr. 5, 2017. http://www.wcc2006.info/fileadmin/files/edinburgh2010/files/News/Afe_Reverse%20mission_edited.pdf.

———. "Transnational Migration and Pentecostalism in Europe." *PentecoStudies: An Interdisciplinary Journal for Research on the Pentecostal and Charismatic Movements* 9:1 (2010) 56–73.

———. *Who Is Afraid of the Holy Ghost? Pentecostalism and Globalisation in Africa and Beyond*. Religion in Contemporary African Series. Trenton, NJ: Africa World Press, 2011.

Adogame, Afe, and Cordula Weisskӧppel. *Religion in the Context of African Migration*. Bayreuth: Bayreuth African Studies, 2005.

Adogame, Afe, and Ezra Chitando. "Moving among Those Moved by the Spirit." *Fieldwork in Religion* 1:3 (2005) 253–70.

Adogame, Afe, and James Spickard. *Religion Crossing Boundaries: Transnational Religious and Social Dynamics in Africa and the New African Diaspora*. Leiden: Brill, 2010.

Adogame, Afe, et al. *Christianity in Africa and the African Diaspora: The Appropriation of a Scattered Heritage*. London: Continuum, 2008.

Aguh, Divine. "Rituals of Healing and Deliverance: The Presbyterian Church in Cameroon and the Pentecostal Challenge (1976–2010)." MA diss., University of Edinburgh, 2010.

Ajani, Ezekiel Oladapo. "Leadership Roles in the Transnationalisation of Nigerian Pentecostal Churches: The Mountain of Fire and Miracles Church in the Netherlands and Ghana." PhD diss., University of Leiden, 2013.

Ajei, Elsie. "Apostle Suleman Johnson's Crusade in Douala: One Killed and 20 Seriously Injured." *Cameroon Concord*, Oct. 21, 2015. https://www.cameroon-concord.com/cameroon?start=1057.

Akoko, Robert Mbe. *"Ask and You Shall Be Given": Pentecostalism and the Economic Crisis in Cameroon*. Leiden: African Studies Centre, 2007.

Akoko, Robert Mbe, and Timothy Mbuagbo Oben. "Christian Churches and the Democratization Conundrum in Cameroon." *Africa Today* 52:3 (2006) 25–48.

Al Jazeera. "Cameroon Teachers, Lawyers Strike in Battle for English." Dec. 5, 2016. http://www.aljazeera.com/news/2016/12/cameroon-teachers-lawyers-strike-english-161205095929616.html.

Anderson, Allan H. "African Initiated Churches of the Spirit and Pneumatology." *Word and World* 23:2 (2003) 178–86.

———. *An Introduction to Pentecostalism: Global Charismatic Christianity*. Cambridge: Cambridge University Press, 2004.

———. "Pentecostal Pneumatology and African Power Concepts: Continuity or Change?" *Missionalia: Southern African Journal of Mission Studies* 19:1 (1991) 65–74.

———. *To the Ends of the Earth: Pentecostalism and the Transformation of World Christianity*. New York: Oxford University Press, 2003.

———. "Towards a Pentecostal Missiology for the Majority World." *Asian Journal of Pentecostal Studies* 1:8 (2005) 29–47.

Anderson, Allan, and Walter J. Hollenweger, eds. *Pentecostals after a Century: Global Perspectives on a Movement in Transition*. Sheffield: Sheffield Academic Press, 1999.

Anderson, Allan, et al., eds. *Studying Global Pentecostalism: Theories and Methods*. Berkeley: University of California Press, 2010.

Angwafo, Peter. *Cameroon's Predicaments*. Langa: Research and Publication Centre in International Governance, 2014.

Arber, Sara. "Designing Samples." *Researching Social Life* 2:1 (2001) 58–82.

Arthur, John A. "International Labour Migration Patterns in West Africa." *African Studies Review* 34:3 (1991) 65–87.

Asamoah-Gyadu, J. Kwabena. *African Charismatics: Current Developments within Independent Indigenous Pentecostalism in Ghana*. Leiden: Brill, 2005.

———. "Anointing through the Screen: Neo-Pentecostalism and Televised Christianity in Ghana." *Studies in World Christianity* 11:1 (2005) 9–28.

———. *Contemporary Pentecostal Christianity: Interpretations from an African Context*. Oxford: Regnum, 2013.

———. "God Is Big in Africa: Pentecostal Mega Churches and a Changing Religious Landscape." *The Journal of Objects, Art and Belief* 15 (May 2019) 390–92.

———. "Pentecostalism in Africa and the Changing Face of Christian Mission." *Mission Studies* 19:1 (2002) 14–38.

———. "'To the Ends of the Earth': Mission, Migration and the Impact of African-Led Pentecostal Churches in the European Diaspora." *Mission Studies* 29:1 (2012) 23–44.

Aseh, N. A. "Splinter Groups within Religious Organisations: Case Study of the Cameroon Baptist Convention Buea." BSc diss., University of Buea, Department of Sociology and Anthropology, 2000.

Atkinson, Paul, and David Silverman. "Kundera's Immortality: The Interview Society and the Invention of the Self." *Qualitative Inquiry* 3:3 (1997) 304–25.

Awasom, N. "Autochthony and Citizenship in Postcolonial Africa: A Critical Perspective on Cameroon." Unpublished seminar paper. Leiden: African Studies Centre, 2001.

Ayuk, Ayuk. "Portrait of a Nigerian Pentecostal Missionary." *Charisma and Christian Life* (2002) 38–49.

Baregu, Mwesiga Laurent, and Christopher Landsberg. *From Cape to Congo: Southern Africa's Evolving Security Challenges*. London: Lynne Rienner Publishers, 2003.

Barrett, David B. "AD 2000: 350 Million Christians in Africa." *International Review of Mission* 59:233 (1970) 39–54.

———. "The Twentieth-Century Pentecostal/Charismatic Renewal in the Holy Spirit with Its Goal of World Evangelization." *International Bulletin of Missionary Research* 12:3 (1988) 119–29.

Barrett, David, and Todd M. Johnson. "Annual Statistical Table on Global Mission: 2002." *International Bulletin of Missionary Research* 26:1 (Jan. 2002) 23.

Basit, Tehmina. "Manual or Electronic? The Role of Coding in Qualitative Data Analysis." *Educational Research* 45:2 (2003) 143–54.

BBC News. "Nigerian Pastors Spread into Cameroon." Last updated Apr. 24, 2007. http://news.bbc.co.uk/1/hi/world/africa/6587833.stm.

———. "Rescue Hopes Fade for Migrants after Boat Capsizes in Mediterranean." Aug. 6, 2015. https://www.bbc.com/news/world-africa-33791920.

———. "South Africa's 'Prophet of Doom' Condemned." Nov. 21, 2016. https://www.bbc.com/news/world-africa-38051923.

Bediako, Kwame. *Jesus and the Gospel in Africa: History and Experience*. Maryknoll, NY: Orbis Books, 2004.

Bennis, Warren, and Burt Nanus. *Leaders: The Strategies for Taking Charge: The Four Keys of Effective Leadership*. New York: Harper and Row, 1985.

Beyer, Engelbert. *New Christian Movements in West Africa*. Ibadan: Safer Press, 1998.

Bielenberg, A. *The Irish Diaspora*. Harlow: Longman, 2000.

Biney, Moses O. *From Africa to America: Religion and Adaptation among Ghanaian Immigrants in New York*. New York: New York University Press, 2011.

Blair, Leonardo. "Pastor Dies from Coronavirus after Laying Hands on Infected Followers, Declaring Them Healed." *The Christian Post*, May 19, 2020. https://www.christianpost.com/news/pastor-dies-from-coronavirus-after-laying-hands-on-infected-followers-declaring-them-healed.html.

Blau, Peter. "Critical Remarks on Weber's Theory of Authority." *American Political Science Review* 57:2 (1963) 131.

Bouyer, Louis. *The Church of God: Body of Christ and Temple of the Spirit*. San Francisco: Ignatius, 2011.

Bowen, T. J. *Adventures and Missionary Labours in the Interior of Africa 1849–1857*. Charleston: Southern Baptist Publication Society, 1857.

Brierley, P. "Evangelicals in the World of the 21st Century." In *Lausanne Committee Forum for World Evangelization*. Pattaya: Thailand, 2004.

Brown, Candy Gunther. *Global Pentecostal and Charismatic Healing*. Oxford: Oxford University Press, 2011.
Bryman, Alan. "The Debate about Qualitative and Quantitative Research: A Question of Method or Epistemology?" *British Journal of Sociology* (1984) 75–92.
———. *Social Research Methods: Second Edition*. New York: Oxford University Press, 2004.
Bryman, Alan, and Robert G. Burgess. *Qualitative Research*. Vol. 2, *Methods of Qualitative Research*. London: Sage, 1999.
Buma, K. *Revival Palaver in Bastos*. Yaoundé: Cockcrew, 1997.
Burawoy, Michael, et al. *Global Ethnography: Forces, Connections, and Imaginations in a Postmodern World*. Berkeley: University of California Press, 2000.
Burgess, Richard. "Bringing Back the Gospel: Reverse Mission among Nigerian Pentecostals in Britain." *Journal of Religion in Europe* 4:3 (2011) 429–49.
Burgess, Robert G. *Field Research: A Sourcebook and Field Manual*. Vol. 4. New York: Psychology Press, 2004.
Burgess, Stanley, and Eduard M. Van der Maas. *The New International Dictionary of Pentecostal and Charismatic Movements*. Rev. and exp. ed. Grand Rapids, MI: Zondervan, 2010.
Caballero, Andrés. "Pray or Prey? Cameroon's Pentecostal Churches Face Crackdown." Apr. 13, 2014. http://www.npr.org/2014/04/13/300975474/pray-or-prey-cameroons-pentecostal-churches-face-crackdown.
Cameroon 2013 Human Rights Report. "Executive Summary." Accessed Sept. 9, 2016. https://2009-2017.state.gov/documents/organization/220302.pdf.
Cartledge, Mark J. *Testimony in the Spirit: Rescripting Ordinary Pentecostal Theology*. Burlington, VT: Ashgate, 2010.
Cassell, Catherine, and Gillian Symon. *Essential Guide to Qualitative Methods in Organizational Research*. London: Sage, 2004.
Castles, Stephen, et al. *The Age of Migration: International Population Movements in the Modern World*. New York: Guilford, 2003.
Centre for the Study of Global Christianity. *Christianity in Its Global Context, 1970–2020: Society, Religion, and Mission*. Gordon Conwell Theological Seminary, June 2013. https://www.gordonconwell.edu/wp-content/uploads/sites/13/2019/04/2Christianityinits GlobalContext.pdf.
Chewachong, Amos Bongadu. "Intra-National Pentecostalism and the Dynamics of Proliferation: The Church of Pentecost UK." MTh diss., University of Edinburgh, 2013.
Chiluwa, Innocent. "Community and Social Interaction in Digital Religious Discourse in Nigeria, Ghana and Cameroon." *Journal of Religion, Media and Digital Culture* 2:1 (2013) 1–37.
Chinedu. "Nigerian Man Beg Bishop Oyedepo to Build Industries Instead of 100,000 Capacity Church Auditorium." YouTube video. Accessed Jan. 8, 2024. https://youtu.be/RgxaeGkq8Io.
Claydon, David. *A New Vision, a New Heart, a Renewed Call: Lausanne Committee Forum for World Evangelization*. Pasadena, CA: William Carey Library, 2004.
Clifford, James. "Diasporas." *Cultural Anthropology* 9:3 (1994) 302–38.
Cole, Ethan. "Nigerian Pentecostalism Thriving on Miracles, Prosperity Promises." *The Christian Post*, Sept. 16, 2007. https://www.christianpost.com/news/nigerian-pentecostalism-thriving-on-miracles-prosperity-promises.html/.

Coleman, James S. "Social Capital in the Creation of Human Capital." *American Journal of Sociology* 94:1 (1988) S95–S120.

Coleman, Simon. "Only (Dis-) Connect: Pentecostal Global Networking as Revelation and Concealment." *Religions* 4:3 (2003) 367–90.

Coppedge, William A. *African Literacies and Western Oralities?* Eugene, OR: Pickwick, 2021.

Corten, André, and Ruth Marshall-Fratani. *Between Babel and Pentecost: Transnational Pentecostalism in Africa and Latin America.* Indiana: Indiana University Press, 2001.

Creswell, John W., et al. *Handbook of Mixed Methods in Social and Behavioural Research.* Thousand Oaks, CA: Sage, 2003.

Dah, J. N. *A Century of Christianity in the Grassland of Cameroon (1903–2003).* Bamenda: Unique Printers, 2003.

———. *A Hundred Years of Roman Catholicism in Cameroon (1890–1990).* Owerri: Nnamdi Printing Press, 1985.

———. *Presbyterian Church in Cameroon: Fifty Years of Selfhood.* Buea: PCC, 2007.

Dahl, Robert A. "The Concept of Power." *Behavioral Science* 2:3 (1957) 201–15.

David Oyedepo Ministries International. "About Us." Accessed Apr. 29, 2014. https://davidoyedepo.org/about.

———. "Books." Accessed Nov. 17, 2016. https://domionlinestore.org/collections/books.

David, Silverman. *Qualitative Research: Theory, Method and Practice.* 2nd ed. London: Sage, 2004.

Dawson, L., and D. Cowan. *Religion Online: Finding Faith on the Internet.* London: Routledge, 2004.

De Matviuk, Marcela A. Chaván. "Latin American Pentecostal Growth: Culture, Orality and the Power of Testimonies." *Asian Journal of Pentecostal Studies* 5:2 (2002) 205–22.

Dempster, Murray W., et al. *The Globalization of Pentecostalism: A Religion Made to Travel.* Oxford: Regnum, 1999.

Denzin, Norman, and Yvonna S. Lincoln. *Handbook of Qualitative Research.* Thousand Oaks, CA: Sage, 1994.

De Witte, Marleen. "Altar Media's Living Word: Televised Charismatic Christianity in Ghana." *Journal of Religion in Africa* 33:2 (2003) 172–202.

Djomhoue, Priscille. "Manifestations of Ecumenism in Africa Today: A Study of the Mainline and Pentecostal Churches in Cameroon." *International Journal for the Study of the Christian Church* 8:4 (2008) 355–68.

Dowden, Richard. *Africa: Altered States, Ordinary Miracles.* London: Granta Books, 2014.

Drønen, Tomas. *Pentecostalism, Globalisation, and Islam in Northern Cameroon: Megachurches in the Making?* Leiden: Brill, 2013.

Dulles, Avery. *Models of the Church.* New York: Image, 2002.

Dyrness, William, and Veli-Matti Kärkkäinen. *A Global Dictionary of Theology.* Downers Grove, IL: InterVarsity, 2009.

Ebaugh, Helen, and Janet Chafetz. *Religion and the New Immigrants: Continuities and Adaptations in Immigrant Congregations.* Walnut Creek, CA: Altamira Press, 2000.

Echu, George. "The Language Question in Cameroon." *Linguistik Online* 18:1 (2004).

Ekwere, Ekemini. "'El Rufai, Either You Revoke the Preaching Law or Die!'—Apostle Suleman Spits Fire." *The Trent: Inform, Empower, Entertain,* Mar. 13, 2016.

Ellis, Stephen, and Gerrie ter Haar. *Worlds of Power: Religious Thought and Political Practice in Africa.* Vol. 1. Oxford: Oxford University Press, 2004.

Enenche, Paul. *Making Full Proof of Ministry: Understanding Your Calling in Life and Ministry.* Destiny Publishers, 2015.

Faith Bible Church. "Who We Are." Accessed Dec. 13, 2016. http://faithbiblec.org.

Faith Tabernacle Canaanland, Ota. "Dominion Publishing House." Living Faith Church Worldwide. Accessed Apr. 3, 2017. http://faithtabernacle.org.ng/aboutus/dph.

Fitzgerald, David. "Towards a Theoretical Ethnography of Migration." *Qualitative Sociology* 29:1 (2006) 1–24.

Flemes, Daniel, and Thorsten Wojczewski. "Contested Leadership in International Relations: Power Politics in South America, South Asia and Sub-Saharan Africa." German Institute of Global and Area Studies, working paper no. 121, 2010.

Flick, Uwe, et al. *A Companion to Qualitative Research.* London: Sage, 2004.

Fombad, Charles Manga. "State, Religion and Law in Cameroon: Regulatory Control, Tension, and Accommodation." *Journal of Church and State* 57:1 (2013) 18–43.

Formum, Z. T. *The Christian and Money.* Yaoundé: Christian Publishing House, 1998.

Foucault, Michel. *Power: Essential Works of Foucault 1954–1984.* Vol. 3. Edited by James D. Faubion. New York: Free Press, 2000.

Fourchard, Laurent, et al., eds. *Entreprises Religieuses Transnationales en Afrique de l'Ouest.* Paris: Editions Karthala, 2005.

Freedom House. *Freedom in the World 2016—Cameroon.* United Nations High Commissioner for Refugees, Aug. 12, 2016. http://www.refworld.org/docid/57b1ad5f102.html.

Gale, Thomas. *World Encyclopaedia of Nations: Cameroon.* 2007. Accessed Dec. 6, 2016. http://www.encyclopedia.com/places/africa/cameroon-political-geography/cameroon#RELIGIONS.

Gaventa, John. *Power and Powerlessness: Quiescence and Rebellion in an Appalachian Valley.* Chicago: University of Illinois Press, 1980.

Gerloff, Roswith. "An African Continuum in Variation: The African Christian Diaspora in Britain." *Black Theology: An International Journal* 4:2 (2000) 84–112.

Gerloff, Roswith, et al. *Christianity in African and the African Diaspora: The Appropriation of a Scattered Heritage.* London: Continuum, 2011.

Gifford, Paul. *African Christianity: Its Public Role.* Bloomington: Indiana University Press, 1998.

———. *Christianity, Development and Modernity in Africa.* London: Hurst, 2015.

———. *Ghana's New Christianity: Pentecostalism in a Globalizing African Economy.* Bloomington: Indiana University Press, 2004.

———. *New Dimensions in African Christianity.* Nairobi, Kenya: All Africa Conference of Churches, 1992.

———. "Trajectories in African Christianity." *International Journal for the Study of the Christian Church* 8:4 (2008) 275–89.

Gilbert, Nigel, and Paul Stoneman. *Researching Social Life.* London: Sage, 2015.

Gille, Zsuzsa. "Critical Ethnography in the Time of Globalization: Toward a New Concept of Site." *Cultural Studies Critical Methodologies* 1:3 (2001) 319–34.

Gille, Zsuzsa, and Seán Ó. Riain. "Global Ethnography." *Annual Review of Sociology* 28:1 (2002) 271–95.

Gitau, Wanjiru M. *Megachurch Christianity Reconsidered: Millennials and Social Change in African Perspective.* Downers Grove, IL: InterVarsity, 2018.

Glaser, Barney G., and Anselm L. Strauss. *The Discovery of Grounded Theory: Strategies for Qualitative Research Observations.* Chicago: Aldine, 1967.

Goliama, Castor Michael. "The Gospel of Prosperity in African Pentecostalism." PhD diss., University of Vienna, 2013.

Goodhew, David, ed. *Church Growth in Britain: 1980 to the Present.* London: Routledge, 2017.

Gornik, Mark R. *Word Made Global: Stories of African Christianity in New York City.* Grand Rapids, MI: Eerdmans, 2011.

Gough, Stephen, and William Scott. "Exploring the Purposes of Qualitative Data Coding in Educational Enquiry: Insights from Recent Research." *Educational Studies* 26:3 (2000) 339–54.

Granberg-Michaelson, Wesley. *From Times Square to Timbuktu: The Post-Christian West Meets the Non-Western Church.* Grand Rapids, MI: Eerdmans, 2013.

Green, Michael. *Evangelism in the Early Church.* London: Hodder & Stoughton, 1973.

Green, Nicola. "Disrupting the Field: Virtual Reality Technologies and 'Multisited' Ethnographic Methods." *American Behavioral Scientist* 43:3 (1999) 409–21.

Haar, Gerrie ter. *Halfway to Paradise: African Christians in Europe.* Cardiff: Cardiff Academic Press, 1998.

Haar, Gerrie ter, and Stephen Ellis. "The Role of Religion in Development: Towards a New Relationship between the European Union and Africa: The Winner of the EJDR Prize 2006." *European Journal of Development Research* 18:3 (2006) 351–67.

Hackett, Rosalind. "Charismatic/Pentecostal Appropriation of Media Technologies in Nigeria and Ghana." *Journal of Religion in Africa* 23:3 (1998) 258–77.

Hackett, Rosalind, et al. "Interview: Rosalind Hackett Reflects on Media in Africa." *Social Compass* 61:1 (2014) 68.

Haley, Garrett. "Cameroon Government Shuts Down over 50 Pentecostal Churches, Plans to Shutter 100 Total." *Christian News*, Aug. 16, 2013. http://christiannews.net/2013/08/16/cameroon-government-shuts-down-over-50-pentecostal-churches-plans-to-shutter-100-total/.

Hammersley, Martyn, and Paul Atkinson. *Ethnography: Principles in Practice.* 3rd ed. London: Routledge, 2007.

Hanciles, Jehu J. "Migration and Mission: Some Implications for the Twenty-First Century." *International Bulletin of Missionary Research* 27:4 (2003) 146–53.

Hannerz, Ulf. "Being There . . . and There . . . and There! Reflections on Multi-Site Ethnography." *Ethnography* 4:2 (2003) 201–16.

Haynes, Naomi. *Moving by the Spirit: Pentecostal Social Life on the Zambian Copperbelt.* Berkeley: University of California Press, 2017.

———. "Pentecostalism and the Morality of Money: Prosperity, Inequality, and Religious Sociality on the Zambian Copperbelt." *Journal of the Royal Anthropological Institute* 18:1 (2012) 123–39.

Hollenweger, Walter J. *Pentecostalism: Origins and Developments Worldwide.* Peabody, MA: Hendrickson, 1997.

———. *The Pentecostals.* London: SCM Press, 1972.

Hovland, Ingie. "Christianity, Place/Space, and Anthropology: Thinking across Recent Research on Evangelical Place-Making." *Religion* 46:3 (2016) 331–58.

Hunt, Steven. "Deprivation and Western Pentecostalism Revisited: The Case of 'Classical' Pentecostalism." *PentecoStudies: An Interdisciplinary Journal for Research on the Pentecostal and Charismatic Movements* 1:1 (2002) 1–32.

Index Mundi. "Cameroon Demographics Profile." Accessed Apr. 5, 2017. http://www.indexmundi.com/cameroon/demographics_profile.html.

The Institute on Religion and Public Policy. *Cameroon Immigration Report 2014*. Accessed Mar. 28, 2014. http://www.justice.gov/eoir/vll/country/Religion_Public_policy/Cameroon%20Immigration%20Report.

Jenkins, Philip. *God's Continent: Christianity, Islam, and Europe's Religious Crisis*. Oxford: Oxford University Press, 2007.

———. *The Next Christendom: The Coming of Global Christianity*. Oxford: Oxford University Press, 2002.

Johnson, Todd M., et al. "Christianity 2017: Five Hundred Years of Protestant Christianity." *International Bulletin of Mission Research* 1:12 (Jan. 2017). https://www.gordonconwell.edu/wp-content/uploads/sites/13/2019/04/IBMR2017.pdf.

Kalu, Ogbu. *African Pentecostalism: An Introduction*. Oxford: Oxford University Press, 2008.

———. "African Pentecostalism in Diaspora." *PentecoStudies: An Interdisciplinary Journal for Research on the Pentecostal and Charismatic Movements* 9:1 (2010) 9–34.

———. "Pentecostal and Charismatic Reshaping of the African Religious Landscape in the 1990s." *Mission Studies* 20:1 (2003) 84–109.

———. "Pentecostalism and Mission in Africa, 1970–2000." *Mission Studies* 24:1 (2007) 9–45.

Kalu, Ogbu, and Alaine M. Low. *Interpreting Contemporary Christianity: Global Processes and Local Identities*. Studies in the History of Christian Missions. Grand Rapids, MI: Eerdmans, 2008.

Kalu, Wilhemina J., et al. *The Collected Essays of Ogbu Uke Kalu*. 3 vols. Trenton, NJ: Africa World Press, 2010.

Kincheloe, Joe L., and Peter McLaren. "Rethinking Critical Theory and Qualitative Research." *Ethnography and Schools: Qualitative Approaches to the Study of Education* (2002) 87–138.

Kindzeka, Moki Edwin. "AU: Return of Nigerian Refugees from Cameroon Should Be Voluntary." *Voice of America News*, July 31, 2017. https://www.voanews.com/a/au-return-of-nigerian-refugees-from-cameroon-should-be-voluntary/3966160.html.

Klaus, Byron D. "Pentecostalism and Mission." *Missiology: An International Review* 35:1 (2007) 39–54.

Knaus, Verena. "Children Drowning in the World's Inaction: UNICEF Geneva Palais Briefing Note on the Increase in Children Taking the Central Mediterranean Sea Migration Route." United Nations Children's Fund, July 14, 2023. https://www.unicef.org/eca/press-releases/children-drowning-worlds-inaction-unicef-geneva-palais-briefing-note-increase.

Knibbe, Kim. "'We Did Not Come Here as Tenants, but as Landlords': Nigerian Pentecostals and the Power of Maps." *African Diaspora* 2:2 (2009) 133–58.

Kollman, Paul. "Classifying African Christianities: Past, Present, and Future: Part One." *Journal of Religion in Africa* 40:1 (2010) 3–32.

Konings, P. "Religious Revival in the Roman Catholic Church and the Autochthony-Allochthony Conflict in Cameroon." *Africa* 73:1 (2003) 31–56.

Kung, Lap-Yan. "Globalization and Ecumenism: A Search for Human Solidarity with Reference to Pentecostal/Charismatism in Hong Kong." *Asia Journal of Theology* 17:2 (2003) 378–402.

Kuponu, Selome. "The Living Faith Church (Winners' Chapel) Nigeria: Pentecostalism, Prosperity Gospel and Social Change in Nigeria." PhD diss., University of Bayreuth, 2007.

Lado, Ludovic. *Catholic Pentecostalism and the Paradoxes of Africanisation: Processes of Localisation in a Catholic Charismatic Movement in Cameroon.* Leiden: Brill, 2009.

Lee, Raymond M. *Doing Research on Sensitive Topics.* London: Sage, 1993.

Lerner, Michael. *Surplus Powerlessness: The Psychodynamics of Everyday Life . . . and the Psychology of Individual and Social Transformation.* London: Humanities Press International, 1991.

Levitt, Peggy. "Local-Level Global Religion: The Case of US-Dominican Migration." *Journal for the Scientific Study of Religion* 37:1 (1998) 74–89.

———. "You Know, Abraham Was Really the First Immigrant: Religion and Transnational Migration." *International Migration Review* 37:3 (2003) 847–73.

Levitt, Peggy, and Nina Glick Schiller. "Conceptualizing Simultaneity: A Transnational Social Field Perspective on Society." *International Migration Review* 38:3 (2004) 1002–39.

Lindhardt, M., ed. *Pentecostalism in Africa: Presence and Impact of Pneumatic Christianity in Postcolonial Societies.* Leiden: Brill, 2015.

Living Faith Church Worldwide. "About Winners' Chapel." Accessed Apr. 10, 2024. https://faithtabernacle.org.ng/about-us/.

Lord, John, and Peggy Hutchison. "The Process of Empowerment: Implications for Theory and Practice." *Canadian Journal of Community Mental Health* 12:1 (2009) 5–22.

Ludwig, Frieder, and J. Kwabena Asamoah-Gyadu. *African Christian Presence in the West: New Immigrant Congregations and Transnational Networks in North America and Europe.* Trenton, NJ: Africa World Press, 2011.

MacTavish, Ron. "Pentecostal Profits: The Prosperity Gospel in the Global South." PhD diss., Lethbridge, Alberta, University of Lethbridge, 2014.

Ma, Julie C., and Wonsuk Ma. *Mission in the Spirit: Towards a Pentecostal/Charismatic Theology.* Oxford: Regnum, 2010.

Makanjououola, Joseph. "St Paul's Teaching on Wisdom and Its Relevance to Anointing for Wisdom in the Living Faith Church." MA diss., University of Ibadan, Nigeria, 2002.

Marcus, George E. "Ethnography in/of the World System: The Emergence of Multi-Sited Ethnography." *Annual Review of Anthropology* 24:1 (1995) 95–117.

Marshall-Fratani, Ruth. "Mediating the Global and the Local in Nigerian Pentecostalism." *Journal of Religion in Africa* 28:3 (1998) 278.

———. *Political Spiritualities: The Pentecostal Revolution in Nigeria.* Chicago: University of Chicago Press, 2009.

———. "Power in the Name of Jesus." *Review of African Political Economy* 18:52 (1991) 21–37.

Masok, Emmanuel. "How Should the Presbyterian Church in Cameroon Respond to Global Pentecostalism?" MTh diss., Presbyterian Theological Seminary Kumba, 2010.

———. "The Revival Crisis in Bastos Yaoundé." BTh diss., Presbyterian Theological Seminary Kumba, 1998.

Mason, Jennifer. "Mixing Methods in a Qualitatively Driven Way." *Qualitative Research* 6:1 (2006) 9–25.

Ma, Wonsuk, and Kenneth Ross. *Mission Spirituality and Authentic Discipleship.* Oxford: Regnum, 2013.

Maxwell, David. *African Gifts of the Spirit: Pentecostalism and the Rise of a Zimbabwean Transnational Religious Movement.* Oxford: James Curry, 2006.

Mberu, Blessing. "Nigeria: Multiple Forms of Mobility in Africa's Demographic Giant." Migration Information Source, 2010. Accessed Jan. 13, 2014. https://www.migrationpolicy.org/article/nigeria-multiple-forms-mobility-africas-demographic-giant.

McCauley, J. F. "Africa's Big Man Rule? Pentecostalism and Patronage in Ghana." *African Affairs* 112:446 (2013) 1–21.

McCracken, Grant. *The Long Interview.* Newbury Park, CA: Sage, 2000.

Mengara, Daniel M., ed. *Images of Africa: Stereotypes and Realities.* Trenton, NJ: Africa World Press, 2001.

Messina, Jean Paul, and Jaap Van Slageren. *Histoire du Christianisme au Cameroun: Des Origines a nos Jours, Approche Ecumenique.* Paris: Editions Karthala, 2005.

Methuen, Charlotte, and Andrew Spicer, eds. *The Church in Sickness and in Health.* Studies in Church History 58. Cambridge: Cambridge University Press, 2022.

Meyer, Birgit. "Christianity in Africa: From African Independent to Pentecostal-Charismatic Churches." *Annual Review of Anthropology* 33:1 (2004) 447–74.

———. "Impossible Representations: Pentecostalism, Vision and Video Technology in Ghana." In *Religion, Media, and the Public Sphere*, edited by Birgit Meyer and Annelies Moors, 290–312. Bloomington: Indiana University Press, 2006.

———. "Make a Complete Break with the Past: Memory and Post-Colonial Modernity in Ghanaian Pentecostalist Discourse." *Journal of Religion in Africa* 28:3 (1998) 316–49.

———. "Mediation and Immediacy: Sensational Forms, Semiotic Ideologies and the Question of the Medium." *Social Anthropology* 19:1 (2011) 23–39.

Mgbonyebi, F. A. *Stories of Great Men of God.* Abuja: Freedom House Publications, 2004.

Mickus, Francis Steven. "A Culture of One: Homogenization across the Star Trek Universe." *Interdisciplinary Literature Studies* 23:3 (2021) 368–88.

Miller, Donald E., et al. *Spirit and Power: The Growth and Global Impact of Pentecostalism.* New York: Oxford University Press, 2013.

Miller, K. D. "Competitive Strategies of Religious Organizations." *Strategic Management Journal* 23:2 (2002) 435–56.

Mills, C. Wright. *The Sociological Imagination.* Oxford: Oxford University Press, 2000.

Moore, David. "Revealed: 8 Incredible Businesses Owned by Nigeria's Richest Pastor, Bishop David Oyedepo." *The Papers*, Nov. 2023. https://thepapers.ng/2023/11/08/revealed-8-incredible-businesses-owned-by-nigerias-richest-pastor-bishop-david-oyedepo.

Mountain of Fire and Miracles Ministries. "Welcome to the Mountain of Fire and Miracles Ministries." Accessed Apr. 15, 2024. https://www.mountainoffire.org/.

Mukonyora, Isabel. "Masowe Migration: A Quest for Liberation in the African Diaspora." *Religion Compass* 2:2 (2008) 84–95.

Mwangi, John, and Loizer W. Mwakio. "The African Traditional Religious Ontology of God, Divinities, and Spirits." In *Phenomenological Approaches to Religion and Spirituality*, edited by E. D. Essien, 21. Hershey, PA: IGI Global, 2021.

Nde, E. B. "The Evolution and Impact of the Pentecostal Movement in Cameroon: A Case Study of Full Gospel Mission Cameroon-Mutengene District, 1960–1997." BA diss., University of Buea, Department of History, 1995.

Niehaus, Isak. *Witchcraft and a Life in the New South Africa*. Cambridge: Cambridge University Press, 2012.

Nofuru, Nakinti. "Rise in Pentecostalism Conversions Makes Cameroonians Wary of Scams." *Global Press Journal*, Aug. 18, 2013. https://globalpressjournal.com/africa/cameroon/rise-in-pentecostalism-conversions-makes-cameroonians-wary-of-scams/.

Northcott, Charlie, and Helen Spooner. "TB Joshua: Megachurch Leader Raped and Tortured Worshippers, BBC Finds." BBC, Jan. 7, 2024. https://www.bbc.com/news/world-africa-67749215.

Northcott, Charlie, et al. "TB Joshua Exposé: How the Disgraced Pastor Faked His Miracles." BBC, Jan. 13, 2024. https://www.bbc.com/news/world-africa-67944614.

Nsom, Joseph. "CAMEROUN: Cameroon: A Francophone Bilingual Country." Accessed June 4, 2015. https://www.camer.be/39483/11:1/cameroun-cameroon-a-francophone-bilingual-country.html.

Nsoseka, Andrew. "Prophet Divine Incarcerated for Sexually Harassing Followers." *Cameroon Postline*, Jan. 30, 2016. http://www.cameroonpostline.com/prophet-divine-incarcerated-for-sexually-harassing-followers. Accessed Jan. 30, 2016.

Nyansako, Ni-Nku. *Cry Justice: The Church in a Changing Cameroon*. Limbe: Pressbook, 1993.

Nyberg, Sørensen. *Living across Worlds: Diaspora, Development and Transnational Engagement*. International Organization for Migration. Geneva: IOM, 2007.

Nye, Joseph. "Public Diplomacy and Soft Power." *The Annals of the American Academy of Political and Social Science* 616:1 (2008) 94–109.

———. *Soft Power: The Means to Success in World Politics*. New York: USA Public Affairs, 2004.

Nzayabino, Vedaste. "Rethinking the Impact of the Church on the Dynamics of Integration of Congolese Migrants in Johannesburg: A Case Study of Yahweh Shammah Assembly." PhD diss., University of Witwatersrand, 2011.

Offut, Stephen. "The Transnational Location of Two Leading Evangelical Churches in the Global South." *Pneuma* 32:3 (2010) 390–411.

Ogunnubi, Olusola, and Christopher Isike. "Regional Hegemonic Contention and the Asymmetry of Soft Power: A Comparative Analysis of South Africa and Nigeria." *Strategic Review for Southern Africa* 37:1 (2015) 152–77.

Olofinjana, Israel. *Reverse in Ministry and Missions: Africans in the Dark Continent of Europe: An Historical Study of African Churches in Europe*. Milton Keynes: Author House, 2010.

Omotoye, Rotimi Williams, and Elizabeth Omoralara Opoola. "The Church and National Development: A Case Study of the Living Faith Church Worldwide (Winners Chapel) in Nigeria." Paper presented at the University of Ilorin, Department of Religious Studies, Kwara State. Accessed Feb. 28, 2017. http://www.cesnur.org/2012/nigeria.htm.

Onyedi, Mathias. "The Prosperity Theology of a New Pentecostal Church: A Case Study of Winners Chapel." MA diss., University of Ibadan, Nigeria, 1998.

Onyinah, Opoku. "Akan Witchcraft and the Concept of Exorcism in the Church of Pentecost." PhD diss., University of Birmingham, 2002.

Orobator, Agbonkhianmeghe E. *Religion and Faith in Africa: Confessions of an Animist.* Maryknoll, NY: Orbis Books, 2018.

Otto, Gala. *Healing Services and Anointing—A Divine Sanction.* Yaoundé: Messie Publishers, 2009.

Oumar, Saidou Baba, and Josue Mbonigaba. "An Assessment of the Performance of the Cameroon Water Corporation for the Period 1967 to 2013." Working paper, Economic Research Southern Africa, Jan. 24, 2014.

Oyedepo, David. *All You Need to Have All Your Needs Met.* Lagos: DPH, 2004.

———. *Born to Win.* Lagos: DPH, 1986.

———. "Faith Tabernacle, Canaanland, Ota, Living Faith Church Worldwide International." Accessed Feb. 23, 2017. http://faithtabernacle.org.ng/.

———. *Making Maximum Impact.* Lagos: DPH, 2000.

———. *The Mandate: Operational Manual of Living Faith Church Worldwide Aka Winners Chapel International.* Lagos: DPH, 2012.

———. *Maximum Impact.* Lagos: DPH, 2003.

———. "Processing Shiloh 2015 Shiloh Sacrifice." Accessed Nov. 22, 2016 https://livingfaithmedia.blogspot.com/2015/12/processing-our-shiloh-sacrifice.html.

———. *Signs and Wonders Today: A Catalogue of the Amazing Acts of God among Men.* Lagos: DPH, 2006.

———. *Understanding Financial Prosperity.* Lagos: DPH, 1997.

———. *Walking in Dominion.* Lagos: DPH, 2006.

———. *Winning the War against Poverty.* Lagos: DPH, 2006.

Parsitau, Damaris Seleina, and Philomena Njeri Mwaura. "God in the City: Pentecostalism as an Urban Phenomenon in Kenya." *Studia Historia Ecclesiasticae* 36:2 (2010) 95–112.

Pasura, Dominic Mazorodze. "Competing Meanings of the Diaspora: The Case of Zimbabweans in Britain." *Journal of Ethics and Migration Studies* 36:9 (2010) 1445–61.

———. "A Fractured Diaspora: Strategies and Identities among Zimbabweans in Britain." PhD diss., University of Warwick, 2008.

Peel, J. D. Y. *Christianity, Islam, and Oriṣa Religion: Three Traditions in Comparison and Interaction.* Oakland, CA: University of California Press, 2016.

Poewe, Karla. *Charismatic Christianity as a Global Culture.* Columbia, SC: University of South Carolina, 1994.

Polsby, Nelson W. *Community Power and Political Theory: A Further Look at Problems of Evidence and Inference.* New Haven, CT: Yale University, 1980.

Portes, Alejandro, et al. "The Study of Transnationalism: Pitfalls and Promise of an Emergent Research Field." *Ethnic and Racial Studies* 22:2 (1999) 217–37.

PPU. "You Will Do Miracles If You Walk in the Footsteps of Jesus, H.E Museveni Tells Born Again Christians." *Consecration, Religion,* Sept. 2023. Accessed Jan. 8, 2024. https://statehouse.go.ug/you-will-do-miracles-if-you-walk-in-the-footsteps-of-jesus-h-e-museveni-tells-born-again-christians/.

Punch, Keith F. *Introduction to Social Research: Quantitative and Qualitative Approaches.* Los Angeles, CA: Sage, 2013.

Pustovitovskij, Andrej, and Jan-Frederik Kremer. *Structural Power and International Relations Analysis: "Fill Your Basket, Get Your Preferences."* St Louis: Federal Reserve Bank of St Louis.

Republic of Cameroon. "Chantal BIYA Foundation (FCB)." Accessed Sept. 14, 2016. https://www.prc.cm/en/the-first-lady/fcb.

The Redeemed Christian Church of God. "Mission and Vision." Accessed Apr. 3, 2017. http://rccg.org/who-we-are/mission-and-vision/?v=79cba1185463.

Richie, Tony. "Translating Pentecostal Testimony into Interreligious Dialogue." *Journal of Pentecostal Theology* 20:1 (2011) 155–83.

Ritchie, Jane, and Jane Lewis. *Qualitative Research Practice: A Guide for Social Science Students and Research*. London: Sage, 2003.

Robeck, Cecil M. *The Azusa Street Mission and Revival*. Nashville: Thomas Nelson, 2006.

Robert, Dana L. *Christian Mission: How Christianity Became a World Religion*. Blackwell Brief Histories of Religion 25. Hoboken, NJ: Wiley, 2009.

Robson, C., and K. McCartan. *Field Research: A Sourcebook and Field Manual*. London: George Allen and Unwin, 1982.

———. *Real World Research*. Oxford: Wiley, 2016.

Rosen, David M. "Leadership Systems in World Cultures." In *Leadership: Multidisciplinary Perspectives*, edited by Barbara Kellerman, 45–67. New Jersey: Prentice Hall, 1984.

Rowan, Kirsty. "'Who Are You in This Body?' Identifying Demons and the Path to Deliverance in a London Pentecostal Church." *Language in Society* 45:2 (2016) 247–70.

Rubinstein, Ernest H. "The 'New' New Catholic Encyclopedia." *Commonweal* 131:18 (2004) 22.

Sahara Reporters. "BBC Investigation Unveils Late Nigerian Pastor, TB Joshua's Atrocities, Life of Abuse, Harassment, Rape, Manipulation, Staged Miracles." Jan. 8, 2024. https://saharareporters.com/2024/01/08/bbc-investigation-unveils-late-nigerian-pastor-tb-joshuas-atrocities-life-abuse.

———. "Oyedepo's Church, Living Faith to Spend N160 Billion on New 100,000-Seater Auditorium." Apr. 15, 2021. https://saharareporters.com/2021/04/15/oyedepos-church-living-faith-spend-n160-billion-new-100000-seater-auditorium.

Sanneh, Lamin. *Whose Religion Is Christianity? The Gospel beyond the West*. Grand Rapids, MI: Eerdmans, 2003.

Schiller, Nina Glick. "Transnational Social Fields and Imperialism: Bringing a Theory of Power to Transnational Studies." *Anthropological Theory* 5:4 (2005) 439–61.

Schiller, Nina Glick, et al. "From Immigrant to Transmigrant: Theorizing Transnational Migration." *Anthropological Quarterly* 61:1 (1995) 48–63.

Seale, Clive. "Quality in Qualitative Research." *Qualitative Inquiry* 5:4 (1999) 465–78.

———. *Researching Society and Culture*. London: Sage, 2004.

Seale, Clive, et al. "Qualitative Research Practice." *Management Learning* 36:3 (2005) 392–93.

Shamir, Boas, et al. "The Motivational Effects of Charismatic Leadership: A Self-Concept Based Theory." *Organization Science* 4:4 (1993) 577–94.

Silverman, David. *Qualitative Research: Theory, Method and Practice*. 2nd ed. London: Sage, 2004.

Smidt, Corwin E. *Religion as Social Capital: Producing the Common Good*. Waco, TX: Baylor University Press, 2003.

Smith, Michael Peter, and Luis Guarnizo. *Transnationalism from Below*. Comparative Urban and Community Research 6. New Brunswick, NJ: Transaction, 1998.

Smith, R. Drew. *Freedom's Distant Shores: American Protestants and the Post-Colonial Alliances with Africa*. Waco, TX: Baylor University Press, 2006.

Stanley, Brian. *The Global Diffusion of Evangelicalism: The Age of Billy Graham and John Stott*. Downers Grove, IL: InterVarsity, 2013.
Stark, Rodney. "Why Religious Movements Succeed or Fail: A Revised General Model." *Journal of Contemporary Religion* 2 (1996) 133–46.
Strathern, Alan. *Unearthly Powers: Religious and Political Change in World History*. Cambridge: Cambridge University Press, 2019.
Swain, Tony, and Garry W. Trompf. *The Religions of Oceania*. London: Routledge, 1995.
Synan, Vinson. *Voices of Pentecost: Testimonies of Lives Touched by the Holy Spirit*. Ann Arbor, MI: Vine Books, 2003.
Tanzanu, P. M. "Practices and Narratives of Breakthrough: Pentecostal Representations, the Quest for Success, and Liberation from Bondage." *Journal of Religion in Africa* 46:1 (2016) 32–66.
Tanku, Tapang Ivo. "Cameroon's President Orders Pentecostal Churches Closed." CNN News, Aug. 15, 2015. http://edition.cnn.com/2013/08/14/world/africa/cameroon-churches.
Taylor, Steven J., et al. *Introduction to Qualitative Research Methods: A Guidebook and Resource*. Oxford: Wiley, 2015.
Tetchiada, Sylvestre. "Nigerians Who Fled Boko Haram Forced Home." UN Relief Web, Aug. 21, 2015. https://reliefweb.int/report/cameroon/nigerians-who-fled-boko-haram-forced-home.
Tettey, Michael. "Pentecostalism and Empowerment: A Study of the Church of Pentecost and International Central Gospel Church." PhD diss., University of Edinburgh, 2015.
Togarasei, Lovemore. "Modern Pentecostalism as an Urban Phenomenon: The Case of the Family of God Church in Zimbabwe." *Exchange* 34:4 (2005) 349–75.
Turner, Bryan S. *The New Blackwell Companion to the Sociology of Religion*. Malden, MA: Wiley-Blackwell, 2010.
Turner, H. W. *The History of an African Independent Church*. Oxford: Clarendon, 1967.
Tweed, Thomas. *Crossing and Dwelling: A Theory of Religion*. Cambridge, MA: Harvard University Press, 2006.
Ukah, Asonzeh Franklin-Kennedy. *African Christianities: Features, Promises and Problems*. Mainz: Johannes Gutenberg University, 2007.
———. "Piety and Profit: Accounting for Money in West African Pentecostalism (Part 2)." *Dutch Reformed Theological Journal Nederduitse Gereformeerde Teologiese Tydskrif* 48:3–4 (2007) 633–48.
———. "The Redeemed Christian Church of God (RCCG), Nigeria: Local Identities and Global Processes in African Pentecostalism." PhD diss., University of Bayreuth, 2003.
———. "Roadside Pentecostalism: Religious Advertising in Nigeria and the Marketing of Charisma." *Critical Interventions* 2:1–2 (2008) 125–41.
Ukuh, Eddy. "Youth Unemployment Challenge in Cameroon." *The Observer*, Aug. 18 2015. https://fuhsharon.wordpress.com/2015/08/18/youth-unemployment-in-Cameroon/.
United Nations. *Charter of the United Nations*. Oct. 24 1945. Accessed Apr. 5, 2017. http://www.refworld.org/docid/3ae6b3930.html.
United Nations Development Programme. "2023 Global Multidimensional Poverty Index." Accessed Mar. 12, 2024. https://hdr.undp.org/content/2023-global-multidimensional-poverty-index-mpi#/indicies/MPI.

———. "Human Development Index, 2016 Report." https://hdr.undp.org/content/national-human-development-report-2016. Accessed Feb. 3, 2016.

United States Department of State. *2013 Report on International Religious Freedom—Cameroon*. July 28, 2014. http://www.refworld.org/docid/53d9079a14.html.

University of Oxford. "COVID-19 Continued to Hit Life Expectancy in 2021 in Unvaccinated Populations and Eastern Europe." Oct. 17, 2022. https://www.ox.ac.uk/news/2022-10-17-covid-19-continued-hit-life-expectancy-2021-unvaccinated-populations-and-eastern.

Waldinger, Roger, and David Fitzgerald. "Transnationalism in Question." *American Journal of Sociology* 109:5 (2004) 1177–95.

Walker, Daniel Okyere. "The Pentecost Fire Is Burning: Models of Mission Activities in the Church of Pentecost." PhD diss., University of Birmingham, 2010.

Walls, Andrew F. "Africa in Christian History: Retrospect and Prospect." *Journal of African Christian Thought* 1:19 (1998) 2–15.

———. "Of Ivory Towers and Ashrams: Some Reflections on Theological Scholarship in Africa." *Journal of African Christian Thought* 3:1 (June 2000) 1–4.

Walls, Andrew F., and Cathy Ross. *Mission in the Twenty-First Century: Exploring the Five Marks of Global Mission*. Maryknoll, NY: Orbis Books, 2008.

Wangira, Dorcas. "Kenya Starvation Cult: 'My Wife and Six Children Followed Pastor Mackenzie.'" BCC News, May 2, 2023. https://www.bbc.com/news/world-africa-65423645.

Wariboko, Nimi. "TB Joshua Scandal: The Forces That Shaped Nigeria's Mega Pastor and Made Him Untouchable." *The Conversation*, Jan. 19, 2024. https://theconversation.com/tb-joshua-scandal-the-forces-that-shaped-nigerias-mega-pastor-and-made-him-untouchable-221421.

Warren, M. A. C., ed. *To Apply the Gospel: Selections from the Writings of Henry Venn*. Grand Rapids, MI: Eerdmans, 1971.

Weber, C. W. *International Influences and Baptist Missions in West Cameroon: German American Missionary Endeavours under International Mandate and British Colonialism*. Leiden: Brill, 1993.

Weber, Jeremy. "Cameroon Orders Military to Close 100 Churches in Major Cities." *Christianity Today*, Aug. 19, 2013. https://www.christianitytoday.com/news/2013/august/cameroon-orders-military-to-close-100-churches-in-major-cit.html.

Weber, Max. *The Theory of Social and Economic Organization*. Translated by A. M. Henderson and T. Parsons. New York: Free Press, 1968.

Wild-Wood, Emma. *Migration and Christian Identity in Congo (DRC)*. Leiden: Brill, 2008.

Williams, Corey. "Multiple Religious Belonging and Identity among the Yorùbá of Ogbomòsó, Nigeria." PhD diss., University of Edinburgh, 2015.

Winners' Chapel International. "Our Mandate." Accessed Apr. 3, 2017. https://winnerschapeledmonton.org/mandate/.

World Bank. "Deep Structural Reforms Guided by Evidence Are Urgently Needed to Lift Millions of Nigerians Out of Poverty, Says New World Bank Report." Press release no. 2022/052/AFW. Mar 22, 2022. https://www.worldbank.org/en/news/press-release/2022/03/21/afw-deep-structural-reforms-guided-by-evidence-are-urgently-needed-to-lift-millions-of-nigerians-out-of-poverty.

World Health Organization, African Region. "Healthy Life Expectancy in Africa Rises by Almost Ten Years." Aug. 4, 2022. https://www.afro.who.int/news/healthy-life-expectancy-africa-rises-almost-ten-years.

Yeh, Allen. *Twenty-First Century Mission, From Everyone to Everywhere: Polycentric Missiology*. Downers Grove, IL: InterVarsity, 2016.

Yufeh, Brenda. "Cameroon: Winners Chapel Donates to Chantal Biya Foundation." *Cameroon Tribune*, Jan. 25, 2010. https://allafrica.com/stories/201001251006.html.

Zimmerman, Marc A. "Psychological Empowerment: Issues and Illustrations." *American Journal of Community Psychology* 23:5 (1995) 581–99.

Zurlo, Gina A. *From Nairobi to the World: David B. Barrett and the Re-Imagining of World Christianity*. Leiden: Brill, 2023.

Index

Page numbers followed by *fig* refer to a figure on that page. Page numbers followed by "n" and another number refer to a specific footnote at the bottom of that page.

Abundant Life Faith Ministries, 190
Accra, 185
Acton, John, 209
Adamawa Region, 101*fig*, 102
Adeboye, Enoch, 83–84, 88, 170–71
Adogame, Afe
    on development efforts, 42
    on growth of Pentecostalism, 105–6
    on hierarchies, 77–78, 186
    on social remittances, 183
    on spiritual worldview of Pentecostalism, 211
Africa, stereotypes surrounding, 29–30
African Gospel Invasion Programme (AGIP), 5, 91, 155
African Initiated Churches (AICs, indigenous/independent Pentecostalism), 17–18, 22, 31
African Pentecostalism
    history of, 17–25, 33–36
    leadership in. *see* charismatic leadership; hierarchies; pastors; prophets
    miracles in. *see* miracles
    missionary efforts in. *see* missions
    prosperity gospel in. *see* prosperity gospel
    as representative of twenty-first-century Christianity, 26–28
    socioeconomic development in. *see* development efforts; humanitarian efforts
    theocratic political elitism in, 49–53, 210
    types of, 31–33, 99
agricultural sciences, 47
Akoko, Robert, 19, 33, 177
Akwaibom, 190
Aladura churches, 18, 22
alcohol, 174–75
Ambassadors of Christ, 189, 192–93
Anderson, Allan, 73, 164
Anglican Church, 198
Anglophone regions, 100, 102
anointing
    African Pentecostal understanding of, 173
    of the body, 161, 167, 167n35
    of objects, 38, 128, 160–61
    in pastoral authority, 65, 66, 74–75
Anti-Homosexuality Act, 52

apocalypticism, 37
Apostolic Church, 17, 19, 94, 96, 168
apostolic succession, 200
area pastors, 104*fig*
"The Ark" project, 44
Asamoah-Gyadu, J. Kwabena, 45, 87, 160–61, 173
Asante, Molefi Kete, 29
Asongyu, George Nfor, 24
Asonzeh, Ukah, 23, 117, 148–49, 184–85
Assemblies of God, 58
assistant pastors, 81
associate bishops, 81
authority
    in charismatic leadership, 82–83, 148–49, 212
    Pentecostal understanding of, 65–69, 74–75, 126
    in Winners' Chapel, 3, 63, 66, 82, 136, 199–201
    See also charismatic leadership; hierarchies; pastors; prophets
Azusa street revival, 133

Bafoussam, 101, 190
Bakary, Issa Tchiroma, 24
Bamenda
    Full Gospel Mission in, 177
    Reinhardt Bonnke's crusade ministry in, 20
    Winners' Chapel in, 24, 102, 104*fig*, 150, 151, 174
barrenness, 128, 134
Barrett, David, 26, 28
BBC (British Broadcasting Corporation), 207–8
Benin City, 21, 35
Bergoglio, Jorge Mario, 28
Bertoua, 101
Bible
    in blood of sprinkling, 141
    as object of spiritual power, 37–38, 40
    in prosperity theology, 38, 138, 139
    real-life testimonies versus, 134, 135
    in sermons, 124
    in spiritual warfare, 38
Bible Pentecostal Church, 94

Bible schools
    in missions, 94, 95–98, 108
    in pastoral training, 34–35, 118, 124, 172, 189, 191
Billy Graham Evangelistic Association, 159n5
bishops, 79, 80–81, 200
Biya, Chantal, 165
Biyamassi-Yaoundé, 150
Black Power, 73
Blau, Peter, 69, 82–83, 212
blood of sprinkling, 141–44
Blyden, Edward Wilmot, 57
board of trustees (BoTs), 79
Boko Haram, 161
Bonaberi
    establishment of Winners' Chapel in, 93, 94–95, 150, 192
    Nigerian missionaries in, 2, 93, 94–95, 117–18, 150, 190
    theocratic political elitism in, 50
    Winners' Chapel services in, 1–2, 141–44
Bonnke, Reinhardt, 20
books, 5–6, 87–88, 89–90, 137–39, 193
boreholes, 162–64, 163*fig*
"born again" transformation, 33, 65, 174–75, 189n93
Botswana, 58
Buea
    business schools established in, 168
    campus ministry in, 189
    Winners' Chapel in, 102, 104*fig*, 150, 187
Bulawayo, 58
business schools, 168
businesses, 160, 177

Caballero, André, 24
Caisse Nationale de Prévoyance Social (CNPS), 179
Call Box, 160
Cameroon
    churches founded in, 188–94, 198
    displaced people in, 161–62
    emigration from, 167–68
    employment issues in, 172, 176–77

INDEX   233

government's relationship with
    religion in, 22–25, 50–51, 178–
    82, 190, 192
history of Pentecostalism in, 17–25
media in. *see* electronic media; print
    media
Nigerian homogenization in, 3–4,
    112, 147–48
Nigerian missionaries in. *see*
    Nigerian missionaries
Nigerian sermons in, 122–25
religious syncretism in, 54–55
in social remittance models, 183,
    184, 185–87
strategic importance of missionary
    work in, 91–93
testimonies in. *see* testimonies
Winners' Chapel hierarchy in,
    103–5, 104*fig*
Winners' Chapel's establishment in,
    4–5, 94, 95–98, 99–100, 105–8
Winners' Chapel's geographic
    distribution in, 100–103, 101*fig*
Cameroonian Pastors Union, 151–54,
    180
Canaanland, 206
    See also Faith Tabernacle; "Shiloh"
    event
Cartledge, Mark J., 126
Castor, Michael, 175
Catholic Church
    as disenchanted form of
        Christianity, 40
    global South and, 28
    hierarchy in, 200
    Pentecostalization of, 19, 32, 192
    relics in, 39
    reverse missions in, 213
    shutdown of Pentecostal churches
        and, 23
Celestial Church of Christ, 78, 105
Central African Republic, 17
Central Region (Cameroon), 101*fig*
Centre for the Blind, 180
Chad, 17, 100, 101*fig*, 104, 190
Chantal Biya Foundation, 165
charismatic gifts. *See* spiritual gifts

charismatic leadership
    African Pentecostal understanding
        of, 65–69, 71–72
    authority in, 82–83, 117, 148–49,
        212
    effectiveness of, 173
    electronic media in, 145
    in Oceanian primal religions, 200
    scholarly conceptions of, 76–77
Charismatic movement. *See* neo-
    Pentecostalism (Charismatic
    movement)
Charismatic Renewal Ministry, 192
Chiluwa, Innocent, 89
Christ Chapel International Churches, 21
Christian Action Faith Ministries
    International (CAFM), 21
Christian Church Outreach, 78
Christian Mission Foundation, 57
Christian Missionary Fellowship
    International (CMFI), 21, 198
Christian Publishing House, 21
Christianity. *See* African Pentecostalism;
    historic mission churches
Church of Pentecost (CoP), 87
Church of Scotland, 8, 124, 213
Cinema Fouato, 1–2
civil unrest, 161–62
classical Pentecostalism, 31, 32, 99, 177
clean water, 162–64, 163*fig*
collective consciousness, 202
colonialism, 13–14, 15, 54
Communion, 127
conception, 128, 134
confirmation, 54
Congo Kinshasa, 103, 105
constitutions, 23, 24, 52–53, 152
contemporary worship, 32
Copeland, Kenneth, 170
Copperbelt, 48
Corten, André, 136
councils, 79
covenant theology, 14
Covenant University, 5, 46–47, 129,
    178n65
COVID-19 pandemic, 29–30, 50–51
crusade ministries, 20, 114, 115, 126

cultural homogenization, 3–4, 59, 119–22, 147–48

David Oyedepo Ministries International (DOMI), 5, 79
deacons, 81, 159n7
Democratic Republic of Congo, 191, 198
demons, 34, 37, 38, 56, 211
development efforts
    clean water in, 162–64, 163*fig*
    medical care in, 50, 66–67, 164–65
    prosperity gospel in, 43–48
    scholarly perspectives on, 40–43, 74, 210
    See also humanitarian efforts
diocesan bishops, 79, 80–81
discipleship, 15–16, 59
disease, 29–30, 50–51, 66, 129–31, 164–65
displaced people, 161–62
district pastors, 81, 104*fig*, 113
Dominion House Publishing (DPH), 5, 87–88
Douala
    church shutdown in, 24
    churches founded in, 189–94
    clean water efforts in, 162–64, 163*fig*
    distribution of Winners' Chapel congregations in, 101
    establishment of Winners' Chapel in, 92, 93, 94–95, 99–100
    Nigerian missionaries in, 93, 94–95, 114, 150, 152
    public health efforts in, 50, 165
    rise of Pentecostalism in, 17
    in Winners' Chapel hierarchy, 104*fig*, 105
    Winners' Chapel remittances from, 185
    Winners' Chapel services in, 1–3
    See also Bonaberi; Ndogbong
Dowden, Richard, 30
Drønen, Tomas, 25, 85–86
Droogers, André, 59
drunkenness, 174–75
Dunamis, 207
Duncan-Williams, Nicholas, 205
Dundee, 213

Durkheim, Emile, 201, 202

Eastern Region (Cameroon), 101*fig*, 102
Ebolowa, 101
Edéa, 17
education. *See* Bible schools; business schools; schools (primary and secondary); universities
elders
    in Full Gospel Mission, 98
    in Israel, 75
    in Winners' Chapel, 81, 146, 147, 159n7
electronic media
    in broadcasting of worship services, 130–31, 139–40, 141–42, 143–45
    in contemporary worship services, 32
    in dominance over international congregations, 137, 139–40, 143–44, 147, 199, 203
    "religionization" of, 89
    in research on African Pentecostalism, 41, 89
    televangelism in, 111–12, 144, 145, 208
Ellis, Stephen, 49
Emmanuel TV, 144, 208
employment opportunities, 166–73, 176–77
empowerment, 73–74, 187–88
Enenche, Paul, 193, 207
English-speaking regions, 100, 102
entrepreneurship, 9–13, 32, 158, 167–71
Episcopal Church, 213
Equatorial Guinea, 100, 101*fig*, 104
Esu, 55
Europe
    COVID-19 pandemic in, 29–30
    decline of religion in, 27, 28, 58–59, 195
    immigration to, 167–68
    missionaries from, 13–14, 15, 17, 20, 33–34, 54–57, 155
    Pentecostalism in, 105, 213
    reverse missions to, 8, 195–99, 212–13
evangelism. *See* missions
exams, 160

INDEX   235

Executive Council (EC), 79
Ezemadu, Reuben, 57

faith, 144, 146
Faith Academy, 5
Faith Bible Church, 94–95
faith healing. *See* healing
Faith Tabernacle, 139, 142, 170
"Faith Theatre" project, 44
Family of God Church, 78
Far north Region (Cameroon), 101*fig*
fire, 86–87
Fitzgerald, David, 60
Fomum, Zacharias, 21
food security, 47
Foucault, Michel, 76, 136
Francis, Pope, 28
Francophone regions, 100, 101–2
freedom of religion, 23–24, 51–52
"Full Gospel", 192
Full Gospel Mission
    in collaboration with Winners' Chapel, 94
    employment opportunities from, 177
    origins of, 17
    prosperity gospel in, 19, 95, 98

Garoua, 102, 177
Gaventa, John, 70
general overseers, 83–84, 186
Ghana
    government's relationship with religion in, 23, 210
    Pentecostal leaders in, 20–21, 204
    prosperity gospel in, 35, 41
    televangelism in, 145
    Winners' Chapel in, 155, 185
Gifford, Paul
    on development efforts, 40–42, 74, 210
    on spread of Pentecostalism in Cameroon, 20
    on Winners' Chapel, 108–9, 185
Gilead Medical Centre, 5
Gitau, Wanjiru M., 44
global North, 8, 27, 29–30, 194–96, 212–13
    See also Europe; North America

global South, 8, 28, 194–96, 212–13
glossolalia (speaking in tongues), 31, 33, 38, 65, 140
God is Love Pentecostal Church, 1, 2
Gospel of Power Chapel, 189–90, 193
grace, 37–40
"Great House Vision", 120
Guti, Ezekiel, 204

Haar, Gerrie ter, 49
Hackett, Rosalind, 89, 147
Hagin, Kenneth E., 34, 169, 170
Hanciles, Jehu, 43
handkerchiefs, 38–39
Harare, 78, 210
Harvest Bible Chapel, 189, 190–91, 193
Harvest Bible Fellowship, 191
Hayford, Joseph Ephraim Casely, 57
Haynes, Naomi, 48
healing
    from "born again" transformation, 175
    by David Oyedepo, 38, 66, 141, 142–43
    eccentric practices in, 36–37
    on Emmanuel TV, 144, 208
    modern medicine in, 67, 129–30, 131, 132
    Nigerian versus Cameroonian testimonies of, 129–32
    in the Pentecostal tradition, 31, 65
    from water, 163–64
hegemony, 201
hierarchies
    in Catholic Church, 200
    in charismatic leadership, 149
    in different types of African Pentecostalism, 31–32, 77–78
    in Redeemed Christian Church of God, 78, 83–84
    Winners' Chapel perspectives on, 122–23, 146–47
    Winners' Chapel's Nigerian dominance in. *see* Nigerian missionaries
    Winners' Chapel's structure for, 79–82, 103–5, 104*fig*

hierarchies (*cont.*)
  in Winners' Chapel's welfare
    program, 159–60
  in Zimbabwe Assemblies of God
    Africa, 204–5
Hill, Clifford, 105
historic mission churches, 19, 23, 36,
    174, 189n93
  See also Anglican Church; Catholic
    Church; Presbyterian churches
"holiness" tradition, 17–18, 99, 108
Hollenweger, Walter, 133
Holy Communion, 127
Holy Spirit
  baptism/transformation from, 31,
    65, 87, 174–75, 189n93
  empowerment from, 73
  guidance from, 84, 163
  in missions, 86–87
  overview of, 65
  in pastoral authority, 65, 66, 70, 75,
    126
  in speaking in tongues, 65, 140
  spiritual gifts from, 38
  in testimonies, 65, 126
homogenization, 3–4, 59, 112, 119–22,
    147–48
hospitals, 66–67, 165, 177, 178–79
Hovland, Ingie, 203
human development, 74
humanitarian efforts
  for clean water, 162–64, 163*fig*
  for displaced people, 161–62
  medical care in, 50, 66–67, 164–65
  scholarly perspectives on, 40–43,
    74, 210
  in welfare, 159–61
  See also development efforts

Idahosa, Benson, 20–21, 34–35, 171
Ikeja Airport Hotel, 108
immigration, 60–61, 167–68, 183, 184,
    198–99
imperial theology, 13–16
indigenization, 155, 191
indigenous African religions, 30–31, 34,
    54–55, 147, 208

indigenous/independent Pentecostalism,
    17–18, 22, 31, 32, 36
Institute of Management and Financial
    Accounting (IMFA), 168
institutionalization, 202
International Central Gospel Church,
    145
International College of Accounting and
    Sciences, 168
intra-African Pentecostalism. *See*
    African Pentecostalism
Islam, 23, 31, 100, 102, 208

James, William, 201–2
job opportunities, 166–73, 176–77
Joda, Tunde, 21
John, Tebah, 189, 192–94
Joshua, T. B., 115, 130, 144, 207–8,
    209–10

Kaduna State, 51–52, 190
Kalu, Ogbu, 41, 56, 110
Kayiwa, Simeon, 205
Kenya, 37, 44, 50, 143
Kincheloe, Joe L., 203
"Kingdom service", 193, 194
Kingship International Pentecostal
    Church, 50
Knorr, Werner, 17
Kum, Ebua, 189, 190–91, 193
Kumba, 20
Kuponu, Selome, 108

Lagos, 108, 121, 185, 211
Landmark University, 46, 47, 178n65
Lanquintinie Hospital, 165
Latin America, 28
leadership. *See* charismatic leadership;
    hierarchies; pastors; prophets
lectionaries, 124
Leverhulme Centre for Demographic
    Science, 29
Levitt, Peggy, 183
Liberation Mandate
  Cameroonian Pastors Union and,
    151, 152, 154
  David Oyedepo as divinely chosen
    for, 66, 82, 85

INDEX

"Great House Vision" and, 120
   humanitarian efforts in, 159
   missions in, 85, 93–94
   overview of, 5–6
Liberty Baptist Theological Seminary, 191
Limbe, 150, 190
Littoral Region, 1–2, 50, 101*fig*
Living Faith Church Worldwide (LFCW). *See* Winners' Chapel
Living Faith World Outreach Centre (LFWOC), 86
Living Word (TV program), 145

Ma, Julie, 108
Ma, Wonsuk, 108
Mackenzi, Paul Nthenge, 37
Maiduguri, 141
Making Full Proof of Ministry (Enenche), 193
Mana, 200
Mandate, The (Oyedepo), 5–6
   See also Liberation Mandate
Manicaland, 58
"Manna from Heaven" program, 97–99, 106
mantle ministry, 38–39
Maroua, 102
Marshall-Fratani, Ruth, 18, 99
materialization, of spiritual grace and power, 37–40
De Matviuk, Marcela A. Chaván, 133
Mavuno Church, 44
Maxwell, David, 58–59, 78, 204
media. *See* electronic media; print media
medical care
   from Full Gospel Mission, 177
   spiritual healing versus, 67, 129–30, 131, 132
   in theocratic political elitism, 50
   from Winners' Chapel, 164–65, 178–79
Mediterranean Sea, 167–68
megachurches, 6, 18, 43–46
Melanesian primal religions, 200
Meyer, Birgit, 18, 109–10, 145, 175
Mickus, Francis Steven, 3, 213

migration, 60–61, 167–68, 183, 184, 198–99
Mills, Atta, 210
Minawao, 162
Ministry Faith Banner, 24
miracles
   from blood of sprinkling, 141, 142–43
   broadcasting of, 115, 144, 208
   in mantle ministry, 38
   in Mountain of Fire and Miracles Ministries, 55
   in pastoral authority, 65, 66
   in societal renewal, 209
   testimonies of. *see* testimonies
   See also healing
missionaries. *See* Nigerian missionaries
missions
   baptism of the Holy Spirit in, 87
   church planting in, 99–100, 105–8
   from Europe, 13–14, 15, 17, 20, 33–34, 54–57, 155
   in history of African Pentecostalism, 9–13, 17–18
   imperial theology in, 13–16
   leadership in, 68–69, 70–71, 75, 150–54
   locations for, 91–93, 104, 105
   as mandate, 7, 14, 15–16, 27, 85–87, 108, 110
   media in, 87–90
   pan-Africanism in, 58–59
   preexisting churches and, 93–95, 97–99, 106–7
   in reverse, 8–9, 194–99, 212–14
   Satellite Fellowships in, 159
Molyko-Buea, 168
Moses, 36, 75
Mountain of Fire and Miracles Ministries (MFM), 55–56
Mozambique, 58
Mumba, Nevers, 205
Museveni, Yoweri, 50
music, 140, 147–48
Muslims, 23, 31, 100, 102, 208
Muténgéné, 17

Nairobi, 50

National Citizens Movement Party (NCMP), 50
National Council, 79, 103
national pastors
    Cameroonian government and, 178
    Nigerians as, 2, 151
    urban-centric focus of, 102
    in Winners' Chapel hierarchy, 104*fig*, 105
National Social Insurance Fund (CNPS), 179
National Water Supply Company of Cameroon (SNEC), 162
Nazarite churches, 18
Nchia, Greenfield, 189–90, 192, 193
Ndifor, Frankline, 50–51
Ndogbong
    establishment of Winners' Chapel in, 100
    humanitarian efforts in, 162–64, 163*fig*, 165
    Nigerian missionaries in, 150
    in Winners' Chapel hierarchy, 104*fig*
    Winners' Chapel services in, 2–3
neo-Pentecostalism (Charismatic movement)
    appeal of, 95–97, 98–99
    growth of, 28
    versus other types of Pentecostalism, 18–19, 65–66
    overview of, 32
    prophets in, 206–12
    transnational influence of, 22
    as urban movement, 92–93
    See also prosperity gospel
new religious movements, 31
Newport-On-Tay Church, 8, 213
Ngaoundere, 102
Nicodemus, 87
Nigeria
    Cameroonian-founded churches in, 198
    displaced people in, 162
    as divinely chosen, 7, 103
    government's relationship with religion in, 23, 48, 49–50, 51–52, 153–54, 208, 209
    media from. *see* electronic media; print media
    as regional hegemon, 35, 111–13
    sermons from, 2–3, 122–25
    in social remittance models, 183, 184–87
    testimonies from, 3, 4, 127–28, 129–32, 199
Nigerian missionaries
    in establishment of Winners' Chapel in Cameroon, 93, 94–95
    in maintaining loyalty to David Oyedepo, 68–69, 104–5, 116–21, 155, 199, 207
    overview of, 113–16
    in tension with Cameroonian pastors, 114, 149–56, 181–82, 190, 203–4
Njafuh, Zach, 94
North America, 28, 33–34, 169–70, 183
North Region (Cameroon), 101*fig*
Northwest Region (Cameroon), 55, 101*fig*
Nye, Joseph, 71, 112, 116

Obakar, Samuel, 17
Oceanian primal religions, 200
offerings, 182, 184, 186, 188, 211
Ojo, Matthews, 98–99
Oladapo, Ezekiel, 72
olive oil, 160–61
Olukoya, 55
Omega Fire Ministries International, 51, 207
Omu-Aran, 178n65
"One Night with the King" event, 141–44
Operation Andrew, 159
Orobator, Agbonkhianmeghe E., 35, 36
orphanages, 169, 180
Osinbajo, Oluyemi Oluleke, 48
Otabil, Mensa, 205
Oyedepo, David
    in church construction efforts, 44, 45
    divine mandate of. *see* Liberation Mandate
    educational background of, 35, 169–70

in electronic media, 130, 139–40,
    141–42, 143–44, 145
entrepreneurial teachings of, 168–69
flamboyant lifestyle of, 20n42
healing by, 38–39, 66, 67
on "Kingdom service", 193, 194
missionary goals of, 93–94, 107
native town of, 178n65
Nigerian missionaries and. *see*
    Nigerian missionaries
photo of, 163*fig*
promise of, 108–9
as prophet, 206–7
sermons of, 2–3, 122–25
"Shiloh" event message of, 187
spiritual authority of, 3, 63, 66, 82,
    199–201
on testimonies, 136
in Winners' Chapel hierarchy,
    79–80, 81–82
writings of, 5–6, 88, 137–39, 193
See also Winners' Chapel
Oyedepo, Faith, 80, 163*fig*
Oyoyo, I. O., 17

pan-Africanism, 57–59, 204
pastors
    alcohol consumption by, 174
    ascetic versus flamboyant living by,
        18–19, 20n42
    authority of. *see* authority
    eccentric practices of, 36–37
    educational programs for, 34–35,
        118, 120–21, 124, 172, 189, 191
    in electronic media, 141–42, 143–45
    employment opportunities
        publicized by, 166
    in entrepreneurial efforts, 167, 168
    exit from Winners' Chapel by,
        188–94
    governments and, 49–53, 153–54,
        178–82
    in hierarchical structures, 81, 84,
        104–5, 104*fig*
    Nigerian missionaries as. *see*
        Nigerian missionaries
    potent religious encounters
        transmitted by, 202
    salaries of, 105, 171
    sermons delivered by, 122–25
    women as, 102
    in Yoruba culture, 147
Peel, J. D. Y., 147
Pentecostal Fellowship of Nigeria
    (PFN), 83–84
Pentecostalism. *See* African
    Pentecostalism
political spirituality, 84
politicians, 49–53, 210
Polsby, Nelson, 68
popes, 28, 200
Portes, Alejandro, 61
positive discrimination, 166
positive thinking, 33
potent religious encounters, 201–2
poverty, 43–48
    See also welfare
power. *See* charismatic leadership;
    hierarchies; pastors; prophets;
    soft power
powerlessness, 69–71
prayer
    in charismatic leadership, 173
    on Emmanuel TV, 144
    at inception of David Oyedepo's
        ministry, 170
    miracles from, 128, 129, 130, 132,
        134, 163
    in missionary selection, 207
    in spiritual warfare, 55–56, 211
    in Winners' Chapel services, 127n35,
        129, 141–44, 160, 167, 211
Presbyterian churches
    Pentecostal converts originating
        from, 17, 21, 160, 189, 192
    Pentecostal converts returning to,
        188
    Pentecostalization of, 19
    reverse missions in, 8
    sermons in, 124
    traditional African religions and, 54
presidents, 50, 79–80, 81, 178
Prince, Derek, 34

print media
    by David Oyedepo, 5–6, 88, 137–39, 193
    in evangelism, 87–88, 89–90
    by Paul Enenche, 193
    in Redeemed Christian Church of God, 7
    testimonies in, 127–31, 133–34
prophesying, 65, 208–9
prophets, 50–51, 205, 206–12
proselytism. *See* missions
prosperity gospel
    appeal of, 95–97, 98–99, 138, 168–69
    criticism of, 97–98
    in David Oyedepo's books, 137–39
    in engagement with business sectors, 168, 177
    flamboyant living in, 20n42
    overview of, 19
    poverty and, 43–48
    rise of, 32, 33–35
    success in, 86, 138
    suffering in, 108–9
    tithing in, 38
    wealth distribution in, 48–49, 53
Prosperity Now (Joda), 21
Provincial Council, 150
public health, 50, 164–65

rational power, 204
Redeemed Christian Church of God (RCCG)
    employment opportunities from, 176
    hierarchy in, 78, 83–84
    missions of, 13, 56, 70–71, 106, 196, 213
    political influence of, 48
    remittances in, 186–87
    Sunday services in, 1–2
    transnational media dissemination in, 7
refugee camps, 162
regional pastors, 104*fig*, 105
regions, of Cameroon, 100–103, 101*fig*
religious freedom, 23–24, 51–52
religious imperialism, 13–16
religious syncretism, 31, 54–55

remittances, 183–87
Renewalists, 28
resistance, 70, 72, 203–4
Reunification Stadium, 114
reverse missions, 8–9, 194–99, 212–14
Richie, Tony, 133
Robeck, Cecil, 133
Roman Catholic Church. *See* Catholic Church
Rowan, Kirsty, 56
El-Rufai, Nasir, 51

Sao Tome, 100, 101*fig*, 104
Satellite Churches, 105, 127, 159–60
satellite imagery, 139–40, 141, 143–44, 208
Schiller, Nina Glick, 61
schools (primary and secondary)
    Full Gospel Mission's ownership of, 177
    supplies for, 160, 161
    Winners' Chapel and, 68, 180, 181–82
    See also Bible schools; business schools; universities
Scotland, 8, 124, 213
secretaries, 80, 81
secularism, 23–24, 51–52
senior pastors, 81
sermons, 2–3, 18–19, 122–25, 137
sexual abuse, 208
Shakahola massacre, 37
Shamir, Boas, 145
"Shiloh" event
    miracles from, 129, 130, 187, 211
    offerings from, 182
    promotion of, 121
    transnational connections forged through, 139–40, 143–44
sickle cell anaemia, 129–30, 131
Sih, Comfort, 134–35
singing, 140, 147–48
small businesses, 160
Smith, Michael, Peter, 60, 85
SNEC (National Water Supply Company of Cameroon), 162
social capital, 166–67, 178–81, 183–87
social remittances, 183–87

INDEX

socioeconomic development. *See* development efforts; humanitarian efforts
soft power, 16, 71–73, 112, 115–16, 203
Soga, Tiyo, 57
Song, Pastor, 189
songs, 140, 147–48
South Africa, 37, 73, 111
South Region (Cameroon), 101*fig*
Southwest Region (Cameroon), 92, 101*fig*, 102
speaking in tongues, 31, 33, 38, 65, 140
spiritual authority. *See* authority
spiritual gifts
    in different types of African Pentecostalism, 31, 32
    in leadership, 71, 118n16
    prophesying as, 208–9
    in prosperity theology, 38
spiritual grace and power, 37–40
spiritual healing. *See* healing
spiritual homogenization, 112
spiritual transformation, 33, 65, 174–75, 189n93
spiritual warfare, 37, 38, 55–56, 211
Stanley, Henry Morton, 29
Star Trek, 3
success, 86, 138
Success Buttons (Oyedepo), 138
Suleman, Johnson, 51–52, 114, 207
surplus powerlessness, 69
Synagogue Church of All Nations (SCOAN), 115, 144, 207–8, 209–10
Synan, Vinson, 126
syncretism, 31, 54–55

televangelists, 111–12, 144, 145, 208
testimonies
    of blood of sprinkling, 142–43
    from Cameroonians versus Nigerians, 3, 4, 127–32, 199
    of finding desirable employment, 187, 211
    of healing water, 163–64
    in the Pentecostal tradition, 65, 125–27
    of personal transformation, 174–75

    practicality of, 132–35
theocratic political elitism, 49–53, 210
Tiko, 150, 190
tithes, 38, 184, 186, 188
Togarasei, Lovemore, 93
tongues of fire (speaking in tongues), 31, 33, 38, 65, 140
Toukea, Nestor, 17
traditional African religions, 30–31, 34, 54–55, 147, 208
traditional authority, 69
transformation, spiritual, 33, 65, 174–75, 189n93
transnational Pentecostalism. *See* African Pentecostalism
Trompf, Garry, 200
Tweed, Thomas, 201

Uganda, 50, 52, 204
Ukah, Asonzeh, 117, 148–49
unction. *See* anointing
UNICEF, 168
Unification Stadium, 191
United Nations, 162
United Nations Development Programme, 74
United States, 33–34, 169–70, 183
Universal Church of the Kingdom of God, 210–11
universities
    campus ministries at, 189
    healing from admission to, 129
    legal issues surrounding, 178–79
    "Shiloh" offerings for, 182
    Winners' Chapel's ownership of, 5, 46–47
University of Buea, 168, 189
urban areas, 92–93, 102, 198

Vatican City, 200
Venn, Henry, 155
vice presidents, 48, 80
Vraie Eglise de Dieu, 17

Waldinger, Roger, 60
Walls, Andrew, 26–27
war, 161–62
water, 162–64, 163*fig*

wealth. *See* prosperity gospel
Weber, Max
   on charismatic leadership, 76–77, 82, 145, 148, 212
   on power, 72, 204
   on religious leadership, 123–24
   on traditional authority, 69
welfare, 159–61
West Region (Cameroon), 101*fig*
Western world. *See* global North
Wild-Wood, Emma, 198–99
Williams, Corey, 31
Williams, Duncan, 21
Winners' Chapel
   Cameroonian government and, 24, 178–82, 190
   Cameroon's geographic distribution of, 100–103, 101*fig*
   churches born out of, 188–94
   divine mandate for. *see* Liberation Mandate
   educational institutions and. *see* Bible schools; business schools; schools (primary and secondary); universities
   employment opportunities from, 166–73, 176–77
   establishment of in Cameroon, 4–5, 94, 95–98, 99–100, 105–8
   humanitarian efforts of. *see* humanitarian efforts
   leadership in. *see* hierarchies; Oyedepo, David; pastors
   media produced by. *see* electronic media; print media
   missionary efforts of. *see* missions
   names of, 4–5
   origins of, 5–7
   sermons in, 2–3, 122–25, 137
   "Shiloh" event of. *see* "Shiloh" event
   social capital of, 178–81
   testimonies in. *see* testimonies
   worship services in, 1–3, 108–9, 127, 141–44, 160, 167
Winners' Chapel Ghana, 155
Wisdom, Pastor, 192
witchcraft, 37, 54, 55
De Witte, Marleen, 145
word of faith, 6, 15, 66, 85
Word of Faith Bible Institute (WOFBI)
   as branch of David Oyedepo Ministries International, 5
   as mission, 95–97, 98
   in pastoral training, 118, 172, 189, 191
World Bank, 33, 45
World Council of Churches (WCC), 210
World Health Organization (WHO), 30
World Mission Agency Inc.. *See* Winners' Chapel
Wum, 102

Yaoundé
   Full Gospel Mission in, 177
   Nigerian missionaries in, 150
   politicians in, 51, 178
   in rise of African Pentecostalism, 17, 21
   Winners' Chapel in, 101, 104*fig*, 165
Yoruba people, 31, 119, 140, 147–48

Zambia, 48, 204
Zimbabwe, 58–59, 78, 93, 204–5
Zimbabwe Assemblies of God Africa (ZAOGA), 58–59, 78, 204–5
Zionist churches, 18
zonal pastors, 104*fig*, 117

www.ingramcontent.com/pod-product-compliance
Lightning Source LLC
Chambersburg PA
CBHW050844230426
43667CB00012B/2133